THE ROLE OF ANIMALS
IN BIOLOGICAL CYCLING OF
FOREST-STEPPE ECOSYSTEMS

THE ROLE OF ANIMALS
IN BIOLOGICAL CYCLING OF
FOREST–STEPPE ECOSYSTEMS

R. I. Zlotin and K. S. Khodashova

English Language Edition edited by

Norman R. French
Natural Resource Ecology Laboratory
Colorado State University

Translated by
William Lewus and W. E. Grant

Dowden, Hutchinson & Ross, Inc.
Stroudsburg   Pennsylvania

Copyright © 1980 by **Dowden, Hutchinson & Ross, Inc.**
Library of Congress Catalog Card Number: 80–12228
ISBN: 0-87933-377-4

82 81 80   1 2 3 4 5
Manufactured in the United States of America.

LIBRARY OF CONGRESS CATALOGING IN PUBLICATION DATA
Zlotin, Roman Isaevich.
  The role of animals in biological cycling of forest-steppe ecosystems.
  Bibliography: p.
  Includes index.
  1. Forest ecology—Russia. 2. Steppe ecology—Russia. 3. Biogeochemical
cycles. I. Khodashova, K. S., joint author. II. Title.
QH541.5.F6Z5513   574.5′2642′0947   80-12228
ISBN 0-87933-377-4

Distributed world wide by Academic Press,
a subsidiary of Harcourt Brace Jovanovich,
Publishers.

Foreword

Stretching across southern Russia from eastern Europe to the Ural Mountains is a belt of fantastically fertile soil called Chernozem, the Russian term that has become standard terminology in soil science. In the heart of this region is an area that has been miraculously protected from cultivation for centuries. Here the Soviet government has established a protected area, the Central Chernozem Reserve, which includes portions of typical steppe and portions of oak forest, which gives the name forest-steppe to this zone. In the Soviet Union, a Reserve is an area that is completely protected. No economic development is allowed, no tourists are allowed, and even scientific workers must have a valid research project and specific permission to work in such an area. The steppe is sometimes considered synonymous with prairie in the American language, due to similar physiognomy. The Russian term steppe, however, refers to a region of grassy vegetation that receives no subsurface water by capillary action, and therefore is a more restrictive term than the American counterpart. The term meadow-steppe refers to a slightly modified region with higher soil moisture.

This book reports on research during eight years of field effort by members of the Department of Biogeography of the Institute of Geography of the Soviet Academy of Sciences. Such studies, which involve numerous investigators representing various disciplines, are referred to in Russian as complex investigations. These and other comparisons between Soviet and American ecology have been extensively reviewed in a chapter to be included in the forthcoming book *Contemporary Developments in World Ecology*, edited by Edward J. Kormondy.

The particular significance of this volume is that it not only represents a multifaceted look at the interactions among biological components in the forest-steppe ecosystem, but that specific quantitative evaluations have been made of the roles of various organisms in affecting productivity and influencing nutrient cycling in the ecosystem. Outbreaks of leaf eating insects that result in almost total but temporary defoliation of portions of the forest were determined to have little effect on the total primary production, but significant influence on the rate of nutrient cycling in the system. Certain large herbivores have definite impact on system structure and are responsible for the migration of nutrients between communities of the forest-steppe ecosystem. Small herbivores, including earth movers or burrowing animals, modify the system locally and have considerable influence on nutrient cycling and water relations in the areas where they are concentrated. Nutrient redistribution is particularly affected by burrowing animals. Decomposition rates have been demonstrated to proceed similarly in both forest and steppe systems, but the role of organisms in this process varies greatly. Experiments are summarized that demonstrate the significance of abiotic decomposition in the steppe. Similar investigations have not been carried out in North American grasslands.

There is a considerable lack of knowledge of Russian scientific work in English speaking countries. The reverse is not the case, however. American and European scientists have as their goal the publication of research results in recognized journals. Journals are circulated widely to individuals and to libraries, including Soviet libraries. Soviet scientists are better versed in foreign languages than most of us. Furthermore, Soviet laboratories usually have one or more full-time translators on the staff. Soviet scientists sometimes publish research results in serial journals, but often important works are published in monograph form with limited numbers of copies, hence they are often unknown outside the Soviet Union. Due to the language barrier and the different mode of publication, there is a great void in our knowledge of the methods and results of Soviet science. The editor and the publisher hope that this edition will help remove this barrier.

The style of writing, as well as the mode of publication of Soviet scientists, is somewhat different than in western countries. This translation is somewhat literal, only a partial effort has been made to convert to the American style. All translations and names have been carefully checked, but errors that may remain are likely the fault of the editor, in spite of the efforts to maintain accuracy. Scientific names are given in the text, or have been added by the editor, or provided in the Appendix.

The authors of the volume, Drs. R. I. Zlotin and K. S. Kodashova, have been extremely generous and helpful to the editor, first in providing the volume and secondly in spending a great deal of time checking the accuracy of certain points of translation, and clarifying their methods of formulation of certain results. Their cooperation, kindness, and enthusiasm have made the effort both profitable and pleasurable. Support from the National Academy of Sciences made it possible to work with Soviet scientists and visit several research sites during three months in 1977 when the editor was an exchangee under the National Academy of Sciences–Soviet Academy of Sciences scientific exchange agreement. Partial but critical support in the form of valuable typing assistance was made available by the Natural Resource Ecology Laboratory under National Science Foundation grants DEB73–02027 A03 and DEB73–02027

A04 under the International Biological Program, for the benefits that would accrue from such translation to the Grassland Biome studies.

NORMAN R. FRENCH

Preface

The mastering of new lands and intensive use of mastered lands leads to essential changes of established natural communities. Under these conditions the internal interactive mechanisms sometimes change so strongly that the function of ecosystems is severely disturbed. This, in turn, often leads to a series of undesirable consequences.

The function of natural communities, or biogeocoenoses as they were called by the founder of the study of biogeocoenosis, V. I. Sukachev, is a result of "interaction of all biogeocoenotic components among themselves and with other biogeocoenoses" (Sukachev 1966, page 15). Thus the necessity of detailed study of all components of the biogeocoenosis and their mutual interrelations.[1]

Among the least studied of the biogeocoenotic processes we consider to be environmental modification by animals. Occupying the highest levels of trophic pyramids, animals transform and disperse material and energy of producers; without their activity it is impossible to have a new cycle of production of organic matter. In addition, animals exert a great influence on the various components of the biogeococnosis. Functioning of the biogeocoenosis is dependent upon the degree and character of zoogenic modification of natural factors. Thus, the role of heterotrophic organisms in the functioning of biogeocoenoses is very great. This was particularly mentioned in the conference resolution on works of biogeocoenotic stations, which took place in Leningrad in December 1971 (Gerosimov et al. 1972).

Environmental modification by animals has long attracted the attention of biologists (Dokuchaev 1883, Formosov 1928, Dimo 1938, Ghilyarov 1939, Lavrenko 1952, and others). A particularly great contribution to the study of animal influence on the environment was the investigations of A. N. Formosov and his students, which began at the end of the 1920s (Formosov 1928, 1929, Formosov and Voronov 1935, and others). However, even now it is difficult to grasp this complicated prob-

[1]The term biogeocoenosis is used by us to designate actual communities, homogenous in structure and occupying a definite area; and the term ecosystem is used in a general sense to designate any broad community type without structural and territorial limitations.

lem in its entirety. In the more complete investigations published here, we examine only partial aspects of the structure of animal populations, particularly to establish the relationship of numbers and biomass of different systematic and ecological groups of animals. Investigations, expecially those of foreign specialists, have analyzed transformation of organic material and energy in separate levels of trophic pyramids. In the International Biological Program the final problem of investigation of secondary productivity is determination of utilization by animals of the annual increment of phytomass (Petrusewicz and Macfadyen 1970). However, the function of animals in the processes of biological turnover remains little studied. Insufficient attention to the importance of heterotrophic organisms is explained, apparently, by a low proportion of zoomass relative to the total organic material and by the characteristic low utilization of primary production by animals.

The subject of the present investigation is determination of the principal effect of animals on the surrounding environment with the goal of explaining participation of heterotrophs in the processes and functioning of natural systems. The materials forming the basis of this monograph were collected during an eight-year field study (from 1963 to 1970) at the Kursk Experiment Base of the Institute of Geography of the Academy of Sciences of the USSR in the Central Chernozem Reserve named for V. V. Alekhin. For verification of the methodological procedures and results from the station investigations, numerous short trips were taken to the southern part of the Russian plains.

As a basis for studying the structure of animal populations, functional groups of animals were selected and trophic relationships with basic structural parts of phytomass were determined: below- and aboveground (annuals and perennials) and aboveground litter. These groups included most of the mass and the characteristic animals of the forest-steppe: leaf-eating insects (the green oak leaf roller), herbivorous rodents (the common vole, the spotted suslik), the consumers of browse (moose, roe deer, hare),[2] root eaters (Spalax microphthalmus) and a complex of saprophagous organisms (microflora and invertebrate saprophages). A functional group approach to the study of zoological components of biogeocoenoses is necessary for the discovery of mechanisms and directions of participation of animals in biogeocoenotic processes.

Selection of the above-mentioned groups was dictated not only by their great significance for the biogeocoenosis, but also by the opportunity for complete evaluation of the general mechanisms of participation of animals in ecosystem function. In addition, the study of their influence facilitates other investigations by estimation of their role in

---

[2]Moose, roe deer, and hare belong to a group of browse consumers by the character of their feeding in the autumnal winter period. We were interested only in their influence on the productivity of the shrub layer of the forest-steppe oak forest.

environmental modification in natural and agronomic communities of various geographic types. The groups of animals considered have wide distribution not only in the region of the forest-steppe zone; closely related systematic and ecological groups of animals are typical of many ecosystems, including those in more humid and more arid regions to the north and south of the forest-steppe zone.

Animal impact on components of the natural environment is most markedly manifested during those particular times when populated or visited by a given group of animals (high densities of leaf-eating insects, colonies of steppe rodents, concentrations of wild ungulates, etc.). Therefore, we concentrated investigations on the regions most densely populated by animals. These regions are not always in the same place, their boundaries are constantly changing. Over a period of time, the animals use all areas of a given biogeocoenosis. The average area of effect of a given group of animals in a biogeocoenosis is not difficult to determine, proceeding from the numbers of animals relative to the area of the section on which their activity is manifested, and the general duration of the active period.

Contemporary autoecology has a set of sufficiently developed techniques that allow assessment of the significance of specific animals utilizing organic materials (Program and Methods of Biogeocoenotic Investigations 1966). Approaches to the study of the role of animal populations in the function of ecosystems have only been outlined. The basic method used by us consists of comparing a similar pair of areas, one the control on which the animals and their activity are eliminated. Description of the techniques of the estimation of the role in biogeocoenotic processes of each functional group is covered in the corresponding sections of this book.

Completion of the present study was helped greatly by the constant aid of the Director of the Central Chernozem Reserve, A. M. Krasnitsky, of scientific coworkers of the Reserve, V. I. Eliseeva, V. V. Gertsik, and the consultant, G. I. Dokhman, and also the scientific coworkers of the Dokutshaev Soil Institute, E. A. Afanasieva and T. P. Kokovina. In the collection and reworking of the materials Z. M. Puzatchenko participated. Great help in the work was given by the leader of the Kursk Experimental Base, D. L. Armand, constant coworkers of the Kursk complex expeditions of the Institute of Geography and student trainees of the N. K. Krupskaya Moscow Pedogogical Institute and the V. I. Lenin Moscow State Pedogogical Institute and the M. V. Lomonosov Moscow State University. To all the above-mentioned individuals the authors give their sincere and deep gratitude.

R. I. ZLOTIN
K. S. KHODASHOVA

Contents

THE ROLE OF ANIMALS
IN BIOLOGICAL CYCLING OF
FOREST-STEPPE ECOSYSTEMS

I

**Characteristics of Natural Conditions
and Groups of Animal Populations in the
Central Part of the Forest-Steppe of
Central Russian Upland**

The major part of the V. V. Alekhin Central Chernozem Reserve where the investigations were conducted is located in the southwestern part of the Central Russian Upland which is a strongly dissected plain about 250 m above sea level. The natural conditions of this part of the forest-steppe zone have been elucidated in sufficient detail by E. A. Afanaseeva (1966), A. M. Semenova-Tian-Shanskaya (1966) and G. I. Dokhman (1968). Therefore, we will give only a general appraisal of characteristics of the ecosystem within these boundaries, and those sections of the reserve which were stations of zoological investigations will be characterized in more detail.

Forest-steppe ecosystems of the Central Russian Upland were formed under conditions of a moderate continental climate[1] with a relatively large quantity of precipitation (about 500 mm per year), a relatively short cold period (October through March), a sufficiently steady snow cover and a moderately hot growing season. The average yearly air temperature is 5.2°C, the soil temperature (at a depth of 0 to 300 cm) 7.8°C. The average monthly temperature of the cold period is -5.6°C, of the warm period is 12.9°C. The coldest month is February (temperature -8.8°C), the warmest month is July (18.9°C). The period with continuous temperatures higher than 5° and 10°C is 188 and 151 days, respectively; the sum of the average daily temperatures higher than 10°C is approximately 2800°C. The precipitation is divided unevenly by seasons: about 60% comes during the warm period and about 20% in May and June. Hard rainfall composes 15-20% of the yearly total. Continuous snow cover lasts 110 days, the snow depth on the watershed in the forest reaches 70 cm, on the steppe 56 cm (Iveronova and Yashina 1971). There is a multi-year cycle of rainfall observed chiefly in dynamics of the quantity during the warm half of the year. According to the data of E. A. Afanaceeva (1966), during the period from 1896 through 1963 in

[1]The climatic data are adopted from the monograph by E. A. Afanaseeva (1966), and also calculated from the data of the meteorological station at the Reserve.

the forest-steppe of the Central Russian Upland there were three
dry and two wet phases. During this time the dry years composed
26%, wet years 20%, and average yearly conditions prevailed 54% of
the time.

The relationship between the yearly quantity of net radiation
balance and the index of dryness is close to 1, which indicates good
conditions for the development of biotic components of the landscape
(Grigoriev and Budiko 1965, Bazilevich, Drozdov and Rodin 1968).

Editor's note:

Radiation balance

$$R = Q(1-\alpha) - I$$

Q = total solar
α = albedo
I = difference between reflection from surface and
reflection back to surface

Index of dryness = R/Lr

R = annual sum of radiation balance (kcal)
Lr = amount of energy needed for evaporation of
annual ppt

Soil in the region of the Central Chernozem Reserve is mainly
typical chernozems, characteristic both of the forest and of the
steppe on gently sloping surfaces and tops of hills. On the slopes
of the ravines are developed podzolic, leached and carbonated
chernozems (Tselishcheva and Daineko 1967). Gray forest soils,
characteristic of the forest ecosystem of other regions of the
forest-steppe zones in the Central Chernozem Reserve, have extremely
limited distribution. They are observed only under oak groves and
on the slopes of the ravines with shallow beds of Cretaceous rock.
The forest-steppe chernozems are distinguished by a high reserve of
humus and nutrients. In the upper meter of the soil profile there
is about 500 tons of humus and 30 tons of nitrogen per hectare
(Afanaseeva 1966).

Plant communities of the forest-steppe are distinguished by high
diversity, complex spatial sturcture and characteristic rhythm of
seasonal development (Golubev 1962, Semenova-Tian-Shanskaya 1966,
Dokhman 1968).[2]

Biological production of the forest-steppe ecosystem is close
to maximum productivity for natural communities of the temperate
zone. Like forest, the meadow-steppe watershed communities annually
produce a similar quantity of phytomass (11-14 tons per ha dry
weight). To the south and north from the forest-steppe the production of phytomass is severely decreased.

The systematic composition and basic numbers of animals in
natural communities of the Central Chernozem Reserve have been
studied quite fully (Ptushenko 1940, Eliseeva 1959, 1965; Gilyarov
1960, Krivolutzky 1962, Arnoldi 1965, Kurcheva 1965, Chernov 1967,
Zlotin 1969a, b, and others). It is interesting to assess the

[2]
Characteristic plant cover is given beyond in the descriptions
of the study areas.

structure of animal populations of the forest-steppe, and to compare
forest-steppe ecosystems with communities of other zones on the
basis of characteristic zoomass. The total zoomass in the watershed
communities of the forest-steppe is between 1.0 and 1.1 tons and in
the ravines between 1.5 and 1.6 tons per ha (live weight), approximately the same quantity as in the broadleaf forest where it is
between 1.3 and 1.5 tons per ha (mixed oak forests on watersheds in
the Orlovskaya district). To the south and north from the forest-
steppe the quantity of total zoomass decreases as does production of
phytomass. So, in true steppe (the northern part of the Ukraine)
the biomass of animals is one-third (300-350 kg per ha) that of
the meadow-steppe ecosystems of the forest-steppe zone. The decrease of the zoomass northward in the mixed coniferous and broadleaf forest transition is less abrupt. In the deciduous forest of
the southern part of the Moscow district zoomass is two-thirds
(700-750 kg/ha) that in the oak forests of the forest-steppe zone.

Zonal changes of zoomass are correlated with analogous changes
of primary production. The total zoomass in the forest-steppe
ecosystem is 3-10 times higher than in forest communities of various
subzones of the taiga, 10-20 times higher than in the tundra, 3-6
times higher than in communities of true (herb-bunchgrass) and dry
(bunchgrass) steppe, 30-40 times higher than in semidesert, and 50-
100 times higher than in clayey and stony deserts (Khodashova and
Zlotin et al. 1967, Chernov, Khodashova and Zlotin 1967).

Characteristic of the animal populations of the forest-steppe
is the similar size of total zoomass (at annual maximum) in forest
and in meadow-steppe ecosystems. This is explained by similar
regimes of temperature and moisture in these ecosystems, which
insures almost identical primary production and reserves of organic
material in the soil. The latter factors, just as the hydrothermal
regime, appear to be the most important parameters of external
environment to the animal populations. Being equivalent in the
forest and steppe watershed ecosystems, they result in development
of identical zoomass quantities. It should be pointed out that the
abundance and activity of microflora in the soil is also similar in
the forest and the steppe (Bondarenko-Zozulina 1955, and also our
observations). The present amplitude of seasonal and multi-year
fluctuation of zoomass in meadow-steppe ecosystems is significantly
larger than in the forest. In many groups of animals, for example
the soil invertebrate mesofauna and inhabitants of the grassy layer,
and also small rodents and insectivores, the seasonal flow of biomass in forest and steppe correlates with the dynamics of moisture
conditions. The corresponding season of high numbers and biomass of
most groups of animals in the oak forest lasts for a month to three
months longer than in the steppe. The amplitude of multi-year
fluctuation of abundance, determined chiefly by the hydrothermal
regime, of the predominant species and groups of animal populations
in the forest ecosystem is one-half of that in the steppe.

The forest-steppe ecosystems differ from ecosystems of other
zones of the Russian plains in terms of systematic composition of
animal populations and in the presence of a significant number of
endemic species and forms of animals which are indigenous representatives of the forest steppe complex (Arnoldi 1965). The animal
population in the forest-steppe is best differentiated into layered
synusia and functional biogeocoenotic groups, formed by multiple
representatives of diverse life forms.

For characterizing structure of animal populations quantitative records were collected of all groups of invertebrates and vertebrates (excluding the most simple) populating all layers of the biocoensis--soil, litter, grass layer, shrub layer. Annual records of numbers were determined during the same phenological period on permanent areas or on line transects. This provided comparative indices of seasonal and annual dynamics of structure of the animal populations.

The number and biomass of invertebrate animals were determined by usual ecological methods with some modification. Soil invertebrate mesofauna were counted by hand sorting of soil cores measuring 25 × 25 or 50 × 50 cm; the soil microfauna was extracted in thermal gradient collectors from soil core samples with a size of 125 or 1000 cc, the abundance of enchytraeid worms and soil nematodes was determined by the funnel method from samples to 8 cc depth and 0.5 to 1.0 cc. In all the studies the depth of soil samples was determined by the limits of animals encountered. Samples were replicated so that the average deviation for each measured group of soil animals would not exceed 20%. The invertebrates of a grassy stand were considered on transects of known area, and also by biocoenometers. The estimated count of the inhabitants of the bark layer was conducted on sample trees or sample branches, with subsequent conversion of the counts to area.

The number of ungulates, hares, birds of prey and mammals, and also some corvid birds were characterized on the basis of absolute records in the entire territory of the reserve (mammals in the winter and summer, birds in the nesting period). The other groups of vertebrates were considered on two permanent transects crossing major forest and steppe lands of the Streletskava area. On these transects was recorded absolute numbers of nesting birds and three times a year (in spring, summer and fall) relative numbers of small mammals (by a 24 hour trap period), and also reptiles and amphibians (transect records).[3] The complete catch of small animals on enclosed areas (0.5 ha), compared with adjoining forest transects, provided coefficients for transformation of indices of absolute and relative abundance, necessary for the estimation of zoomass in various types of forest-steppe ecosystems.

In the forest-steppe, just as in other humid landscapes of the temperate zone, invertebrates predominate. More than 90% of the zoomass is concentrated in the soil layer. Aboveground invertebrates compose 1.4 to 2.5% of the total zoomass (Tables 1 and 2).

Complexes of invertebrates are very heterogeneous, particularly in steppe communities. A distinct layer is formed here by the inhabitants of grassland. The most characteristic and numerous groups are the herbivorous insects: grasshoppers (Acrididae), cicada (Cicadodea), caterpillars (Noctuidae, Geometridae), sawfly (Tentredionidae), bugs (Pentatomidae, Lygaeidae, and others), leaf beetles (Curculionidae, Chrysomelidae), and also predaceous and parasitic arthropods--spiders (Aranei), phalangids (Opiliones), locusts (Tettigoniidae), hymenopterans (Ichneumonidae, Braconidae, Chalcidodea) and a series of others.

[3]Dynamics of numbers of vertebrates was studied jointly with the zoologist of the Central Chernozem Reserve, V. E. Eleceeva.

Table 1. Structure of animal populations in forest-steppe watershed ecosystems, kg/ha (average values, live weight).

Group of animals	Soil biomass		Aboveground biomass	
	Oak forest	Meadow steppe	Oak forest	Meadow steppe
Invertebrates				
Saprophagous	974	929	4	2
Phytophagous	20	33	15[a/]	25
Predators, parasites	7	4	3	2
Vertebrates				
Phytophagous	0.1	0.2	10	4[b/]
Predators	--	--	1	1

[a/] In years of outbreak of oak leaf roller the biomass reaches 150 kg/ha, and proportionate weight of phytophages is 10% to 18% of zoomass quantity.

[b/] In preagricultural period the biomass was essentially 5 times larger because of the ungulates, large rodents, and birds.

Table 2. Relationship of biomass of basic trophic groups of animals (percent).

Group of animals	Oak forest	Meadow steppe
Saprophagous	94.6	93.0
Phytophagous	4.3	6.2
Soil-inhabiting (including *Spalax*)	1.9	3.3
Aboveground invertebrates	1.4	2.5
Aboveground vertebrates	1.0	0.4
Predators, parasites	1.1	0.8

In the forest ecosystem invertebrate inhabitants of the grass stand are significantly less numerous; there cicadas predominate, bugs, and spiders. The major biomass of aboveground invertebrates is essentially inhabitants of the tree-shrub layer. Among the dominant groups are included the larvae of butterflies (Tortricidae, Geometridae, Noctuidae, Lasiocampidae), sawfly, some bugs, gall gnats (Cecidomyidae) and spiders.

The major soil fauna is composed of earth worms. In the oak forests the representatives are *Lumbricus, Dendrobaena, Eisenia*; in steppe watersheds *Eisenia, Allolobophora* (Gilyarov 1960). Earthworms account for 80-90% of the total zoomass and about 94% of the biomass of soil animals. In the steppe ecosystem the second place in biomass belongs to the free-living soil nematodes and the millipeds--diplopods, and in the forest communities it belongs to diplopods and enchytraeids. As to representatives of the micro-arthropod complex--Collembola and mites, in the meadow steppe they are twice as numerous as in the oak forests. Among the complex of soil animals in the steppe ecosystem herbivorous insect larvae are very characteristic (Elateridae, Scarabaeidae, Curculionidae, Asilidae) and predaceous millipedes (Geophilidae). In the oak forest the phytophages are much less numerous; they are represented primarily by lepidopteran larvae (Noctuidae). In numbers of predators and parasites here predominate the millipeds (Lithobiidae) and nematodes (Mermithidae) (Table 3).

The vertebrate share of total zoomass in forest steppe eco-systems is essentially 0.5 to 1.1%. The vertebrate fauna of the Central Chernozem Reserve is not rich in species composition nor in number (Ptushenko 1940, Eliseeva 1959, 1965, 1967a, b). In the steppe there no longer remain any marmots or large steppe birds, in the oak forests there are no mammals living in burrows, and very few hole-nesting birds (Eliceeva 1968). This is related to the small area of the reserve, surrounded by vast territories of agri-cultural land, and also to young oak forests that were periodically severely cut.

In the steppe the basic vertebrate population is composed of the mole-rat, common vole, spotted ground squirrel, larks (field and steppe), the meadow wheatear, the lively lizard, the steppe viper, the green frog and the burrowing toad.[4] About 90% of the zoomass of vertebrates belongs to rodents. The number of nesting birds does not exceed 2-3 pairs per hectare.

In the oak forests the ungulates predominate in biomass--moose and roe deer; the second place is occupied by rodents--red forest voles (*Clethrionomys glareolus*), forest mice (*Apodemus sylvaticus*), and yellow throated mice (*A. flavicollis*). The most conspicuous birds include the ortolan bunting (*Emberiza hortulana*), white-throat (*Sylvia communis*), garden warbler (*S. borin*), tree pippit (*Anthus trivialis*), chaffinch (*Fringilla coelebs*) and thrush nightingale (*Luscinia luscinia*). Of the reptiles the most common are the *Lacerta agilis* and *Anguis fragilis*. About 90% of the zoomass of vertebrates belongs to mammals (of this total 65% belongs to ungulates). The remaining types are insignificant. For example,

[4]Editor's Note: *Spalax micropthalmus, M. arvalis, Citellus suslicus, Alauda arvensis* and *Melanocarypha calandra, Saxicola rubetra, Lacerta agilis, Vipera ursini, Bufo viridis, Pelobates fuscus*.

Table 3. Structure of soil invertebrate fauna in forest-steppe
          watershed ecosystems, g/m^2 (average values, live
          weight).

Group of animals	Oak forest	Meadow steppe
Saprophages	97.4	92.9
Including:		
Lumbricids	91.2	82.9
Nematodes	1.5	5.6
Diplopods	2.1	2.7
Enchytraeids	1.6	<0.1
Collembola	0.4	0.4
Oribatid mites	0.2	0.4
Other mites	0.1	0.2
Phytophages	2.0	3.3
Including:		
Larva of flies	0.1	0.4
Beetles	0.1	1.1
Predators and parasites	0.7	0.4
Including:		
Mites	0.1	0.1
Myriapods	0.4	0.1

the number of nesting birds in an open oak forest does not exceed 10 pairs per hectare (7% of the biomass) and only in small sections of dense oak forest with thick undergrowth does it reach 20 to 22 pairs (Table 4).

As in the steppe, predators in the forest are small in number. Most often one meets the fox (*Vulpes vulpes*), badger (*Meles meles*) and the steppe polecat (*Mustela eversmani*). In the steppe nest annually the hen harrier (*Circus cyaneus*), and in the oak forest the black kite (*Milvus korschun*), the buzzard (*Buteo buteo*), honey buzzard (*Pernis apivorus*), and goshawk (*Accipiter gentilis*). For analysis of the functional tophic structure of the animal pop- ulation it is expedient to examine the relationship of three basic groups of animals: saprophages, phytophages and representatives of the third tophic level--predators and parasites. For forest-steppe ecosystems, just as for many other humid communities, the domi- nance of saprophagic animals is characteristic (93-95% of the total zoomass). The portion of phytophages is significantly lower. In this situation in the meadow steppe ecosystem the apportioned weight of the herbivorous animals is relatively higher (6%), than in the oak forests (4%). Predatory and parsitic animals account for almost 1% of the general zoomass.

The animal saprophages play a very essential role in the func- tional compartment of ecosystems we call "plant-soil." Partici- pating in the mineralization of plant litter, saprophages facilitate entrainment into the biological cycle of various organic compounds and chemical elements, which ensures the sequential cycle of pro- duction of organic material. The biomass of saprophages undergoes important zonal changes; to the south from the forest-steppe their absolute significance and proportional weight decrease.

The role of phytophages in the functioning of the ecosystem is determined mainly by their impact on primary production. Phyto- phages perform a basic trophic change, by which is accomplished the transfer of organic material and energy from primary producer photosynthetic plants to a branching hierarchy of heterotrophic organisms. The significance of the phytophagous animals in con- sumption of primary production to a certain degree correlates with their proportion of the total zoomass. The biomass of phytophagous animals increases as humidity decreases and reaches a maximum in the semi-desert and desert regions. The abundance of phytophagous organisms in the forest steppe zone is characterized by middle values (Chernov, Khodashova and Zlotin 1967).

A special place in the trophic group of phytophagous animals belongs to forms utilizing green parts of plants. Of these types in humid ecosystems the invertebrates predominate; in the dry steppe, semi-desert and desert communities the function of this trophic level is accomplished primarily by vertebrates--mammals (rodents and ungulates).

At the present time in the forest steppe zone the dominant position among herbivorous animals belongs to the insects, with certain varieties consuming green parts of certain types of plants. A relatively narrow trophic selection by many herbivorous insects serves as an adaptation to a more complete utilization of phytomass production.

It should, however, be kept in mind that in the pre-agricultural period, when biomass of herbivorous vertebrates was significantly

Table 4.   Structure of vertebrate fauna in forest-steppe
watershed ecosystems, kg/ha (average values, live
weight)[a].

Groups of animals	Oak forest	Meadow steppe
Systematic group		
Mammals	10.0	4.7
Ungulates	7.2	--
Hares	0.6	0.3
Rodents	2.0	4.2[b]
Insectivores	0.1	0.1
Carnivores	0.1	0.1
Birds	0.8	0.4
Passerines	0.7	0.3
Others	0.1	0.1
Reptiles	<0.1	0.3
Amphibians	<0.1	0.1
Trophic group		
Phytophages	9.9	4.4
Root eaters	0.1	0.2
Foliage eaters	7.9	3.7
Seed eaters[c]	1.9	0.5
Predators, including insect eaters	0.9	0.8

[a] Biomass of mammals, reptiles, and amphibians--in the summer
period, birds in the nesting period.

[b] 3.7 kg/ha of the biomass belongs to the common voles (*Microtis
arvalis*) and spotted ground squirrel (*Citellus suslicus*).

[c] In the oak forest in the winter period the majority of foliage
eaters (7.8 kg/ha) change to browse eaters.

greater, their participation in the function of forest-steppe ecosystems (especially the steppe ecosystem) was higher and possibly no
less important than the role of insects. This can be judged by the
influence exerted by the separate types and groups of vertebrates on
the productivity of virgin steppes (Formosov 1928, Formosov and
Voronov 1939, Lavrenko 1952, Kucheruk 1963).

Predatory and parasitic animals occupy the highest level of the
tophic pyramid and for this reason fulfill the role of regulators in
the ecosystem, limiting the development of heterotrophs of the first
order. In this way, the role of these animals is an indirect participation in the processes of biological cycling and is manifested
in the fluctuation of abundance of phytophages and saprophages,
thereby exerting an indirect impact on the function of ecosystems.

Forest Ecosystems. The forest of the Central Chernozem Reserve
is represented primarily by communities of oak (*Quercus robur* L.).
The area occupied by forest at the Streletskaya section is 47%, and
at the Kazatskaya section 33% of the reserve area. Periodic high
density of the oak leaf roller and also the role of browsing mammals, of *Spalax*, and of forest saprophagous animals was studied
primarily on the Streletskaya section, in the Dubroshina and Soloviatnik
areas which are separated by a large ravine--the Tolsti Log. The
total area of these lands is about 390 ha. Brief observations were
conducted as well in the lands of Petrin Forest (440 ha) and the
forest of Dedov Vesely (190 ha) in the eastern part of Streletskaya
and in the Kazatskaya section (490 ha), and also in small oak forests
of up to 10-15 ha which one encounters on the slopes of steppe
ravines.

In the lands of Dubroshina and Soloviatnik 69% of the forest
area is occupied by middle-aged (40-50 years) oak grove growth, 3%
by aspen and 28% by forest plantation (oak saplings from 5-30 years
in age) with an insignificant mixture of the *Evonymus europaeus,
Pirus communis,* the tartar maple (*Acer tartarica*), elm (*Ulmus* sp.)
and several other species.

In the classification of forests of the Central Chernozem
district according to conditions of growth, suggested by N. P.
Kobranov (1925), among standing timber of the Central Chernozem
Reserve are identified oak forest, occupying watersheds and nearby
watershed slopes, and ravine oak forests confined to the steppe
ravines. As a separate type one should identify plantations of the
forest ravines. The oak forests of the reserve have a park structure and are characterized by sequences of high density forest with
clearings of various sizes and shapes. Closed timber stands are
usually developed on the slopes of the forest ravines.

Study areas were placed near experimental areas, on which are
conducted complex multi-year investigations by the coworkers of the
Central Chernozem Reserve and the Kursk Experimental Base of the
Institute of Geography of the Academy of Sciences of the USSR. The
study area of Dubroshina[5] occupies the upper half of the near
watershed slopes with a very weak southern exposure. Composition of
the plantings is nearly 100% oak, with admixture of pear, willow,
and crab apple trees; the age is about 40 years; estimated production class of the forest is IV to V (scale from I to V, best to

[5]The description of areas in the Dubroshina and Tolsti Log is from
the year 1964. The characteristics of the area in Soloviatnik is
according to information in A. M. Krasnitsky (1967).

poorest production); the average diameter breast high is 20.6 cm; the average height 11 m; density 0.6 (scale 0.1 to 1.0); the number of trunks per ha is 830. The origin is by growth from shoots; the trees belong at least to the third generation (at least two previous cuttings). The plantings are of uniform size. In the undergrowth are individual pear trees, crab apple trees, rowan, bird cherry tree, and linden tree. The undergrowth is weakly developed and consists of the spindle, blackthorn, dogrose, buckthorn, hawthorn, honeysuckle and other bushes. In the grass canopy predominates common goutweed, in places one meets lily of the valley and *Brachypodium* association.

The study area in the Soloviatnik occupies a watershed surface and upper near watershed part of the slope of northern exposure. The structure of forest in this land is more complicated, and the estimated production of standing timber is higher (I-II). Composition of the forest community is the same as Dubroshina, but the importance of accompanying species is a little higher. The age is about 40 years; the average diameter breast high is 21.9 cm; the average height is 16 m; density 0.7-0.8; the number of trunks per ha is 770. The origin is from seeds (the first shoot generation). The layer of undergrowth is well developed and consists of spindletree (*Evonymus europaeus* and *E. verrucosus*) and to a lesser degree of bird cherry, rowan, blackthorn, hawthorn, Guelder rose, and cherry. In the grass canopy common goutweed predominates. There are the usual associations of nettle and smallreed.

In Tolsti Log the study area occupies the middle and lower parts of ravine slopes with northern and southern exposure in the region called "Big Proseka." The forest communities in this ravine have the following composition: 90% oak, 10% aspen, individual crab apple trees, pear, and goat willow; in the next lower layer, especially on the northern slopes, there is aspen. The age is 30-40 years; diameter breast high is 13.2 cm; the height is 10 m; density is 0.7-0.8; the number of trunks per ha is 980. The layer of undergrowth is expressed indistinctly and is formed of spindle, Guelder rose, cherry, and wild almonds. The grass canopy is represented by the association of goutweed and also liverleaf and nettle (Zozulin 1955, 1959).

Watershed and ravine oak forests of the Kazatskaya section have the most complicated composition. They are characterized by the presence of a secondary woody canopy, in which in addition to oak, the usual species (pear, crab apple, and willow) are mixed, and also Norway maple and linden. In the undergrowth, besides other bushes, hazel nut is common. In the grass canopy there are goutweed, nettle and herbs.

Under the watershed oak forests is developed the typical leached chernozem. On the slopes of the ravine they change to podzolic-chernozem, and on the bottoms are formed steppe-chernozem soils (Tselitscheva and Daineko 1967).

Meadow steppe ecosystems. In these ecosystems were studied biogeocoenotic activity of the herbivorous rodent, *Spalax*, and a complex of steppe saprophages. On each of the sections of the Central Chernozem Reserve the grass ecosystem occupies no less than half of the area. Study areas were on watersheds and near watershed slopes. According to the system of land use all steppe sections were divided into two types: mowed and unmowed. The main study area was in the mowed section, on which the grass canopy has been mowed three years out of four. The fourth year mowing did not take place.

The correlation of herbs and graminoid vegetation in the mowed section is approximately the same (Semenova-Tian-Shanskaya 1966). A herb and straight brome grass (*Bromus erectus*) association predominates. Besides the edificator (environment-forming plant) straight brome grass, other graminoids are common: sheep's fescue, smooth brome grass, wheatgrass, quack grass, and meadowgrass. Among the herbs predominate milfoil, spring adonis, veronica, and dropwort. Often one meets legumes (*Vicia tenuifolia* Roth., *Trifolium pratense* L., *T. montanum* L., *Orobus pannonicus* Kramer, *Onobrychis arenaria* (Kit.) D.C.).

The meadow steppe grassland differs in its micro-complexity. On the watershed is usually smallreed and feather grass association. On the surface of the soil in mowed steppe there is developed a continuous mossy cover consisting of *Thuidium abietinum*. The litter layer is indistinct.

The unmowed, completely reserved, sections of the steppe have existed since 1935. They are occupied by the smooth brome grass-herb-spear grass groups (Golubev 1962). Herbs and legumes here are very insignificant. The following grasses predominate: feather grass and narrow-leaf grasses, bush grass, straight brome grass and smooth brome grass, and meadow grass; the mossy cover is lacking. The unmowed section differs from the mowed section in having an accumulation of a thick layer of steppe litter.

Under the meadow steppe grassland there is formed thick typical chernozem. In the colonies of the steppe rodents they are changed by digging of the marmot (Tselishcheva and Daineko 1967).

II

The Role of Basic Functional Biocoenotic Groups of Animals in Biological Cycling of Forest-Steppe Ecosystems

II-1

Leaf Eating Insects

The role of herbivorous insects in the biocoenotic process was studied in the case of the green oak leaf roller (*Tortrix viridana* L.) and a complex of accompanying leaf-eating lepidopterans. The range of the oak leaf roller covers a very wide territory--from Leningrad region in the north to the semi-desert Caspian Sea region in the south (Djanybek). The green oak leaf roller is a monophage and its distribution is limited by oak forest.

In recent years mass outbreak of the leaf roller was observed over a large part of its range; particularly intensive in the forest-steppe zone--on the territories of Kursk, Voronej, Orlovsk, and other adjacent administrative regions, and also in the strips of forest of the steppe zone. Considering the exceptionally wide region involved, this outbreak can be called pandemic.

Mass reproduction of the green oak leaf roller in the Kursk oak forest was accompanied by a noticeable increase in other representatives of the Tortricidae (*Cacoecia crataega* Hb., *C. xyloleuca* L. and others), and also the *Euproctis chrysorrhoea* moth, and several types of cutworms, looper moths (Noctuidae, Geometridae) and saw flies (Tenthredinidae). In separate years, differing by cool and wet springs, high abundances of aphids and thrips (Thysanoptera) were observed. Other leaf-eating insects often observed included Melilontids: in the ravine oak forests *Phyllopertha horticola* L., and in the watershed oak forest *Melolontha melolantha* L. However, in the period of larval development of the green oak leaf roller participation of the accompanying species in the total biomass of leaf eating insects was usually less than 1% and only sometimes reached 2-5%.

In the central forest steppe of the mid-Russian upland the last outbreak of the leaf roller started in 1963. Having formed in that year, the centers manifested themselves most intensely in 1964. During the period of investigation (1964-1970) there were 2 years of decreased numbers and 5 years with high abundance of leaf-eating insects.

REASONS FOR OUTBREAKS OF LEAF EATING INSECTS

The reasons for increased reproduction of needle eating and leaf eating insects were studied clearly and sufficiently (Vorontsov 1963). Without giving a detailed analysis of all the varied factors determining the beginning of the outbreak of the green oak leaf roller, we will examine only the possible conditions for the appearance of high density. This will allow estimation of the degree of participation of leaf eating insects in biocoenotic processes, excluding other external factors.

The main cause of the outbreak of the oak leaf roller was apparently change in the solar activity, leading to a significant deviation in weather conditions. The latter influenced the physiological state of trees, which facilitated successful reproduction of the leaf roller.

The most characteristic manifestation of deviation in weather conditions is the change of average yearly and monthly precipitation and change of the temperature regime. As already pointed out, according to the data of E. A. Afanaseeva (1966), in the central part of the forest steppe of the mid-Russian upland during the period from 1896 through 1963 there were two humid and three dry phases. Examination of data from the meteorological station of the Reserve allowed us to establish that the dry phase is still continuing, and its manifestation after 1963 has become more noticeable. As affirmation of the increased dryness of the climate in the forest steppe of the mid-Russian upland one can use the decreased discharge of ground waters and the lowering of their level, and also the sharp decrease of outflow of rivers (Afanaseeva 1966).

To show the connection of mass increase of the oak leaf roller with weather conditions, we analyzed some climatic indicators of the period of mass increase (1963 through 1970) and of the preceding period of equal duration (1955 through 1962). We calculated for these periods an average yearly quantity of precipitation and the quantities during warm and cold seasons, and separately the precipitation which fell in May and June, that is, during the months of larval development of the leaf roller and the most intensive vegetation growth of oak (Table 5). For the same period we calculated degree-days of warm periods of each year (Table 6).

The data presented in Tables 5 and 6 show the essential changes of weather during the last 20 years. The period before the outbreak of the leaf roller population differs by having relatively high humidity during the warm time of the year and relatively low temperatures. The years of increased density of the leaf roller coincide with a relatively dry and hot period. Precipitation of the warm six months decreased by 11%, and the quantity during May-June in comparison with 1955 through 1962 decreased by 15%. There was a particularly sharp decrease of humidity in May: by 28% in comparison with the multi-year average and a 41% increase in comparison with 1955 through 1962. The sums of positive temperatures higher than 0 and 10 degrees were respectively 2% and 6% higher than the multi-year aveage indicators and 5-11% more in comparison to the period before the outbreak, and the general duration of the warm period--greater respectively by 11 and 15%.

It should be noted that the yearly total precipitation in the periods differed little from the multi-year norm. The difference

Table 5. Average quantity of precipitation and deviation from
          long term average.

Months	1947-1970 Long term average (mm)	1955-1962 mm	% of long term average	1963-1970 mm	% of long term average
May	53	65	123	38	72
May through June	114	112	99	37	85
April through Sept.	325	326	100	289	89
Oct. through March	239	226	95	276	115
Year	564	552	98	565	100

Table 6. Sums of temperatures of various gradings by periods.

Index	1947-1970 Long term average (°C)	1955-1962 °C	% of long term average	1963-1970 °C	% of long term average
Sum of temperatures higher than 0°					
May	426	405	95	441	104
May through June	897	869	96	914	102
Year	2842	2783	98	2918	102
Sum of temperatures higher than 10° during the year	2478	2350	95	2620	106
Duration of period with temperatures higher than 10°, number of days	151	144	95	170	111

was observed only in distribution by seasons: the quantity of precipitation in the warm period, including May and June, was less than the multi-year average.

For normal growth of oak the humidity in May and June is most essential, since this period is the time of active physiological processes accompanying accumulation of organic material by the phytomass. For this reason decreased precipitation during these months affects oak growth unfavorably.

According to our calculations, beginning with the 1940's, thickness of the annual growth rings of trees in various forest lands of the Reserve continuously decreased. Simultaneously there was a sequential reduction of the quantity of spring-summer precipitation, an increase of average temperature and an increase of duration of the warm season of the year. Changes of the growth increment of oak, synchronized with the analagous fluctuations of climate, were also observed in the central part of the forest steppe by M. I. Skriabin (1946) and by S. I. Kostin (1960). Thus, increased dryness facilitated lowering of the intensive growth process in the forests.

The trees, weakened by dryness, have a lower resistance to the harmful leaf eating insects (Vorontsov 1963). The biochemical composition of the green part of the phytomass essentially changes, in particular by increases of soluble sugars, starch and other albuminous components, which favors the growth of leaf eating insects and facilitates mass increase (Taranukha 1952, Amirkhanova 1962, Molchanov 1970).

Numerous phytophagous forest insects, as a rule, are thermophylic and xerophylic, and for this reason the dryness and the increased temperature positively influence their development.

Consequently, one can consider as prerequisite for the beginning of the outbreak of the oak leaf roller in the Kursk oak forest is the anomolous development of some meteorological factors during several years and their extreme deviation during the year of this outbreak (Fig. 1) and the disruption of the physiological composition of the trees. The hypothesis of the great role of the trophic interaction in the appearance of the outbreak is confirmed by the fact that the abundance of larval leaf rollers on trees was proportional to the degree of decreased growth increment. That is, it was an indicator reflecting the physiological state of the tree (there were fewer larvae on the trees whose diameter increment toward the beginning of the outbreak decreased less).

In passing we will show that significant deviation in the weather was preceded by a previous short outbreak of the oak leaf roller, observed in the Central Chernozem Reserve in 1950 and 1951. In 1948 and 1949 the average temperature in May was higher, and the quantity of precipitation lower, than the multi-year average. This outbreak was, apparently, disrupted extremely by the rainy and cold weather in May of 1951. In the forests of the Voronez Reserve near Kursk where in 1926 and in 1951 through 1955 there also appeared high densities of the oak leaf roller, outbreaks were caused by deviation of the quantity of May precipitation in the direction of dryness in the years before the outbreak (Egorov, Rubtsova, and Solozhnikina 1961).

The method of investigation of the impact of the leaf roller on biological productivity was as follows. At selected areas for observation we determined the number of trunks per hectare, and by

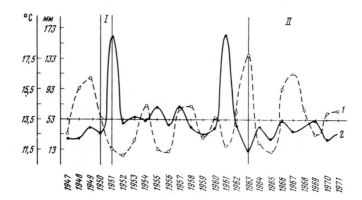

Figure 1
Perennial dynamics of air temperature (1) and precipitation (2) of oak leaf roller (I, II).

measuring their diameters they were separated into tree size classes. For each size class in the forest we selected about 10 (not less than 6) trees for study. In the spring of 1964 at the beginning of vegetation growth two workers independently determined the quantity of branches separately in the upper, middle and lower parts of the crown on these trees. As sample branches we used those with length of about 2 m and diameter at the base of 5-7 cm. By calculation we obtained the total branches from the various parts of the crown per hectare. On the sample branches we determined the number of 1-year old shoots. Their number on one branch fluctuated from 120 to 260, and averaged 150.

For determining the increment of leaves on these shoots from each layer of the crown we cut 1-2 branches, from which, depending on the abundance of foliage and number of leaf-eating insects, were collected 100 or 200 1-year old shoots. The shoots were taken in polyethylene sacks to the laboratory, weighed in fresh condition, and the foliage was separated from stems. Both were dried to a contant dry weight.

In 1964 and 1965 the growth of shoots and foliage was determined 2-3 times a month during the entire vegetation period (from May through October), and in the other years the records were collected in several basic phenological periods, coinciding with the beginning of growth of shoots, with a period of maximum defoliation of the crown, with the beginning and ending of the second (additional) growth.

During each period of observation on one area there was selected from 6-18 sample branches from each of 2-6 trees. The localities of high density of the oak leaf roller are usually characterized by a relatively homogeneous structure, and for this reason such a quantity of trees is sufficient for satisfactory precision. The error of average indicators in our records was as a rule lower than 20%.

For determining the area of the foliage surface we used the method of cutting from 100 to 200 leaves, representing a mixed sample.

Growth of tree trunk diameters was determined with an increment borer. The wood cylinders were extracted either from the south west side of the tree or on four mutually perpendicular radii. The width of the yearly growth ring was measured under a binocular microscope (MBS-1) with the precision of 0.05 to 0.1 mm. The results were analyzed by analysis of variance (Plokhinsky 1961). Similarly, determination of diameter increase in main branches of the oak was estimated, and also in the shrub species of the undergrowth.

Determination of productivity of the grass layer was conducted during the period of maximum vegetative growth in areas of 0.25 m^2 size with 5-10 replicates. The plants taken in the sample were divided by species and weighed wet and dry. Simultaneously, a large series (50 to 200 samples) of representatives of the dominant species were measured according to height, stage of phenology was noted and leaf area index was measured. For calculation of total root biomass of grass stands we extracted soil cores from a 30 cm layer of soil, in which there is concentrated more than 80% reserve of the roots of grass. The roots were washed with water on soil sieves, after which their constant dry weight was determined.

The productivity of root biomass of the grass layer was estimated by the method which considers the yearly production of the roots of grasses in the forest to be equal to 1/3 of their total live biomass (Rodin, Remezov and Basilevitch 1968).

Estimation of the reserve of litter and the yearly fall of leaves was conducted annually in the spring and fall. Sample quadrats were of 25 × 25 or 50 × 50 cm, with 6 to 12 replicates in various sections of the forest. The aboveground plant residues were divided into fractions of fresh litterfall of oak leaves, old leaf litter, and twigs.

In localities with high densities of leaf rollers, and in control areas (no leaf rollers), observations were carried out of temperature and humidity at the height of 1 m and at the surface of the soil (at a height of 5 cm). The 24-hr course of these meteorological elements was registered by automatic recorders. In addition, minimum and maximum temperatures of the surface of the soil were recorded. The illumination was measured by a light meter (Luxmeter, U-16).[1]

The abundance of leaf-eating insects was determined simultaneously with samples of the green phytomass. The larvae were divided into five size groups, corresponding approximately to the basic age groups. An average live weight was calculated for each age group of the larvae, and also for pupae and imago, by weighing of 30 or more samples. At the end of summer or fall, beginning with 1966, we estimated the abundance of eggs of oak leaf rollers on the sample branches which were cut from several (2 to 8) trees from the various layers of the crown. The indices of abundance and biomass of leaf rollers were calculated the same as biomass of foliage, proceeding from the total quantity of sample branches and annual twigs in the forests, and were conducted on an area of 1 ha.

In the laboratory we determined an index of food consumption and assimilation by average age larvae of the leaf roller. In field conditions, simultaneously with calculation of biomass of larvae, we

[1]137,000 lux = 1.98 calories · cm^{-2} · minute^{-1}.

estimated the mass of their excrement with special cages. The calculation of biomass of larvae with these two methods gave similar results. The indexes obtained allowed us to calculate utilization of the green phytomass by the larvae of the leaf roller and the quantity of excrement produced during the entire period of feeding activity.

CHARACTERISTICS OF THE DYNAMICS OF OUTBREAKS
AND PECULIARITIES OF THEIR DISTRIBUTION

Among the stages of development of the leaf roller the most critical is the larval stage since the larvae are the most sensitive to external influences. Larval development of the oak leaf roller continues for 2-3 weeks and in the Kursk region usually finishing in May. For this reason, in order to characterize the dynamics of outbreaks of the leaf roller, we give for each year hydrothermic conditions during this month.

1963. The beginning of the outbreak took place in a hot and dry spring. Average temperature for May was 4.3 degrees higher, and precipitation was 74% (39 mm) lower than the multi-year average (Fig. 1). Localities of high density of leaf rollers occupied the larger part of the oak forests of the reserve. Defoliation of the oak crowns and numbers of larvae were average. Oak groves of ravines were free of outbreaks. Growth of larvae finished toward the middle of May, and already on the 17th of May the first pupae appeared (personal communication, V. I. Eliseeva). Mass hatching took place in the beginning of the third 10-day period of May. The mass flight of imagos was observed in the first 10-day period of June.

1964. The boundaries of the outbreak areas were completely formed. Temperature in the spring was 1.5 degrees lower than the multi-year average. Humidity conditions were close to average. However, more than half the precipitation had fallen in the first 10-day period of May, before the beginning of the larval hatch, which was observed in the middle of the month. During the time of larvae development there was good weather with brief periods of rains. These conditions favored a rapid growth of larvae, a widening of the area of outbreak and significant defoliation to the crowns of the trees. The larvae in the beginning ate the leaves on the upper branches, and then migrated into the lower parts of the crowns. In the Dubroshina lands more than 90% of the trees were completely devoid of foliage, regardless of the relatively low abundance of larvae. In the watershed oak forests of Soloviatnik complete defoliation was observed in 60% of the trees. Forest ravines had little defoliation of the crowns, and the abundance of leaf-eating insects in them was very low. At the end of the first 10-day period of June on the watershed mass hatching of the leaf roller began, and approximately 10 days later the first imagos appeared. Intensive second growth of leaves coincided with the appearance of the imagos.

1965. The entire area of outbreak divided into sections with various degrees of defoliation. The weather in May was characterized by low temperature (2° lower than the multi-year average) and by a small (29 mm) quantity of precipitation (lower by 45% than the norm). Particularly cool was the first 10-day period of the month (7°C). Precipitation was divided unequally among 10-day

periods: the first and the third 10-day periods were dry (6-7 mm),
but in the second 10 days there was more than 15 mm of precipitation.
      Hatching of the larvae on the watershed began the 11th or 12th
of May. At this time the buds of the oak had swelled, but had not
yet opened. The larvae could not penetrate them and died. Only
several larvae gnawed openings in the buds and fed upon them. There
was observed a migration of larvae of the first stage to the lower
branches, however there the buds were still more dense. Rapid growth
of leaves in the watershed oak forest took place at the end of the
second 10 day period in May. Hatching of the larvae of the leaf
roller continued for more than a week, and for this reason many of
them were able to feed in the open buds. As a consequence of the
prolonged period of unfolding of the leaves and failure of the
hatching time to coincide with opening of the buds, defoliation in
the watershed was small. In many of the trees defoliation was
lacking. Fast growth of foliage was facilitated by favorable conditions of humidity in June.
      During the first two 10 day periods more than 70 mm of pre-
cipitation fell. Significant defoliation of the crowns was observed
only on the forest margin, where the larval hatch and the opening of
the buds occurred in a shorter time span and was relatively
synchronous.
      In the forest ravine, the larvae also appeared earlier than the
swelling and opening of the buds (May 13). On the 17th of May there
was a strong frost; minimum temperature in the ravine forest were
-5°C. The frost destroyed all the foliage of the trees growing in
the lower part of the ravines, and in the middle only part of the
foliage was preserved on the upper branches. All larvae living on
shoots destroyed by frost perished from hunger, since second growth
began a week after the frost. The cold itself, apparently, did not
affect the larvae: live larvae were observed in the dead buds
several days after the frost.
      Mass pupation of the leaf roller took place on the 4th and 5th
of June, and on the 25th of June the flight of the imagos began.
Intensive growth of new foliage on defoliated trees began soon after
pupation, and by the first half of July the area of the leaf surface
in the forest with high density and in the undamaged trees equalized.
      1966. In the hot and moderately hot weather there occurred an
intensive development of high leaf roller density. The temperature
in May was 2°C higher than the multi-yearly average, and precipitation corresponded to the normal (53 mm). High temperature
(12°C) and the absence of rain in the last 10 day period of this
month made conditions favorable for massive and simultaneous
hatching of the larvae, which occurred at the end of April.
      Death of larvae was small: about 30% of all first age larvae
pupated. However, despite the favorable conditions for larval
growth, defoliation in the outbreak locality was noticeably smaller
than in 1964 because of the small number of larvae. Full defoliation in the land of Dubroshina was noted only in 70% of the trees,
· and in the land of Soloviatnik in 30 to 40%. Hatching of the larvae
was somewhat late in comparison with the opening of the buds. This
disparity increased on the average, particularly in the lower layers
of the crowns. The larvae were feeding on the opening foliage and
could not cause important harm. Strong defoliation was noted only
in the upper layer. The branches of the middle layer were little

defoliated, and of the lower layer very weakly.[2] Considering the
relationship of branches in the various layers of the crown, the
general degree of defoliation in the outbreak localities may be
considered average.

Vertical migration of the larvae, caused by insufficient food,
was observed only in the larvae of the older ages on separate parts
of the outbreak areas of the watershed. Mass pupation in watershed
oak forest began on May 20th, and soon thereafter in the damaged
trees began a second growth of vegetation. At the end of May there
occurred a mass flight of imagos.

In the ravine oak forest hatching of the larvae was noted on
the 10th of May and coincided with bud opening. However, a strong
frost on the 19th of May destroyed young shoots on the lower and
middle branches. Larvae of the leaf roller survived only in the
upper layer, which suffered little from the frost.

1967. The entire outbreak occupied all the watershed oak
forests of the reserve. Weather in May was favorable for growth of
the leaf roller. Temperature was 3°C higher than the average.
High temperatures continued during the entire month. A monthly
quantity of precipitation was 26% (by 14 mm) lower than normal. All
of April and the first 10 day period of May was sunny, almost without
rain. Daily maximum temperatures in May reached 30°C.

Hatching of the larvae of the leaf roller on the watershed
occurred in the beginning of May and coincided with opening of the
oak buds. In the second 10 day period of May, following destruction
of the shoots on the upper layers, there was observed a migration of
larvae of the middle age group to the lower layers of the crown.
Death of larvae was relatively small: pupae were only 20% of all
larvae hatched.

In watershed oak forests they damaged 90% of the trees, in 80%
there was complete defoliation of the entire crown. On the 15th of
May second growth of vegetation began on the upper branches, abandoned by the larvae, and after the 20th of May, during pupation of
the leaf roller, new shoots began on branches of both the middle and
lower layers.

Development of buds and the hatching of larvae in the ravine
oak forests took place only 2-3 days later than in the watershed
area. However, the quantity of larvae was insufficient for
noticeable harm to the leaves. An average degree of defoliation was
observed in approximately 50% of the trees and then only in the
upper layers of the crown. Development of the leaf roller in
ravines was very successful. After the 20th of June imagos approached
the egg laying stage.

In the Dubroshina mass appearance of imagos began on the 2nd of
June. Male imagos turned out to be twice as abundant as females.
During the night of the 9th of June a mass departure of imagos
beyond the boundaries of the watershed oak forests was observed.
Accumulations of moths were seen near electric lights at distances
of more than 1 km from the Reserve. The relationship of sexes in
these accumulations was 11:1 in favor of males.

[2]The proposed evaluation of the degree of defoliation was based on
the following indexes: very strong damage--more than 70% of the
shoots defoliated, strong damage--50% to 70%, average damage 30% to
50%, weak damage 10% to 30%, and very weak damage less than 10% of
the shoots.

1968. The outbreak areas as before occupied all the watershed oak groves. During the last 10 day period of April and in May the weather was warm and moderately rainy. The temperature in May was 0.7°C higher, and precipitation 17% lower than normal (44 mm). Hatching of the larvae of the leaf roller in watersheds began on the 26th of April and preceded development of the buds by 2 or 3 days. However, this did not show a noticeable impact on development of the larvae. About 20% of all larvae reached the pupal stage. Vertical migration of the larvae was not observed. In watershed oak forests about 60% of the trees had their crowns defoliated completely. In the remaining trees shoots were destroyed only in the upper parts of the crown, and in the middle and lower branches little damage was noted. For watersheds as a whole defoliation can be characterized as moderately strong. At the end of May began massive pupation began, and on the 9th of June the first imagos appeared.

Special high density areas occurred in forest ravines. The spread of imagos, observed in 1967, caused a significant infestation of the ravines by the egg laying of the leaf rollers. Warm weather, the lack of spring frost, and also coincidence of the times of hatching of larvae and the beginning of oak vegetation growth facil- itated successful development of leaf rollers in ravines. In trees growing in the middle part of the ravine slopes, the upper branches were defoliated to some extent, on the branches of the middle layer only the upper shoots were consumed (weak damage), and in the lower branches the damage was almost lacking.

1969. In May unusually cool weather with short periods of rain was observed; the monthly quantity of precipitation was normal. The temperature was 0.9°C lower than the normal. Hatching of the larvae began in the second 10 day period of May and preceded the opening of oak leaves, which in combination with cool and wet weather caused a significant lowering of the numbers of leaf rollers: less than 10% of the hatched larvae pupated. The outbreak area in the watershed was divided into parts showing various degrees of damage. More than half of all the trees showed no visible damage of the shoots, and in the others damage was primarily in the upper branches. Very little damage was noted in Soloviatnik and the Tolsti Log gorge. Pupation of the larvae in watershed forests began on the 7th of June.

1970. The temperature in May was 0.4°C higher, and the quan- tity of precipitation was 49% lower than normal (27 mm). The first 10 day period of May was particularly dry and hot (17°C). At this time hatching of larvae began, which coincided with the stage of bud opening. All of this facilitated successful growth of the larvae. Mortality of leaf rollers during the period of hatching until the end of pupation did not exceed 70%.[3] However, general damage to the foliage in Reserve oak forests was insignificant because of the low numbers of larvae. The data on distribution of damage in the layers of the crown in various forest habitats and the results of the counts for trees with various degrees of damage are given in Tables 7 and 8.

[3]Abundance of pupae of the leaf roller was calculated according to the data of the entomologist of the Reserve, Y. S. Tseytgamel. Usually from the larvae of the first age until the pupae only 2% to 15% of all individuals survive (Vainschtein 1950, Steger 1960).

Table 7.   Damage of various layers of the crown of oaks in 1970.

Forest type, layer	Degree of damage (%)				
	Strong	Average	Weak	Very weak	None
Watershed oak forest					
Dubroshina					
Upper	33	37	25	4	1
Middle	5	20	57	12	6
Lower	--	3	20	40	37
Kazatskaya					
Upper	7	35	28	25	5
Middle	--	9	23	57	11
Lower	--	--	5	17	78
Ravine					
Tolsti Log					
Upper	3	15	27	24	31
Middle	--	5	21	27	47
Lower	--	--	7	18	75

Table 8. Damage of trees in various forests in 1970.

| Forest | Degree of damage (%) | | | | |
	Strong	Average	Weak	Very weak	None
Watershed					
Dubroshina	8	28	50	13	1
Kazatskaya	--	9	40	43	8
Ravine					
Tolsti Log	--	5	23	41	31

Observations of the dynamics of numbers of leaf rollers during the period of outbreak allows us to draw some conclusions regarding the influence of various factors on development of this species. A. I. Vorontsov (1963), based on the results of laboratory experiments by Schütte (1957), came to the conclusion that the most important conditions for successful outbreak of the oak leaf roller is the synchronous development of buds and hatching of the larvae. Schütte showed that the largest quantity (above 70%) of larvae of the first age group will survive if they fall on buds of the oak during the short period when the latter are beginning to open. If the larvae fall on closed buds or on developing foliage, then the survival rate is sharply decreased. Schütte thought also that this coincidence of open buds and hatching of larvae cannot be considered the only condition of successful development for leaf rollers. Our observations did not reveal a close tie between the outbreak and synchrony of hatching of larvae of the leaf roller and the open bud stage (Table 9).

Of great significance for successful outbreak are weather conditions in the period of larvae growth. It was shown above that the outbreaks occurred in the years of increased dryness and higher temperature in May (Fig. 1). Development of the leaf roller was most effective in 1966, 1967, 1968, and 1970, when in the initial period of larval growth there was dry and warm weather. In 1966 and 1968 the appearance of larvae did not coincide with the stage of open buds, but their biomass reached high levels during the entire outbreak (120-140 kg/ha live weight). Mortality of leaf rollers in the period from hatching to pupal stage in 1966 and 1968 was 62 to 82%.[4]

[4]The proportion of larvae which perished from parasitic insects usually was less than 1%. This index, just as the destruction of larvae of the leaf roller by birds, changes slightly in various years of outbreak. The differences in the mortality in the years is connected with the indirect impact of weather conditions and fungus disease of larvae, observed during humid years.

Table 9. Indices of effectiveness of oak leaf roller development in lands of Dubroshina.

Year	Number of eggs and larvae at moment of hatching, millions of specimens per ha	Number of pupae, millions of specimens per ha	Mortality of larvae (%)	Maximum biomass kg/ha (live weight)	Coincidence of hatching of larva with the open bud stage	Deviation of meteorological elements during May from long term average (%)	
						Temperature	Precipitation
1964	9.0 [a/]	1.7	82	87	coincides	-10	-13
1965	8.4 [a/]	1.1	87	96	early	-15	-45
1966	8.6 [a/]	3.0	65	142	late	+15	0
1967	14.4 [b/]	3.4	76	89	coincides	+23	-30
1968	12.4 [b/]	2.5	80	126	early	+5	-17
1969	11.2 [b/]	0.7	94	22	early	-7	0
1970	4.2 [b/]	1.6	62	65	coincides	+3	-48

[a/] Number of larva (1964-1966)

[b/] Number of eggs (1967-1970).

In 1965 and 1969, when a cold period began during the time of larval hatching, accompanied by rain, mortality of larvae rose to 87% to 94%.

The above allows us to hypothesize that successful development of the oak leaf roller is determined chiefly by weather conditions during the period of larval hatching and to a lesser degree depends on the close phenological coupling of the appearance of larvae and open bud stage in the oak. The lack of the latter only increases the impact of unfavorable weather, as in 1965 and 1969.

The main outbreak locality of the oak leaf roller with high numbers in all growth stages and with maximum damage to the crowns was confined to watershed oak forests. The number of leaf rollers in the various sections was dissimilar, the degree of damage to foliage also varied correspondingly.

The oak leaf roller, as already noted, is highly dependent upon temperature and humidity, and for this reason its larval development is more successful in open warm and dry oak forests. The same opinion is held by B. A. Winestein (1949), who studied the peculiarity of distribution of leaf-eating insects in the oak forests of the south Ukraine.

In the Central Chernozem Reserve the outbreak areas of leaf rollers were most steady in the region of Dubroshina in Petrin forest and the forest of Dedov Vesely on the Streletskaya section, where the forests were open (closure 50-70%).

In oak forests with a higher closure the abundance of leaf rollers and the degree of defoliation of oaks was usually signif- icantly lower, and the outbreak areas themselves differed by having non-homogeneous structure. Thus, in Soloviatnik (80% closure of forest) during the years of outbreak damage to the leaves was weak as a rule, and the indices of maximum number and biomass of leaf rollers were 2-4 times lower than in Dubroshina. Completely de- foliated trees were observed primarily on more open locations.

The dissimilar appearance of outbreak areas and also the low number of leaf rollers in Soloviatnik are not only due to less favorable microclimatic conditions in closed forests. The oak forests in this region are of seed origin; they are more resistant to phytophagous animals than shoot forests (Vorontzov 1963). Besides this, the watershed oak forests of Soloviatnik have a more compli- cated structure, and for this reason a greater variety of predators occur which limit the number of leaf rollers. The abundance in Soloviatnik of nesting insectivorous birds was twice as large as in Dubroshina (personal communication of V. I. Eliseeva). Here also large ant hills of the *Formica* type are common. In the Voronez Reserve one colony *F. polyctena* Forst bring in a day about 6000 larvae and pupae of the oak leaf roller (Smirnov 1966). In Dubroshina ant hills of *Formica* are found only locally, and the small hills of the ants *Lasius niger* are widespread. They feed on the oak, pri- marily through sugary secretions of the dendrophilic aphids.

A special place in watershed oak forests is occupied by young plantings (5-10 years), and by oak undergrowth. Growth of foliage in young oak trees with a height up to 3 m begins one to two weeks later than in the middle-aged trees. For this reason the young plantings and undergrowth usually are not damaged by the oak leaf roller, hatching of which coincides with the beginning of foliation of adult trees. Individual damage is observed only in those years when the larvae, having completely destroyed the foliage on the

large trees, move down or fall on the undergrowth. However at this
time the foliage on the young oak trees is already well developed,
and the larvae cannot feed normally on them.

Special outbreak centers of the leaf roller occur in forest
ravines. Ravine oak forests suffer insignificant damage to the
crowns and usually show only locally high density and biomass of
leaf-eating insects. A similar picture was observed in recent years
in the entire range of the oak leaf roller to the south of Moscow.[5]
In forest ravines of the Central Chernozem Reserve there never
occurred complete zoogenic defoliation and only in certain years
with hot and dry weather in May and June did some of the trees have
defoliated branches of the upper layer. Abundance of the leaf
roller in ravine oak forests is significantly less than abundance in
watershed oak groves: the abundance of eggs in the forest ravines
was on the average about 5 times less, and the difference in maximum
biomass of larvae was 35 times less.

During comparison of dynamics of various growth stages of the
leaf roller on watersheds and in ravines the following picture is
revealed. In years with cool and relatively rainy weather during
spring and summer (1969), with low abundance of leaf rollers, the
seasonal dynamics of abundance in both biotopes is similar. In dry
and hot years (1970) the biotopic differences in abundance of leaf
rollers is approximately the same as in the cool and wet years
(Table 10).

The data in Table 10 show that a constant difference between
watershed and ravines is evident for the entire yearly cycle of
development of the leaf roller. Some decrease in the difference in
quantity of imagos is explained by their active migration before
laying of the eggs.

However, a completely different situation results in years when
spring frost occurs (1964, 1965, 1966). In those years the maximum
biomass of the leaf roller in ravines is 9-35 times less than in the
watershed areas, since spring cold spells connected with periods of
an anticyclonic regime always have stronger influence in ravines
where cold air flows nightly from the watersheds. Stratification
facilitates the preservation "of lakes of cold air" in the morning
hours (Geiger 1960). Nightly minimum temperatures damage the young
leaves of the oak, and as a result the larvae starve and a significant part of the population perishes.

There can be an impact of winter frost on the abundance of the
oak leaf roller on ravine forests. There are indications that
temperatures lower than a -30°C continuing for several days are
ruinous for the egg-carrying leaf roller (Belgovski 1959, Egorov,
Rubtsova and Solozenikina 1961). Such low temperatures were not
observed during the period of outbreak of leaf rollers in the Kursk
oak forests. However, negative gradients of temperature between the
watersheds and ravines were preserved on clear days and in the
beginning of spring, when development of eggs had already begun and
their resistance to low temperatures decreased. Thus on the 19th of
March 1965, when the weather at night was cloudy, with fog and a
slight wind, temperature on the watershed and in the ravines was
similar (-4.5°C), and on the 21st of March when the night was clear

[5]High abundance in watershed forest and a small number in ravine
habitat are characteristic for the many species of leaf-eating insects.

Table 10.   Dynamics of abundance of different age groups of leaf rollers
            (yearly averages).

Index	Oak forest		Difference between watershed and ravine, number of times
	Watershed	Ravine	
1968			
Number of egg clusters, millions/ha (average 2 eggs/cluster	5.7	1.6	3.6
1969			
Maximum biomass of larvae, kg/ha (live weight)	22.0	6.0	3.7
Abundance of imagos (number/sample branch)	9.0	5.0	1.8
Number of egg clusters, millions/ha	2.6	0.7	3.7
1970			
Maximum biomass of larva, kg/ha (live weight)	65.0	21.0	3.1
Number of egg clusters, millions/ha	7.9	2.4	3.3

with no wind, the temperature on the watershed raised to -2°C but in
the ravines lowered to -5.5°C. In years without an early spring
frost the difference in abundance of leaf rollers in the ravines and
on the watersheds was obviously determined by other factors.

Microclimatic observations conducted in the summer of 1967 did
not reveal significant differences in the average monthly and 10-
day period of temperature and humidity, there was no significant
difference between the 24 hour average. But the 24 hour course of
temperature and humidity was of slightly different character in the
ravines than in the watersheds (Table 11).

From Table 11 it follows that the essential difference is only
in duration of high nightly humidity, which in the ravines was
longer by 1.5 to 3.5 hours than in the watersheds. The data allow
us to hypothesize that one of the factors limiting development of
the oak leaf roller in ravines is the peculiar regime of humidity,
since the leaf rollers possess a high sensitivity to conditions of
humidity.

INFLUENCE OF OUTBREAK OF INSECTS ON FOREST PRODUCTION

One may consider the quantity of the annual primary production
as an indicator of ecosystem function. The participation of animals
in biogeocoenotic processes is determined by their impact on the
productivity of phytomass. The oak leaf roller, appearing as a
specialized phytophage-consumer of the foliage of oak[6] shows direct

[6] In the case of a shortage of oak foliage--the larvae of the leaf
    roller can feed on leaves of some other woody and shrub species
    in addition, and also on plants of the grassy layer. However, as

Table 11. Average daily and nightly temperature and humidity in the summer
           of 1967 (at a height of 1 m).

Index and location	20-25 June	6-11 July	20-25 July	3-8 August	Average (June-August)
Temperature in the day (°C)[a/]					
Watershed	18.2	20.4	22.0	20.7	20.3
Bottom of ravine	19.6	22.0	22.9	23.4	21.9
Temperature in the night (°C)[b/]					
Watershed	12.6	13.9	14.8	13.6	13.7
Bottom of ravine	12.1	12.9	11.6	12.8	12.2
Relative humidity in the day (%)[a/]					
Watershed	77.8	57.2	64.4	54.6	63.5
Bottom of ravine	69.6	45.2	51.8	50.2	54.4
Relative humidity at night (%)[b/]					
Watershed	93.2	83.4	84.8	91.4	89.4
Bottom of ravine	97.6	91.2	98.2	98.6	96.4
Difference between ravine and watershed in duration of the time period with increased humidity, number of hours	1.5	3.0	3.5	3.0	

[a/] 1000 to 1800 hr

[b/] 2200 to 0600 hr

impact on photosynthetic processes and also on generative organs.
The remaining components of forest phytocoeosis show mainly indirect
influence of the leaf roller.

Study of the biogeocoenotic role of the oak leaf roller during
the period of outbreak was conducted primarily in watershed oak
forests (land of Dubroshina). A high number of leaf rollers in this
forest, and also the presence of separate forest localities and
separate trees which were not damaged by the leaf roller during the
years of outbreak and could therefore serve as a controls, facilitated the problem.

Influence on the Production of Foliage. Appearance of larvae
of the oak leaf roller during years of outbreak takes place in
watershed oak forests between the end of April and the middle of May
as the leaf buds of oak trees begin to open. At this time the sum

a result of such forced eating the reproductive capability of an
imago leaf roller decreases sharply.

of mean 24 hour temperatures reaches 200°C. The hatched larvae
penetrate the separated glumes into the buds, move to the bases (the
point of growth) and begin to feed.

Usually the oak buds develop very rapidly (Fig. 2). Within a
month after the beginning of leaf growth on damaged trees, the

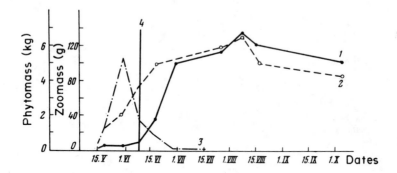

Figure 2
Dynamics of growth of leaf biomass of oak and biomass of oak leaf
roller (average values per tree, 1964). 1-leaf biomass damaged
trees (dry weight); 2-leaf biomass undamaged trees, (dry weight); 3-
biomass of leafroller (live weight); 4-beginning of pupation.

shoots almost develop their complete leaf surface. Further increase
of weight is primarily due to thickening of the leaves. Development
of young shoots is strongly retarded by larval damage to the growth
centers.

Characteristically, limited growth of oak leaves at the beginning of leaf development is due chiefly to indirect impact of the
larvae. Direct consumption of the foliage production is relatively
small. Thus, on 19 May 1964 the biomass of larvae (2nd-3rd instar)
in watershed oak forest was 25 g per tree. During the period of
hatching until 19 May the larvae consumed 65 g of fresh foliage.
On the average 900 g of leaves remained on the trees, while the
biomass of leaves on the undamaged trees averaged 5600 g. Consequently the decrease of growth increment of shoots in damaged trees
due to larvae of the leaf roller was 84% (production only 16% of
control). Of the total loss up to 19 May, only 1.1% of the leaf
production was consumed. During the entire period of larval development (up to 9 June) the oak leaf rollers consumed 1.5 kg of
phytomass. Together with net growth this composed 2.9 kg of raw
material. The average growth of foliage on the control trees at the
beginning of pupation was 11 kg. Thus, during the entire feeding
period the larvae of the leaf roller lowered the growth of leaves by
74% (production 26% of control), but they consumed only 13% of the
leaf production.

Consequently, a significant decrease in production of leaves,
which can be observed during the period of larval development in the
centers of outbreak, is due not to the quantity of foliage consumed,
but to mechanical disturbance of points of growth in developing
organs.

Reduction of the rate of growth of foliage in damaged trees is very great. The relationship of maximum biomass of leaf rollers to the quantity of leaf biomass at the time of maximum leaf roller biomass can serve as an indicator of impact of the oak leaf roller on the growth of oak leaves. This relationship, often called the index of influence of animals on the food base, was different in various years of outbreak.

The most intensive interaction between plants and the leaf rollers appeared during years with hot and dry weather in the spring and summer season. Such weather facilitates a high intensity of feeding by larvae of the leaf roller and, in addition, slows the growth of shoots. Thus, in 1964 and 1966-1968 production of leaves was 10-20 times higher than the maximum zoomass (usually it is 100-300 times higher). A peculiar situation with resulting strong damage of watershed oak forests was observed in 1964, when after the second larval molt occurred mass migration to branches of the lower layer, resulting in defoliation of the entire crown. This year was characterized by the greatest index of influence. The relationship between maximum zoomass and the biomass of leaves was 1:12. In the remaining years with hydrothermic conditions favorable for the development of the leaf roller (1966 through 1968) the differences of zoomass and phytomass were somewhat larger, vertical migrations of larvae were not so significant, and the damage to leaves was average or great. During years with a cold and wet spring (1965, 1969) there was minimum influence and very weak damage to the crowns of oaks. Vertical migration in these years was not characteristic; the larvae ate the shoots primarily only in the upper parts of the trees (Table 12).

Degree of defoliation of oak crowns in outbreak localities depends also on the abundance of larvae. However, the connection between degree of defoliation and this index is not linear and essentially less important than the weather conditions. In fact, different degrees of damage can be observed in years with similar biomass of leaf rollers. Thus, in 1965 and 1967 differences in zoomass were almost non-existent, but damage to the crowns differed by 2 units (on a scale of 6 units, see footnote p. 25).

The upper layer of the oak crowns was always damaged to the greatest degree. Here conditions for the development of all age stages of the oak leaf roller were most favorable: maximum heat and illumination, minimum humidity (especially during the period of embryonic and larval development), high content of carbohydrates and nutrients in the leaves. For this reason in the upper half of the crown there is an abundance of egg clusters and larvae of the youngest ages, and also maximum survival. Consumption of shoots of the middle layer of the crown is characterized by medium damage. As a rule, each successive layer, beginning from the upper, is damaged 1 unit less.

Due to damage caused by the oak leaf roller, during 3-4 weeks of larval development there is little increase of area of assimilation surface in the outbreak localities. Even during years with low degree of defoliation the increase of leaf area in the outbreak localities was significantly less than the increase of leaf area on the undamaged localities. By the time of maximum zoomass the total area of leaves in trees damaged by the leaf rollers was more than 30 times less than in the control localities, and the maximum difference reached 120 times.

Table 12. Characteristics of watershed outbreak areas (average index per tree).

Year	Maximum zoomass, (g)[a]	Biomass of leaves, (g)[a]	Relationship of zoomass and phytomass	Degree of defoliation[b]
1964	32	400	1:12	Very strong
1965	36	2700	1:73	Weak
1966	54	900	1:16	Average
1967	33	720	1:22	Strong
1968	48	900	1:19	Strong
1969	10	3200	1:320	Weak
1970	23	No data	No data	Weak

[a] Air-dry weight

[b] The proposed evaluation of the degree of defoliation was based on the following indices: very strong damage (more than 70% of the shoots defoliated), strong damage (50% to 70%), average damage (30% to 50%), weak damage (10% to 30%), and very weak damage (less than 10% of the shoots).

At the same time the period of strong defoliation is relatively short; it is equal to the period of larval development of the oak leaf roller, which averages 25 days. Soon after the beginning of pupation, and some times a few days earlier[7] (the average time of pupation occurs at the end of May and the beginning of June in the Kursk oak forest) the second growth of damaged trees begins. A few days before this increased turgidity of shoots in the damaged trees is observed (Fig. 3). Secondary growth begins from dormant buds on the old lignified shoots and branches of the second and third order. In addition, many new buds develop on stems, the growth of which is almost unaffected by leaf rollers. For this reason, at the beginning of the second growth the stems have attained a length of 8-10 cm (average 2-4 cm) and have up to 6-10 new buds each. These buds soon open and provide the beginning of new shoots. The growth of buds, consumed during the first growth, usually renew themselves after pupation of the leaf roller.

For this reason the number of new buds at the beginning of secondary growth seems greater than at the beginning of first

[7] The larvae of the oak leaf roller finish feeding a few days before pupation.

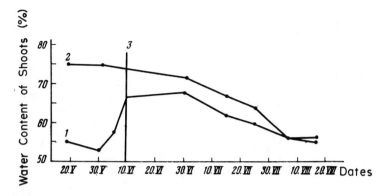

Figure 3
Dynamics of water content of young shoots (average values, 1964).
1-damaged trees; 2-undamaged trees; 3-beginning of pupation.

growth. This can be considered a special adaptation to recovery
from zoogenic defoliation.

Second growth begins in the upper layer, since there pupation
occurs several days earlier, and gradually moves lower enveloping the
entire crown (Table 13).

Table 13. Dynamics of growth of shoots in different layers
           of the crown in damaged trees in watershed oak
           forest in 1964 (air-dry weight of 100 shoots (g)).

Layer	May		June			July	August		October
	19	30	9	18	30	25	7	17	4
Upper	8	4	12	53	145	145	190	180	150
Middle	10	13	7	45	134	163	170	200	140
Lower	22	31	27	38	130	200	200	170	130

Growth of secondary foliage occurs very quickly. Due to the
high intensity of physiological processes, characteristic for young
unthickened shoots, the difference between biomass of leaves and the
area of photosynthetic surface in damaged and control trees quickly
disappeared (Fig. 4, see also Fig. 2). The rate of the average
daily increase of biomass and area of leaves can serve as an index
of the rate of growth of shoots. During 2 weeks after the beginning
of the secondary growth in outbreak localities this value was 0.2 kg
and 4 m^2, and on the control localities 0.1 kg and 1.2 m^2, per
tree. For comparison, the index of growth of control trees at the
beginning of leaf growth will be equal to 0.14 kg and 1.8 m^2 per
tree, which corresponds to 1.4 and 2 times lower than in the damaged
trees at the beginning of the second growth.

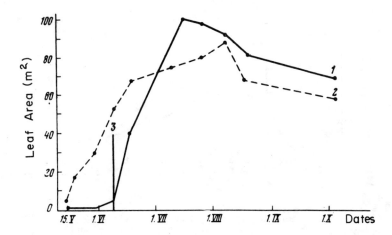

Figure 4
Dynamics of leaf area index of oaks (average values per tree, 1964).
Explanations of 1-3, see Figure 3.

As a result, at the beginning of July biomass of foliage and
the index of leaf area in the damaged and control trees is equal,
insuring almost complete compensation for zoogenic disturbance.   In
autumn both in the outbreak localities and in the control sections
production of leaf biomass of oak is approximately the same.   Thus,
in 1964 the maximum biomass of foliage in the outbreak localities
in August was about 10% greater than in the control trees, and in
1967 and 1970 it was 20% and 11% less, respectively.   These data
lead us to believe that on the average during the outbreak production of leaves was approximately 10% lower in the outbreak localities
than on the control sections.

The seasonal dynamics of the leaf area index (Fig. 4) shows
that in the damaged trees the total area of leaf surface can noticeably
exceed the index in the control oaks.   This is explained by the
lesser thickness of the secondary foliage.   Thus, on 17 June 1964,
average weight of 1 cm^2 done of leaf from undamaged trees was 7.6
mg, and after second growth of damaged oaks it was 4.2 mg.   This
difference remained until the end of July.   Future growth of young
leaves was chiefly by changing thickness, and for this reason at
about the end of July the difference in the weight per unit leaf
surface in the damaged and undamaged trees disappeared.

Total area of the photosynthetic leaf biomass during the entire
vegetative season in these groups of trees was practically the same.
Thus, from 15 May through 4 October 1964 the sum of the areas of
leaves during each day on the control section was equal to 8660 m^2
for one tree, and in the outbreak localities 8770 m^2.   Consequently,
despite the relatively continuous defoliation of the upper canopy of
the forest in the outbreak localities, second growth completely
compensated for the loss of leaf area.

Also a result of second growth is an increase in the duration of the vegetation period of oaks in the outbreak localities, which lengthens the duration of photosynthetic activity. The leaf fall in autumn in damaged trees occurs 10 to 14 days later than in the control trees. Chemical analysis of fresh oak leaves collected in the middle of October, 1964, revealed that the nitrogen content in second growth was 1.3 times greater and potassium 1.8 times higher than in the leaves of undamaged oaks. This suggests that translocation of nutrients from the leaves occurs later in outbreak localities due to a longer period of photosynthesis.

Annual production of leaf biomass in the outbreak localities during the period of outbreak of leaf rollers is given in Table 14. Determination of net production of leaves was from records of their biomass on sample branches taken from various layers of the crown before the period of falling of leaves. A separate estimate of net production was taken from litter fall of oak leaves (the average on 10-16 areas with a size of 1/16 m^2). In the last instance a correction was made for the portion of winter leaves and the unrecorded summer litter fall; the mass of these fractions on the average compose, according to the data of A. M. Krasnitsky (1967), 10% of the total litterfall. The portion of total production of leaves used by the larvae of the leaf roller is calculated, proceeding from

Table 14. Consumption of annual foliage production by larvae of oak leaf roller.

Year	Production of oak leaves (g/m^2) (air-dry weight)			Portion of total production of leaves consumed by larvae of leafroller (%)
	Net production	Consumption by larvae	Total production	
1963	324[a]	?	?	?
1964	307[a]	48	355	13
1965	300	28	328	8
1966	285	60	345	17
1967	254	40	294	14
1968	233	80	313	22
1969	199	10	209	5
1970	162	25	187	13
Average	258	41	290	13

[a] According to data of A. M. Krasnitsky (1967).

the dynamics of zoomass during each day of larval development and the coefficient of use of the leaf biomass per unit of weight of body.

As seen from Table 14, during the outbreak there was a sequential decrease in the primary production of leaves. The 1970 leaf growth, in comparison with 1963, decreased by half. Before the outbreak the watershed oak forest annually produced about 350 g/m^2 (Gertsik 1959). Consequently, during the period of outbreak the average net production of leaves of the upper layer decreased 26%. From the table it follows that replacement of leaves consumed by the larvae of the leaf roller composed on the average 13%. This value is close to the quantity of foliage consumed by other phytophagous organisms (Shvartz 1967).

Since the annual increment of green biomass of oaks on the control sections exceeds net production in the outbreak localities by 10% on the average, then it averages 284 g/m^2. Total production of leaves in the outbreak centers is on the average 290 g/m^2. Consequently during the period of outbreak of leaf rollers damaged and undamaged sections of the watershed oak forests produce approximately the same biomass of leaves.

Impact on the Growth of Branches. The development of stems, corresponding to the annual growth of trees in height, is realized primarily at the expense of reserve mobile materials, carried from previous years (Kramer and Kozlovski 1963). In deciduous species accumulation of mobile materials occurs at the end of summer (Polyakova 1954). Therefore, consumption of leaves of oak during the spring period apparently should not be accompanied by significant reduction of the yearly growth of stems. It is known that outbreak of mass reproduction of many types of leaf-eating insects does not result in limited growth of trees in height. Usually the change of growth in height due to various external factors (in particular weather, and by man) is manifested to a much smaller degree than the change of growth in thickness (Vorontsov, Golosova and Mozolevskaya 1966).

In the autumn of 1970 the study of the annual increment in length and weight of stems was undertaken. Essential differences in weight increment of various categories of trees in the Kursk oak forest was not observed, and total annual production was practically the same; 820 and 800 g per tree or 66 and 65 g/m^2 (air dry wt), respectively. A small different was noted only in the layer distribution of stem growth (Table 15).

In undamaged trees the length of the yearly shoots noticeably increases down the crown; on the branches of the lower layer the length is 1.5 times greater on the average than on the upper branches. In damaged trees this tendency is preserved; however, the increase of linear growth of shoots in the lower layer is less evident than in the controls.

Growth of branches by weight shows an inverse relationship; it decreases downward along the crown, corresponding to the changes of growth of leaves and main branches. More equal growth of shoots by weight and by length among various layers of the crown in undamaged trees may be explained by more uniform light penetration through the crowns of the defoliated trees, resulting in all layers of the crowns receiving similar amounts of illumination.

Table 15.   Crown layer distribution of growth increment of stems
(% of growth in the upper layer)[a].

Layer	Length		Weight	
	Control trees	Damaged trees	Control trees	Damaged trees
Upper	100	100	100	100
Middle	132	101	85	93
Lower	148	107	61	73

[a] From measurement of more than 4,000 stems.

    Influence on Growth of Trunk Wood. During studies of the
dynamics of production of forest ecosystems a basic index is the
growth increment of trunks. About half of the yearly production
of phytomass in average aged forest-steppe oak forest is in the
form of growth increment to trunks (Molchanov 1964). Growth increment of trunks occurs primarily at the expense of products of photosynthesis accumulated during the current vegetative season (Elagin
1962, Kramer and Kozlovski 1963). Partial and in some years complete
defoliation of the crowns of oaks in the centers of mass reproduction of the oak leaf roller should disturb the course of growth
processes in damaged trees, since the loss of the leaf surface
occurs in late spring when conditions of radiation and hydrothermic
regimes are favorable for intensive photosynthesis. Therefore, one
can hypothesize that the mass reproduction of the leaf roller is
accompanied by limited productivity. In Soviet literature there are
numerous examples of decreased production of oak wood in years of
outbreak of the oak leaf roller (Turchinskaya 1963, Vorontzov 1963,
Ierusalimov 1965, Mozolevskaya 1965, Vorontzov, Golosova and
Mozolevskaya 1966, and others).
    Reviews of various methods for determining zoogenic losses of
growth increment in trees are given by A. I. Vorontzov (1963) and I.
A. Turchinskaya (1963). Mostly two methods are used. One is
based on comparison of growth in damaged trees and control trees,
and the other on a comparison with the average growth of damaged
trees during the period preceding the outbreak. The latter approach
is most often used, and is based on the assumption of relatively
constant growth increment during several successive years (Vorontozov
Ierusalinov and Mazolevskaya 1967).
    In watershed oak forests of the Central Chernozem Reserve the
growth increment of damaged trees during all the years of outbreak
(with the exception of 1965) was noticeably lower than in control
trees (Table 16). The growth increment of weakly damaged trees
decreased by 8-52% and in the strongly damaged trees by 44 to 75%.

Table 16.   Growth of oak in diameter (mm at a height of 1.3 m)[a/].

Year	Control trees			Weakly damaged trees				Strongly damaged trees			
	M ± m	CV (%)	m (%)	M ± m	CV (%)	m (%)	% from control	M ± m	CV (%)	m (%)	% from control
1969	4.8 ± 0.35	19	7.3	3.7 ± 0.45	28	12.1	77	1.8 ± 0.28	26	15.5	38
1968	3.8 ± 0.17	16	4.8	3.5 ± 0.50	37	14.3	92	1.7 ± 0.32	62	18.8	47
1967	7.5 ± 0.31	11	4.1	3.6 ± 0.28	21	7.8	48	2.0 ± 0.22	37	11.0	27
1966	6.9 ± 0.29	12	4.2	3.6 ± 0.31	23	8.6	52	2.2 ± 0.18	28	8.1	32
1965	4.5 ± 0.35	21	7.8	6.2 ± 0.70	30	11.2	139	4.9 ± 0.59	39	12.0	109
1964	5.0 ± 0.45	25	9.0	4.3 ± 0.45	27	10.4	86	2.7 ± 0.26	31	9.6	54
1963	5.9 ± 0.85	40	15.7	5.2 ± 0.54	27	10.3	88	3.3 ± 0.32	33	9.7	56
Average	5.5 ± 0.40	20	7.3	4.3 ± 0.46	28	10.7	78	2.7 ± 0.31	37	11.5	49
1962	5.9 ± 0.48	21	8.1	5.7 ± 0.45	20	7.9	96	3.9 ± 0.51	43	13.1	66
1961	10.1 ± 0.94	24	9.3	7.6 ± 1.29	44	16.2	75	5.0 ± 0.53	35	10.6	49
1960	10.6 ± 1.76	37	16.6	7.0 ± 1.09	40	15.6	67	3.9 ± 0.43	31	11.0	37
1959	8.0 ± 0.68	14	8.5	6.4 ± 0.92	37	14.4	80	4.7 ± 0.37	22	7.8	59
1958	11.7 ± 0.68	16	5.8	5.9 ± 0.93	31	15.8	50	6.4 ± 0.85	39	13.3	55
1957	12.0 ± 0.85	17	7.1	6.3 ± 0.90	28	14.3	52	6.8 ± 0.97	41	14.2	57
Average	9.1 ± 0.90	21	9.9	6.5 ± 0.93	33	14.3	72	5.1 ± 0.61	35	11.9	56

[a/] M = average linear growth of trunk wood, m = error of the mean, CV = coefficient of variation.

In 1965 in the damaged trees an increase of growth in diameter was observed, apparently as a result of a special combination of weather conditions (rainy May), low number of leaf roller larvae, a peculiar phenology of their hatching, and also a positive reaction of trees under weak damage of crown by leaf rollers in the initial stage of the outbreak.

From the first method of calculation we determined that during outbreak times the average decrease of growth in weakly damaged trees was 22% and in strongly damaged trees 51%. The average index of decrease of growth for all damaged trees was equal to 37% (given here and below the differences in the indices of growth are reliable to the 0.95 level of significance). The same result is obtained by using the control as an average increment in damaged trees before the outbreak (second method); in the weakly damaged trees growth during the outbreak when compared with a period of the same duration before it decreased by 34%, and in strongly damaged trees by 47%, for an average of 40% (Table 17).

Applying both methods gives the impression that the sharp reduction of growth increment was a result of outbreak of the leaf-eating insects. However, comparison of the course of growth of average age forest during and before the period of outbreak showed

Table 17.   Dynamics of average growth in diameter of trees in a
            watershed oak forest (average index per tree at a
            height of 1.3 m).

Period	Control trees (mm)	Damaged trees[a]		
		Weak	Strong	Average
1957–1962	9.1	$\dfrac{6.5}{28}$	$\dfrac{5.1}{44}$	$\dfrac{5.8}{36}$
1963–1969	5.5	$\dfrac{4.3}{22}$	$\dfrac{2.7}{51}$	$\dfrac{3.5}{37}$
Decrease of growth for 1963–1969 (%)	39.0	34.0	47.0	40.0

[a] In the numerator--the growth in mm, in the denominator--%
decrease in relation to control trees.

that decrease of growth during the observed period was a general
tendency, inherent not only in the damaged trees but to the same
degree in undamaged trees (Fig. 5).

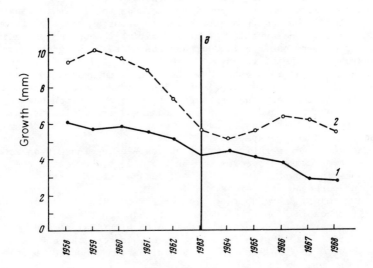

Figure 5
Dynamics of growth increment of oak trunks (diameter at a height
of 1.3 m). 1-damaged trees; 2-undamaged trees; 3-beginning of
outbreak of leaf roller. The curves are smoothed by the moving
average method.

Study of dynamics of growth of oaks on various forest sections of the Central Chernozem Reserve revealed a significant decrease during the outbreak in varied groups of trees independent of their age, degree of damage of crowns by larvae of the leaf roller and of hydrological type of forest. Thus, in seed-produced watershed oak forest of Soloviatnik with average damage during the outbreak growth decreased on the average by 45%, and in the ravine very weakly damaged oak forests decreased by 29 and 25% (respectively, on the slopes of southern and northern exposures).

It is highly characteristic that lowering of growth in the latter years was observed not only in the middle-aged forests but also in the young cultures of oak. At this time in the 19th year culture, damage on the average decreased the growth by 57% and in the 9 year old forests, which during all the years of outbreak were completely undamaged, growth was lower by 41%.

From this we conclude that the sharp decrease of growth in years of outbreak of the oak leaf roller may be explained not so much by zoogenic defoliation and losses of the second leaf growth or by the age dynamics of growth, but by other external factors.

Apparently a general lowering of productivity of tree stands was caused, in the first place, by deviation of hydrothermic indices from the norm. They created necessary prerequisites for the beginning of outbreak of the oak leaf roller and some other species of leaf-eating insects. Differentiation of forests according to trees with various degrees of damage was predetermined by the previous condition of the trees. Thus, in strongly damaged trees growth before the outbreak was lower by 44%, and in weakly damaged trees the growth was 28% lower than in the control trees.

When we used the above mentioned methods for determination of zoogenic losses of wood production in the outbreak areas of leaf-eating insects, the dynamics of growth during the period preceding the outbreak were not considered, and the decrease of growth during the years of damage of trees was described exclusively on the basis of the activity of the pest. However, the cited graphs in many investigations of multi-year fluctuations of production of trunk wood show convincingly that the decrease of growth often begins long before the outbreak and that in the undamaged trees similar changes can be observed (Turchinskaya 1963, Ierusalimov 1965, Vorontozov, Golosova and Mozolevskaya 1966).

The degree of negative impact of leaf-eating insects on wood production of damaged species can be revealed by comparing the difference in growth of undamaged and damaged trees during the period of outbreak and before.[8]

In strongly damaged trees, in comparison with the control trees, the difference in growth before the outbreak constituted 44%, and during the period of outbreak increased to 51% (indices are reliable to the 0.99 level of significance). Consequently, the decrease of growth due to leaf rollers in a given situation constitutes only

[8]In damaged and control trees the degree of decrease of growth before the outbreak is practically the same (Fig. 5). This provides the basis for believing that the changes in degree of difference between the damaged and undamaged trees during the period of outbreak may be explained by the influence of phytophagous animals.

7%. In the group of weakly damaged trees decreased growth in comparison with control trees during the period of outbreak was not
observed. The average value for all data of zoogenic decrease of
growth increment for all damaged trees was 1% (the difference is
reliable to the 0.95 level of significance).

In trees of ravine oak forests occupying more favorable habitat
because of conditions of humidity, decrease of growth increment during
the observed period was relatively small. This also indicates the
significance of climatic conditions.

For determining the dynamics of forest productivity we calculated
indices of growth on a cross sectional area using the usual forest
assessment method (Sergeev 1953). The dynamics of growth of middle-
aged trees according to this index correspond to the yearly fluctuations of radial growth, but the degree of decrease in various
categories of trees during the study period is notably less than
when determined by yearly increase of thickness of the trunks.
There is a relatively constant coefficient between the changes of
diameter and of cross sectional area which can be used for conversion of an index of radial growth to index of area growth (Vorontzov,
Golosova and Mozolevskaya 1966). Thus, the decrease of radial
growth during the outbreak in comparison to the preceding period
constituted 39% in undamaged trees, 34% in weakly damaged trees,
47% in strongly damaged trees (Table 17), and according to cross
sectional area 23, 20, and 41%, respectively (Table 18). The
decrease of growth in the cross sectional area in damaged trees due
to leaf-eating insects is somewhat greater: in strongly damaged
trees by 15% and on the average for all damaged trees by 6%.

The growth of trees in volumetric and weight units was determined in accordance with methods recommended by A. A. Molchanov and
V. V. Smirnov (1967). The average zoogenic loss of trunk wood in

Table 18. Dynamics of average growth of cross sectional area
of trees in a watershed oak forest (average index
per tree at a height of 1.3 m).

Period	Control trees (mm)	Damaged trees[a]		
		Weak	Strong	Average
1957–1962	19.5	$\frac{14.8}{24}$	$\frac{12.9}{34}$	$\frac{13.9}{29}$
1963–1969	15.0	$\frac{11.9}{21}$	$\frac{7.5}{49}$	$\frac{9.8}{35}$
Decrease of growth for 1963–1969 (%)	23.0	20.0	41.0	30.0

[a] In the numerator--the growth in mm, in the denominator--%
decrease in relation to control trees.

the centers of outbreak of the oak leaf roller constituted 0.2 kg of dry material per tree. The same value, expressed in percent of average production of wood in damaged trees during the years of outbreak, is about 6%. From this, it is possible to conclude that it is unimportant to conduct control measures for the green leaf roller in the Kursk oak forests, since losses of economically valuable production in forest ecosystems as a result of zoogenic defoliation are very small.

Another result of the outbreak of leaf-eating insects can be death of damaged forests. However, evidence of the influence of leaf-eating insects on the composition of deciduous forests is yet insufficient, and the reasons for the dying of oak, in spite of numerous special investigations, are unclear (Tarkhanova 1963, Mozolevskaya 1965).

Dying of oak forests in the forest steppe zone has been observed for the last 30 years (Skryabin 1946). The majority of investigators of this phenomenon came to the conclusion that the reason for death is the periodic drought, which strengthens the impact on the forest of such external factors as leaf-eating insects and trunk pests, fungus and vascular diseases, intensive grazing by domestic animals, unsuccessful methods of planting (Vorontzov 1963). In the Reserve forest it is apparently drought which in the majority of cases is the primary cause of death, and infestation by pests only intensifies this process.

Observations of death of oak in the Central Chernozem Reserve began in 1964. In the first years of outbreak of the oak leaf roller (1963–1965) loss of trees was not noted, only sequential dying of branches of the lower layer (Krasnitsky 1967, and our observations). In the fall of 1965 in the outbreak locations of the oak leaf roller intensive loss of branches from the trunks of the lower layer was observed in approximately 10% of the middle-aged trees. Dying of trees became noticeable in 1966. Later the quantity of dead trees gradually increased, and reached 16% in 1970. On the undamaged sections of the watershed oak forest death of the oaks in the years of outbreak was not noticed. In undamaged trees only the lower branches died.

It is highly characteristic, that in the outbreak localities of the oak leaf roller not only the weakest and most strongly damaged trees died, which had minimum growth, but also the less strongly damaged oaks which had more growth.

In watershed forests of Soloviatnik the number of dead trees of was just as large. In the fall of 1970 about 18% died completely and yet about 5% had many dead branches in all layers of the crown; for this reason, it appears these trees are also doomed to die. The dying of trees in very small numbers admittedly was also observed in the ravine oak forests. In forests of Tolsti Log in 1967 the quantity of dead oaks constituted 0.2% , and in 1970 increased to 1%. The reason for the insignificant death in the ravine oak forests may not be explained, apparently, by the low abundance of leaf rollers and weak damage of crowns[9], but by a more favorable regime of humidity in dry years for the growth of trees in ravines.

[9]In ravines complete defoliation of the crown of oaks is often observed as a result of damage of young shoots by early spring frost. However, these weather disruptions of the crown are not accompanied by notable decrease of growth.

Thus, the death of trees in average aged watershed oak forest of the Central Chernozem Reserve cannot be a consequence only of crown damage by leaf-eating insects but is chiefly the result of the same climatic changes which cause a sharp decrease of growth of forest tree communities. A similar conclusion of the impact of the oak leaf roller on the tree stand was reached by E. G. Mozolevakaya (1965) who noted that the outbreaks of this pest do not lead to a mass dying of reserve forests in central Europe, since second growth compensates for the loss of foliage.

In spite of the fairly large death in watershed oak forests of the Central Chernozem Reserve in 1970, decrease of the average growth of trunk wood during the entire outbreak when branch fall is considered constituted about 6%.

Influence on Production of Branches. Contribution of branches to the total production of wood in the oak forests of the Central Chernozem Reserve is relatively small. Main branches account for about 10% of the total production of wood.

Determination of growth of this fraction was made by cutting a section from the middle of sample branches from each layer of the crown with 5-8 replicates. The number of annual rings in all the branches examined was approximately the same (15-21), allowing them to be in one age group.

The dynamics of radial growth in branches was very similar to the growth of trunk diameter (Fig. 6). During recent years main branches in control areas showed a sharp decrease of growth just as in the leaf roller outbreak areas. This had begun long before the outbreak of the oak leaf roller.

The absolute growth of branches in undamaged trees was somewhat higher than in the damaged trees. However, this difference was not

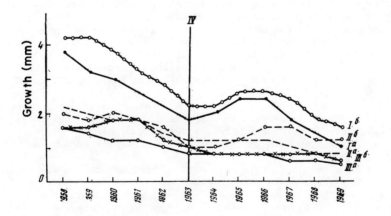

Figure 6
Dynamics of growth increment in diameter of main branches of various layers of the oak canopy. I-upper layer; II-middle layer; III-lower layer; IV-beginning of outbreak of oak leafroller; a-damaged trees, b-undamaged trees (a and b are general for layers 1 to 3). The curves are smoothed by the moving average method.

statistically significant. Only in the upper branches did it reach
a significant level (P = 0.90). Average growth of branches in the
various layers of control trees was lower by 45–50% and in the
damaged trees by 48–54%. Consequently, the growth of branches
decreased more significantly than the growth of trunks. It is
highly characteristic that decrease of growth is less in higher
layers of the crown than in lower layers. Growth of the branches of
the lower layer decreased by 50–54%, of the middle layer by 46–50%,
and of the upper layer by 45–48%. This peculiarity coincides with
the vertical changes of absolute maximum quantity of growth, being
greatest in the upper branches and significantly less in the middle
branches and still less in the lower branches (Table 19). Such
distribution of changes in amount of growth is caused by differences
in intensity of physiological processes in the various layers of the
crown of the growing trees (Kramer and Kozlovsky 1963, Molchanov
1964).

Determination of zoogenic losses of growth of branches was also
carried out by comparing the absolute value of the average linear
growth in damaged and control trees before and during the outbreak.
However, such calculation of losses due to the activity of leaf-
eating insects is highly conditional, since the growth of branches
in damaged trees before the outbreak was somewhat less, and for this
reason the increased difference during the period of outbreak may
be due to variations in the dynamics of growth in the preceding
period in addition to damage by leaf-eating insects.

The decrease of average radial growth of branches in damaged
trees, in comparison with the control trees, was 5% for the upper
layer and 7% for the middle and lower layers. It is interesting
to note that the degree of decrease of growth is inversely related
to losses of leaf biomass and leaf surface.

Regarding the dynamics of growth of sample branches in cross
section we observed that the upper branches have a larger diameter
than the branches of the middle and especially of the lower layers.
For this reason in the upper branches during the period of outbreak
there is an increase of growth of the cross sectional area, and in
the others it decreases, but not so significantly as the trunk
radius. The decrease of growth during the outbreak constitutes 3%
in the upper branhces, 12% in the middle branches, and 21% in the
lower branches (Table 20).

The total decrease of growth of main branches in damaged trees
during the time of outbreak in comparison with the control trees
was calculated according to the various layers. It was 8%, and
that was almost as much as the zoogenic decrease of production of
trunk wood (6%).[10]

Along with the changes of growth of branches during the period
of outbreak there was a peculiar modification of the structure of
the crown: There was an intensive clearing of branches from the
lower half of the crown. In damaged trees death of the branches
began in the lower layer in 1964 and was accompanied by an increase
of branches in litter (Krasnitski 1967). In 1965 about 10% of all
the trees in the outbreak areas had dead lower branches. By 1968
their dying was noted in 25 to 30% of the oaks; simultaneously there

[10]The calculated weight indices of production of branches in damaged
   and control trees in periods compared are given below.

Table 19. Dynamics of average growth in diameter of main branches in watershed oak forest[a].

Period	Upper layer		Middle layer		Lower layer	
	Growth (mm)	% of control	Growth (mm)	% of control	Growth (mm)	% of control
1955–1962	$\dfrac{3.80 \pm 0.18}{3.32 \pm 0.44}$	-13	$\dfrac{1.90 \pm 0.16}{2.00 \pm 0.24}$	+5	$\dfrac{1.60 \pm 0.16}{1.48 \pm 0.18}$	-8
1963–1970	$\dfrac{2.10 \pm 0.16}{1.72 \pm 0.14}$	-18	$\dfrac{1.02 \pm 0.14}{1.00 \pm 0.16}$	-2	$\dfrac{0.80 \pm 0.14}{0.68 \pm 0.10}$	-15
Change of growth for 1963–1967 (%)	$\dfrac{-45}{-48}$		$\dfrac{-46}{-50}$		$\dfrac{-50}{-54}$	

a/ In the numerator--growth of control trees, in the denominator--growth of damaged trees.

49

Table 20. Dynamics of average growth in cross section of main branches in watershed oak forest[a/].

Period	Upper layer		Middle layer		Lower layer	
	Growth (cm²)	% of control	Growth (cm²)	% of control	Growth (cm²)	% of control
1955–1962	$\frac{0.97 \pm 0.05}{0.65 \pm 0.08}$	−33	$\frac{0.59 + 0.05}{0.64 \pm 0.07}$	+8	$\frac{0.31 \pm 0.03}{0.35 \pm 0.04}$	+13
1963–1970	$\frac{1.22 \pm 0.09}{0.78 \pm 0.06}$	−36	$\frac{0.52 \pm 0.07}{0.50 \pm 0.08}$	−4	$\frac{0.26 \pm 0.04}{0.24 \pm 0.04}$	−8
Change of growth for 1963–1970 (%)	$\frac{+26}{+20}$		$\frac{-12}{-22}$		$\frac{-16}{-32}$	

a/ In the numerator--growth of control trees, in the denominator--growth of damaged trees.

began a dying of branches of the middle layer. At the end of 1970 the dying off reached a maximum. Healthy crowns in the centers occurred in only 5% of the trees. In 41% of the trees there were dead lower branches, in 33% both lower and middle, and in 5% the dying had touched the whole crown. Completely dying crowns were observed in 16% of the trees. In undamaged trees, just as in the oaks of the ravine forests, dying off of branches did not occur.

A reverse type of dying, namely from the lower branches to the upper layer of the crown, allow to hypothesize the possibility of a peculiar mechanism, directing this process. It is known that photosynthesis is much more intense in the upper branches. Removal of a large part of the lower branches of healthy trees does not limit total growth of trunks in diameter (Kramer and Kozlovski 1963). The lower layer of the oak crown is characterized by relatively higher respiration and lower net production (Alekeeva 1956, quoted according to Molchanov 1964). Thus, in the upper branches loss due to respiration constitutes about 30% of total photosynthesis, and in the lower 50%. Intensity of photosynthesis of the lower part of the crown is so low that it cannot compensate for losses of respiration and this leads to death (Tselniker 1967).

For this reason the loss of less productive lower branches during the period of sharp decrease of growth can apparently be looked at as an adaptation hindering the lowering of the total photosynthesis at the expense of transfer of necessary resources to the more productive upper layer.

Influence on Production of Roots. Methods of determining production of roots of woody plants are very poorly developed. Indices of root productivity were calculated from the relationship between the yearly growth of trunk wood and all of the woody roots of middle age oaks of Telterman forest (Molchanov 1964). According to the data of A. A. Molchanov the annual production of woody roots of 40 to 60 year old forests constitutes about 20% of the trunk growth. The assumption accepted by us about synchronous changes of growth of these fractions of woody phytomass is based on the data of Kamenetskaya (1970), which established the presence of a direct proportional relationship between growth of trunk wood and of roots. Calculation of production of roots of oak before and during the outbreak period of oak leaf rollers showed a 26% decrease in the control trees and 30% in the damaged trees.

We now look at the dynamics of productivity of the entire woody layer and will try to calculate the impact of leaf-eating insects on reduction of growth (Table 21). The data in Table 21 show that in the outbreak localities average production of the tree stand was lower than in the undamaged plantings before and during the outbreak. The decrease of total growth increment on these sections of oak forest, excluding dead trees, turned out be be approximately the same; on the control section during the period of outbreak production decreased by 266 g/m^2 and in the outbreak localities by 235 g. Regarding the natural death of trees the total annual production in the centers constituted 804 g/m^2; in this case the decrease of growth during the outbreak in comparison to the preceding period increased to 283 g/m^2.

The difference in the growth increment of damaged and control forests allows us to calculate the impact of leaf-eating insects on reduction of the total production of the forest community. Before

Table 21. Annual production of woody layer (g/m^2, air-dry weight).

Fraction of the woody layer	Control	Outbreak[a]
Trunk		
In the period of outbreak	486	329
Before outbreak	655	467
Roots		
In the period of outbreak	97	66
Before outbreak	131	93
Branches		
In the period of outbreak	129	92
Before outbreak	107	91
Annual shoots[b]		
In the period of outbreak[c]	349	365
Before outbreak	435	436
Total production of the tree stand		
In the period of outbreak	1061	852
Before outbreak	1327	1087
Decrease of production during period of outbreak	266	235

[a] Without natural dead fall.

[b] Foliage and stems.

[c] Foliage production is included in the green foliage eaten by the leaf roller larvae.

the outbreak the average increment of outbreak areas was lower by
17% than in the control section. During the period of outbreak this
difference increased to 19%. Consequently the decrease of growth
connected with the activity of larvae of leaf roller was 2% (about 4
g/m^2). If to the value of zoogenic decrease of growth we add losses
due to natural tree death, the difference is still not great, up to
7%. The dying of trees noticed in recent years of outbreak was
accompanied by an insignificant decrease of the average growth
increment.

Small zoogenic losses of production of the woody layers in
outbreak areas of oak leaf rollers is due to the brief period of
defoliation (3 to 4 weeks). During this time about 30 to 40% of the
annual increment of wood is formed in the oak (Ermich 1956, Elagin
1962). However, the period of defoliation coincides with the growth
of early spring wood, which occurs primarily at the expense of the
reserve biochemical materials accumulated by the plant in preceding
years (Raskatov 1948, Vikhrov 1954, Elagin 1962, Grudzinskaya 1962).
Annual fluctuations in the growth of early wood usually do not occur;
this is also indicated by the data of E. G. Mozolerskaya (1965).

Dynamics of growth increment are determined by the changes of
thickness of the zone of late (summer) wood which, under the influence of changing environmental conditions, undergoes significant
fluctuations (Grudzinskaya 1962). For this reason defoliation of
the crowns of oak in the spring period is obscured by the initiation
of late wood and apparently does not decrease the annual increment
of wood in damaged trees. Besides this, as was shown above, the
total photosynthesizing area of leaf in damaged and undamaged trees
is the same.

In damaged trees intensity of the growth processes can increase
due to increased concentration of CO_2 in the air.[11] Under com-
parable illumination a two-fold increase of CO_2 concentration increases the rate of photosynthesis of the oak by almost 7 times
(Molchanov 1964).

It is highly indicative also that oak of the late form, whose
vegetation begins 2 weeks later than the trees of the early form,
have similar production by autumn (Kobranov 1925) since physiological processes proceed more intensively (Shutyaev 1964).

All of this testifies to the presence of complex adaptations of
forest-steppe oak forests to damage by the leaf-eating insects which
maintain production of forests.

Influence on Seed Production. The impact of leaf-eating insects
on seed production of oak forests is manifested in direct and indirect forms. The direct influence includes eating by the larval
leaf roller of the generative tissues, and the indirect the possible
decrease of photosynthate reserve which serves as a source for fruit
production.

Observations showed that the generative organs (flower buds and
flowers) are strongly damaged only in some years of outbreak of leaf
roller (for example, in 1964), when as a result of complete defoliation the larvae were starving and in the search of forage they
moved around the crown consuming the remaining leaves and the
flowers. Usually the larvae did not touch the flowers and the

[11]The arrival of zoogenic litter on forest litter (excrements,
bodies of larvae, gnawed leaves) sharply increases diffusion of CO_2.

damage caused by them to the generative organs was not great.
Damage of the generative organs by the leaf roller can be considered
an unusual phenomenon. Accumulation of products of photosynthesis
which permit fruit production occurs in the second half of summer
when as a result of a second growth in damaged trees complete leaf
surface is restored.

     For this reason the spring zoogenic defoliation does not
effectively decrease accumulation of assimilates necessary for
flowering and seed production the following year. In fact, intensive flowering and satisfactory harvest of acorns were observed in
the outbreak localities in 1965 and 1967 despite the fact that in
the preceding years spring defoliation of the crowns was very great.
Even in 1970 the damaged trees produced a supply of acorns, which
was not large. Defoliation of the crowns in ravine oak forests as a
result of spring frost also did not limit seed production and
usually there was good production of acorns there. Thus, there
is potential for natural seed renewal of forest in the outbreak
localities.

IMPACT ON UNDERGROWTH LAYERS OF THE ECOSYSTEM

     Participation of leaf eating insects in the function of forest
communities is not limited to their impact on damaged species.
Defoliation of the upper cover of the forest in the years of outbreak leads to changes of the biogeocoenotic processes which occur
in undergrowth. In particular, productivity of undergrowth changes
sharply and also that of the accompanying woody species of the
forest floor (Ierusalimov 1965, Vorontzov, Ierusalimov and
Mozolevskaya 1967).

     In forests damaged by the oak leaf roller deviations in light,
radiation, hydrothermic and gas regimes are observed and in the
regime of nutrient cycling. Conditions of illumination in the
outbreak localities approach those of open sections to some degree.
Measurements on 21 May 1967, when the decrease of the leaf surface
in the outbreak locality approached 70% in comparison with the
control section, showed the following. At 1000 to 1100 hours the
quantity of solar radiation penetrating to the grass cover was
38.5 ± 1.40 thousand lux or 60%; on the control section it was
6.6 ± 0.69 thousand lux, or 10% of the value in open areas. Radiation penetrating to the surface of the litter in the outbreak
center was 7.2 ± 0.71, or 23% and on the control section 1.2 ± 0.22
thousand lux or 4%. Consequently damaged crowns during the period
of greatest defoliation allowed 6 times more light to penetrate
than the undamaged crowns. During the period from maximum defoliation to foliage renewal there is 50% more light on the undergrowth layers in the sources of outbreak than on the control section
(Vorontzov, Ierusalimov and Mozolevskaya 1967). After production
of second growth the illumination in the outbreak localities and in
the control sections became approximately the same.

     In closed oak forest undergrowth plants suffer a lack of light.
Species of the shrub and grassy layers in the southern taiga and
the forest-steppe oak forests show a sharp decrease of photosynthesis at the beginning of complete foliation of the tree stand
(Malkina 1964, Mitina 1969). According to the data of I. S. Malkina

(1964) in the oak forests surrounding Moscow decrease of illumination leads to lowering by 4 to 5 times the rate of photosynthesis
of lungwort and by 4 times for sedge, and twice for the rowan,
hazelnut and lily of the valley. Maximum photosynthesis in goutweed
in forest steppe oak forest occurs with a light intensity of about
40 thousand lux (Mitina 1969). About the same quantity of light
penetrates under the upper layer during the period of defoliation of
the forest-steppe oak forest.
    The difference in absolute quantity solar radiation absorbed by
the grass stand can be used as an indicator of the intensity of
assimilation of the grassy layer in the area of outbreak of the oak
leaf roller. As was pointed out, in the outbreak centers it is
approximately 30,000 lux and on the control section about 5000 lux.
But the transmitting capability of the grass canopy on both sections
is the same (82% of the incoming radiation is absorbed), determined
by its similar structure which is primarily wide-leaf herbs.
    As a result of the differences in radiation conditions damaged
forests are heated more than the undamaged oak forests and the
thermal regime in the outbreak locality is similar to the open
sections.
    Temperatures at the height of 1 m are higher in outbreak
localities than on the control section during all hours of a 24 hr
period. A very significant difference (2.3°C) is observed during
the daytime hours, when the sun is high in the sky. In the morning
and in the evening the air in the outbreak localities is warmer by
1.5 to 1.7°C. At night temperatures become equalized, but still
remain higher on the damaged sections by 0.6°C. On the average
during a 24-hr period the temperature at a height of 1 m in damaged
forests is higher by 1.5°C, where a positive difference is noted
during 21 hours, and only during 3 hrs of the 24-hour period (from
0200 until 0500) is the temperature lower than on the control
sections. Maximum temperature at the height of 1 m in the outbreak
localities was higher by 2.8°C, and minimum temperature was higher
by 0.9°C than in the healthy forests. The amplitude of 24 hr fluctuations of temperature in damaged oak groves was greater by 1.9°C.
    Temperature under the grass canopy at a height of 5 cm has a
somewhat different diurnal variation. The grassy layer in the
outbreak localities holds a significant part (about 80%) of the
heat. For this reason the difference in daily temperature under the
grass stand of the outbreak localities and of the control areas is
less than at the height of 1 m, being 1.4°C. There is even less
difference in the evening hours, 0.2°C. At night the grass layer
allows a larger fraction of the long wave radiation from the soil to
escape. As a result in the outbreak localities the layer of air
near the soil cools more rapidly and the difference in comparison
with the control section becomes negative (-1.9°C). Minimum temperature in the outbreak localities at this height is 2.4°C lower
than in the undamaged forests. A negative difference between the
center and the control section (-0.8°C) is preserved in the morning
hours. As a result, in a 24-hr period in the outbreak centers
during 15 hrs the temperature under the grass stand is lower and
during 9 hrs it is higher than in the control section (Table 22).
    Rapid cooling of the ground layer of air facilitates stable
stratification in the night and morning hours resulting in a high
temperature gradient. If we compare the difference in temperature
at night and in the morning at heights of 100 cm and 5 cm in the

Table 22. Differences in average temperatures in May 1967.

Level above soil surface (cm)	Hours (X100)	Temperature (°C)		
		Control section	Outbreak locality	Difference
100	6–10	20.6	22.3	+1.7
	11–15	27.4	29.7	+2.3
	16–20	24.9	26.4	+1.5
	21–5	18.2	18.8	+0.6
	24-hr average	22.8	24.3	+1.5
5	6–10	19.4	18.6	−0.8
	11–15	26.1	27.5	+1.4
	16–20	23.7	23.9	+0.2
	21–5	17.7	15.8	−1.9
	24-hr average	21.7	21.4	−0.3

outbreak localities and on the control section, then we note that the gradients in the first instance is 3 to 3.7°C and in the second 0.5 to 1.2°C. The average 24 hour temperature under the grass stand on both sections is almost the same; in undamaged areas it is higher by 0.3°C. Maximum temperature in the outbreak localities is higher by 1.9°C, and for this reason the amplitude of 24 hr fluctuation here is greater by 4.3°C than in the control areas.

Consequently the temperature at a height of 1 m in the outbreak localities is much higher than in the undamaged plantings. Maximum differences attain several degrees. In the grass canopy a positive difference is observed only during the daytime and evening hours, which apparently facilitates more intensive assimilation in this layer of the damaged areas. Along with this the lower temperature at night can decrease respiration as a result of which total production of the grass layer in damaged forests increases.

Relative humidity was measured simultaneously with determination of the temperature regime at these heights (Table 23). Relative humidity above the grass canopy (at a height of 100 cm) in damaged forests during the greater part of the 24-hr period is less than on the control section. Only during 2 hours at night (from 3 to 5 a.m.) was the air at this height in the outbreak localities more humid.

Table 23. Differences in average relative humidity in May 1967 (%).

Level above soil surface (cm)	Hours (X100)	Temperature (°C)		
		Control section	Outbreak locality	Difference
100	6-10	55	50	-5
	11-15	41	28	-13
	16-20	50	41	-9
	21-5	58	56	-2
	24-hr average	51	44	-7
5	6-10	72	76	+4
	11-15	48	49	+1
	16-20	65	71	+6
	21-5	77	87	+10
	24-hr average	66	71	+5

The 24-hr amplitude of humidity at a height of 1 m in the leaf roller outbreak centers was 19% greater than on the control section. In the grass canopy the reverse was observed. In the damaged forests relative humidity is noticeably higher than in the undamaged and this difference is preserved for 21 hrs of the 24-hr period. The fluctuation of 24-hr relative humidity in the grass canopy is less significant than at the 1 m height. In damaged forests it is 7% greater than in the control areas.

A higher content of water vapor in the ground layer of air during the daytime and evening hours can be explained by increased evaporation of moisture from the soil and from the leaf surface of the grass canopy in the outbreak locality during the day, and at night due to a sharp fall of temperature leading to saturation of moisture of the lower layer of air. Dew formation on the damaged section is observed much more often than in the control section in which the undisturbed upper foliage layer exerts a screening effect lessening the flow of radiation of the soil. Thus, the grass canopy in the outbreak localities has a more favorable humidity condition.

We did not make observations of soil moisture. However, detailed investigations of the dynamics of soil water regime of the forest-steppe zone published by A. A. Molchanov (1964), by A. F. Bolshakov (1961) and E. A. Afanaceeva (1966) permit comparison of characteristics on damaged and control sections.

As is known, in forest-steppe forests the moisture is used primarily in transpiration, which in average age grass stands account for more than 70% of the total water use (Molchanov 1964).

Transpiration by leaves is a function of their mass and surface area (Polyakova 1954). Besides this, as shown above, the water content of young damaged shoots is lower than in the healthy trees. For this reason during the period of defoliation removal of water from the root zone in damaged forests is slower, lessening the competition for moisture between grass seedlings, underbrush and woody roots.

In outbreak localities lower layers of vegetation receive a supplementary supply of condensation moisture in the form of dew. In the damaged forests according to our measurements the quantity of dew is 50 to 70% greater than on the control area. In addition, the crowns of trees lacking leaves let a larger part of the spring-summer precipitation through. In oak forests of the Central Chernozem Reserve the upper layers retain on the average 17% of the liquid precipitation (Gertzik 1957). During continuous weak rains (1 to 2 mm) the crowns of the trees hold up to 50% of the precipitation.

The decrease of the thickness of undergrowth observed in the outbreak localities facilitates further moistening of the root zone of the soil. Special experiments have shown that a 3-fold increase of undergrowth (from 120 to 360 g/m^2) lowers water penetration by 6 to 8 times. During continuous rain (up to 10 mm) undergrowth of such density stops almost all falling precipitation. We conclude that the plants of the subordinate layers in outbreak localities of the oak leaf roller develop in conditions of more favorable water regime than in the undamaged forests where they have strong competition from the healthy trees.

In years of mass reproduction of leaf rollers a large quantity of excrement, of dead insects and of leaf debris falls to the forest undergrowth and soil. On the average this litterfall during the period of outbreak is equivalent to a little more than 10% of the net production of leaves.

Zoogenic litterfall has a high content of nutrients such as nitrogen, phosphorus, and potassium. In comparison with autumn leaf litterfall, excrement of the leaf roller contains 3 times the phosphorus and almost twice the potassium and nitrogen, and in remains of the green leaves the content of nitrogen is almost 4 times higher. There are high amounts of nitrogen in the animal litterfall (bodies and exuvia of the leaf roller); its quantity reaches 11% which is 10 times greater than the content of nitrogen in autumn leaf litterfall. The quantity of nitrogen and phosphorus applied to the surface of the soil in outbreak localities during the period of defoliation is about 35% of the content in oak leaf litter, and the quantity of potassium is 26%. Zoogenic litterfall decomposes very quickly and plants of the subordinate layers receive a large supplementary supply of easily assimilated minerals. Total annual contribution of nitrogen, phosphorus and potassium from zoogenic litterfall damaged tree stands is higher by 17%, 21%, and 13%, respectively, than in the control forests. Consequently, in the outbreak centers of oak leaf rollers the plants of the lower layers have more favorable nutrient conditions than in healthy forests.

These nutrient additions to the undergrowth change the gas regime in the ground layer of air. Excrement enhances development

of microorganisms which leads to a sharp increase of CO_2 emission
from the surface of the undergrowth. Special experiments on diffusion of CO_2 from undergrowth with leaf roller excrement showed
that emission of CO_2 is several times greater than from the clean
undergrowth[12]. Especially significant increases (from 3.6 to 4.5
times) of CO_2 output from undergrowth with excrement is observed
during the first several days. Later it decreases noticeably but
still remains 2 to $2\frac{1}{2}$ times higher than for clean undergrowth. The
surface of the undergrowth in the outbreak centers of leaf rollers
is warmer by several degrees, and daily maximum temperature is up to
10 degrees higher than in the undamaged forests. This undoubtedly
speeds up the process of diffusion of CO_2 into the atmosphere since,
according to our calculations, an increase of substrate temperature
by 10 degrees increases respiration by 1.8 to 2.5 times.

Stratification of the ground layer of air on the damaged sections decreases turbulence which leads to relatively high concentrations of CO_2. This in turn stimulates photosynthesis of the
grass canopy.

In this way, in years of outbreak of the oak leaf roller,
defoliation of the upper layer of the forest improves conditions
for development of lower layers. Hydrothermic radiation, gas regime,
and nutrients under the canopy in the outbreak localities are more
favorable for the growth of plants of the lower layers than in
damaged forests.

Influence on Growth of Underbrush. In order to study the
dynamics of growth of representative species of underbrush we
examined 33 specimens from 11 species of woody types. Results of
changes of growth in diameter are given in Table 24. Average growth
of underbrush species increased in the outbreak centers by 10%;
however, this increase is not statistically significant.

If we consider the growth of underbrush stems in cross sectional area, then there is a clearer picture; according to this
indicator average growth for all species during the years of damage
was 0.9 ± 0.09 cm^2, and prior to the outbreak it was 0.4 ± 0.02 cm^2.
Hence, during the latter years there was a 56% increase of growth
(significant at the level of 0.999).

The underbrush is poorly developed in the study areas of the
Central Chernozem Reserve. Consequently normal variations of production here have little influence on the dynamics of total production of the forest community. Together, in forests of complex
composition the losses of growth of the dominant species during the
outbreak of leaf-eating insects can be completely compensated by
production of other woody species of the first and second layers and
of the underbrush (Vorontzov, Ierusalinov, and Mozolevskaya 1967).
Average growth of wood in damaged forests according to cross sectional area of the trunk remains equal to the average growth during
the years preceding the outbreak (in the same location).

Consequently outbreaks of monophagous leaf-eating insects
facilitate intensive growth of the accompanying woody species of

[12]Experiments were conducted in the laboratory for 2 to 6 weeks
with a constant temperature and humidity of the substrate. The
undergrowth was placed in glass jars with a capacity of 0.5 l.
Quantity of CO_2 was determined by the absorption method (Zlotin,
Kalandadze and others 1970).

Table 24.   Average indicators of growth in diameter of underbrush in damaged
watershed oak forests (mm, at a height about 1 m).

Type	Number of samples	1955–1962	1963–1970	Change of growth (%)[a]	Level of significance of differences
European bird-cherry	3	0.9 ± 0.07	1.7 ± 0.22	+47	0.01
Honeysuckle	4	0.5 ± 0.03	0.9 ± 0.12	+44	0.02
Warty spindle	3	0.5 ± 0.04	0.8 ± 0.07	+37	0.01
Pear	4	1.0 ± 0.04	1.4 ± 0.11	+28	0.02
Apple	3	0.9 ± 0.03	1.2 ± 0.11	+25	0.02
Field maple	2	1.0 ± 0.04	1.2 ± 0.21	+17[b]	0.10
Spindle	3	0.9 ± 0.05	0.9 ± 0.06	±	--
Hawthorn	2	0.9 ± 0.06	0.8 ± 0.10	-12[b]	0.10
Rowan	3	0.9 ± 0.04	0.7 ± 0.03	-28	0.01
Blackthorn	5	1.0 ± 0.06	0.7 ± 0.04	-43	0.01
Linden	1	1.1 ± 0.06	0.7 ± 0.06	-56	0.01

[a] Reliability of indicators is greater than 0.98.

[b] Indicators not significant.

undergrowth, which leads to forest community dynamics of high quality with more complex structure and better able to withstand external influences, as a result of the increased variety of woody and bush species. A. I. Vorontzov, E. I. Ierusalinov, and E. G. Mozolevskaya (1967) think that autoregulation of total productivity in a forest ecosystem is characteristic only of mixed forests with a significant variety of species. In their opinion, this is not observed in pure stands or in tree stands with a significant pro- portion of damaged species. However, loss of growth of trees in pure stands of oak groves of the Central Chernozem Reserve during years of outbreak is almost completely compensated for by increased productivity of the grass layer.

Influence on Development of the Grass Layer. As a result of changes of the external environment under the upper layer of the damaged oak forest basic vegetative and generative phenophases in the grass canopy are accelerated. Thus, in the period of maximum development of the green biomass the number of specimens of goutweed reaching the generative stage in the outbreak localities is always significantly greater (1.4 to 1.8 times) than in undamaged localities. *Clematis* undergoes a complete cycle of development only on the damaged sections, and on the control sections occur primarily veg- etative shoots; the flowering plants are solitary (Table 25). Other representatives of the spring-summer ephemeral complex (bitter

Table 25. Contribution of plants in different stages of
development in the period of maximum green biomass
$(\%)$[a].

Stage of development	Goutweed			Clematis		
	1966	1967	1970	1966	1967	1970
Vegetative	$\frac{59}{43}$	$\frac{80}{63}$	$\frac{62}{46}$	$\frac{70}{--}$	$\frac{90}{--}$	$\frac{--}{--}$
Generative	$\frac{41}{57}$	$\frac{20}{37}$	$\frac{38}{54}$	$\frac{30}{100}$	$\frac{10}{100}$	$\frac{--}{100}$

[a] In the numerator--on control section, in the denominator--
on outbreak centers.

vetch, cow wheat, the wonder violet and others) are significantly
more successful in damaged localities.

During the outbreak of leafeating insects there are significant
changes of structure of the grass canopy. In the outbreak centers
variety of grasses increases, accounted for chiefly by light-loving
and nitrogen-loving representatives of the varied groups of grasses.
Thus, on the study areas where phytomass was recorded in the outbreak centers, there were 23 species of these plants, and on the
control section only 15. In the latter many of the species were of
low abundance.

For the damaged sections the most characteristic plants are cow
wheat, geranium, veronica, strawberry, dropwort, inula, wild chervil,
and spring vetchling. Shade-loving types, such as the lily-of-the-
valley, become rare and are seen only in shade on the north sides
of tree trunks, and also under weakly damaged trees. Nitrogen
enrichment of the soil and thinning of crowns results in damaged
forests becoming choked with several ruderal species; poison ivy,
elder, raspberry.

Thinning of tree stands is accompanied by intensive flowering
of many grasses and shrubs. The male imagos of the leaf roller feed
especially on nectar of chervil and the European prickwood. Flowers
of these species are much more abundant in the outbreak localities
than in the undamaged sections and produce noticeably more nectar.
This favors a high level of reproduction by the imago of the oak
leaf roller.

Average height of the grass canopy changes insignificantly
during consumption of the oak crowns by the leaf-eaters. The height
of vegetative parts of goutweed, which forms the major leaf surface
in the outbreak localities, is somewhat greater than on the control
section. The height noticeably increases where crowns suffer weak
or average damage. Where crowns are strongly damaged there is a
significant development of height of plants (clematis, chervil) that
form the upper layer of the grass canopy, limiting the growth of

vegetative organs of goutweed. In addition, the height of the
generative stalks of goutweed and clematis in the outbreak localities is 1.3 to 1.5 times greater and the degree of difference increases according to the degree of defoliation of the upper layer
(Table 26).

Table 26.   Average height of shoots of goutweed in
            the period of maximum vegetative biomass
            in 1970 (cm).

| Section | Shoots | |
	Vegetative	Generative
Control	44.0 ± 0.4	99.8 ± 0.9
Weak damage	52.5 ± 0.5	126.0 ± 1.1
Average damage	47.8 ± 0.5	127.5 ± 1.3
Strong damage	41.8 ± 0.5	129.0 ± 1.5

Average weight of the majority of species of grass flora in
damaged forests is sharply increased. For example, the average dry
weight of the vegetative shoots of goutweed on damaged sections is
1.2 ± 0.15 g, and on the control only 0.6 ± 0.05 g. Clematis and
chervil in the outbreak centers are 5 to 6 times larger.
    The productivity of the soil-forming species and of the entire
grass layer in the damaged section noticeably increases. The production of the aboveground phytomass of the grass canopy determined
during the period of maximum vegetative growth differs notably in
various years of the outbreak. However, in the outbreak centers the
growth of green phytomass in comparison with the control sections is
always 2 to 2.3 times higher (Table 27).
    The total area of leaf surface of the grass layer at the time
of maximum vegetative biomass in the damaged section was 2.1 to 2.5
times greater than on the control section. As a result the total
cover of the grass canopy in the undamaged forests was about 50%,
and in the outbreak centers it was up to 70 to 80%, in some instances attaining complete shading of the soil.
    The dominant plant of the grass canopy is goutweed, the im-
portance of which is preserved during almost the entire cycle of the
outbreak. However, in the outbreak locality its contribution to the
total phytomass noticeably decreases in comparison with the control
section, and the weight of codominant species from this group of
varied grasses increases proportionately.
    Changes in the structure of phytomass during the period of
outbreak of the oak leaf roller becomes particularly obvious when
our results are compared with the data of V. V. Gertzik (1959) for
the same section of the watershed oak forest and with those for the
year 1957 (Table 28 and 29).

Table 27. Maximum standing crop of green vegetation and area of leaf surface in watershed oak forest (g/m², air-dry weight)[a].

Year	Goutweed	Clematis	Monocots	Others	Total	Leaf surface (m²/m²)
1966	$\frac{58}{164}$	$\frac{0.2}{39}$	$\frac{22}{12}$	$\frac{21}{21}$	$\frac{101}{236}$	$\frac{1.22}{3.06}$
1967	$\frac{75}{118}$	$\frac{--}{23}$	$\frac{--}{8}$	$\frac{11}{44}$	$\frac{86}{193}$	$\frac{1.17}{2.46}$
1968	$\frac{96}{92}$	$\frac{--}{28}$	$\frac{0.1}{41}$	$\frac{6}{102}$	$\frac{102}{233}$	$\frac{1.22}{2.77}$
1970	$\frac{124}{148}$	$\frac{--}{24}$	$\frac{2}{4}$	$\frac{16}{107}$	$\frac{142}{283}$	$\frac{1.65}{3.50}$

[a] In the numerator--on control section, in the denominator-- in the outbreak locality.

Table 28. Contribution of different plants to green biomass (%).[a]

Year	Goutweed	Clematis	Monocots	Others
1966	$\frac{57}{69}$	$\frac{<1}{16}$	$\frac{22}{6}$	$\frac{21}{9}$
1967	$\frac{87}{61}$	$\frac{--}{12}$	$\frac{--}{4}$	$\frac{13}{23}$
1968	$\frac{94}{27}$	$\frac{--}{12}$	$\frac{<1}{17}$	$\frac{6}{44}$
1970	$\frac{87}{52}$	$\frac{--}{9}$	$\frac{1}{1}$	$\frac{12}{38}$

[a] In the numerator--on the control section, in the denominator--in the outbreak area.

Table 29.   Structure of aboveground phytomass of the grass canopy[a].

Year	Goutweed	Other types of herbage	Monocots	Legumes	Total
1957	$\frac{81}{84}$	$\frac{10}{10}$	$\frac{5}{5}$	$\frac{0.5}{<1}$	$\frac{96.5}{100.0}$
1966–1970					
Control	$\frac{88}{82}$	$\frac{13}{12}$	$\frac{6}{5}$	$\frac{0.3}{<1}$	$\frac{107.3}{100.0}$
Outbreak	$\frac{123}{52}$	$\frac{97}{41}$	$\frac{16}{6}$	$\frac{0.6}{<1}$	$\frac{236.6}{100.0}$

[a] In the numerator--g/m^2, dry weight, in the denominator--%.

As seen in Table 29, the structure and productivity of the grass canopy before the outbreak (1957) and during the period of outbreak of the oak leaf roller on the undamaged sections were preserved almost unchanged, but in the outbreak center there was a modification of internal structure and sharply increased production of green phytomass.

In forests damaged by leafeating insects characteristic dynamic changes of species codominants occur which are determined by yearly changes in spring-summer weather, by the type and degree of defoliation of the canopy by the leafeating insects, and also by competitive interrelationships of the plants. Among the codominants in various years of outbreak were included such species as clematis, cow wheat, chervil, short-leaf grasses, and some others.

Changes in leaf surface structure also indicate the peculiar phytocoenotic dynamics of the grass canopy in damaged forests. The proportion of goutweed leaf surface in the grass canopy in outbreak centers is significantly less than on the undamaged section. Surface area of goutweed in various years of outbreak constituted 25% to 55% of the total, when in the control forest it was 56% to 92%.

In the outbreak centers of the oak leaf roller biomass of the belowground layer of grass canopy also changes. The general reserve of roots in a layer 0 to 30 cm, where more than 80% of the total quantity is concentrated, is 2 times greater in the outbreak areas than on the control section--609 and 264 g/m^2, respectively (average values). Along with this the root index (the relationship of root biomass to aboveground parts of the grasses) is similar: on both sections the quantity of roots is 2.5 times the biomass of the aboveground parts.

The average production of the grass canopy during the period of outbreak of the oak leaf roller including both aboveground and

belowground biomass constituted 430 g/m^2 (dry weight) in the outbreak centers and 188 g/m^2 on the undamaged sections. Thus, production of the grass canopy in the outbreak localities during the
outbreak was 2.3 times greater than the control section.

Influence on Development of Undergrowth. Under the canopy of
the trees in the centers of outbreak of oak leaf rollers conditions
favorable for the appearance and development of undergrowth are
formed. In closed forest-steppe forests the oak undergrowth usually
experiences a shortage of light (Kryzhanovski 1954, Malkina 1965).
Light saturation and optimum conditions for photosynthesis in undergrowth occurs at a light intensity of 8 to 9 thousand lux (Molchanov
1964).

Oak sprouts usually appear in middle or late May. During the
second year of development growth of oak seedling slows sharply
because of lack of light. Later, if thinning of the upper canopy
does not occur, many sprouts perish (Kornakovski 1904, quoted in
Malchanov 1964).

Thinning of the upper canopy is a necessary condition for the
growth of oak seedlings in the forest-steppe. This retards somewhat
the appearance of new shoots, but later helps their growth. During
establishment of favorable light conditions the shoots begin to grow
intensively, their growth in height increasing up to 10 times
(Risin 1970). It is also characteristic that shade resistance of
oak seedlings increases under improved water conditions and soil
moisture (Karmanova 1970, Risin 1970), lowering competition in the
ground layer. Consequently, during the years of outbreak of the oak
leaf roller the light of the upper layer and favorable conditions of
water and mineral supplies facilitate successful development of oak
seedlings.

During the period of outbreak in the damaged forests the via-
bility of seedlings was high. Length of annual shoots usually was
20 cm, and in this case it reached 60 cm. This allows us to hypothesize that the change of species composition of forests in the
outbreak centers of oak leaf roller will not occur, despite the
dryness of the watershed forest observed in recent years. Just the
opposite, an intensive growth of seedlings in the outbreak centers
can lead to forests produced from seedlings more resistant to unfavorable impact. In addition, there may be an increase in com-
plexity of community structure due to associated woody species and
bushes, thereby increasing stability of the ecosystem.

The Dynamics of Total Production. In Table 30 are shown all
indicators of dynamics of the primary production of forest ecosystems. From the Table it follows that on the damaged sections production is almost the same as on the undamaged: the total difference
between them is 15 g/m^2.

Attention is drawn to the fact that in the first years of
outbreak (up to and including 1965) the total growth of phytomass in
the outbreak localities was noticeably higher than on the control
section, and later it became significantly lower. During recent
years of outbreak, beginning with 1968, the total production in the
outbreak localities and on the control section differed insignificantly (Fig. 7).[13] Differences in the dynamics of total growth of

[13]The data on productivity of the grass layer in 1964 and 1965 were
presented by V. D. Utekheen and for 1963 they were calculated as
the average of the indexes from the adjacent years.

Table 30.   Average production of organic matter in phytomass
(g/m^2, air-dry weight).

Layer	Control section	Outbreak locality	Difference
Tree-stand			
Before outbreak	1327	1087	
At the time of outbreak[a]	1061	804	−257
Grass layer			
Before outbreak	158	158	
At the time of outbreak	188	430	+242
Total			
Before outbreak	1485	1245	
At the time of outbreak	1249	1234	
Decrease of growth during the outbreak	236	11	
% from growth before outbreak	16	<1	

[a] Including the portion of natural death of trees.

phytomass are explained by the course of growth of forests. Annual
fluctuations of production of the grass layer are very small.
Linear regression indicates the similarity of both sections in total
production during the entire period of outbreak. But if we compare
the values for the undamaged and damaged tree stands up to and
during the outbreak, then they appear highly different. It is
characteristic, that in the control forests productivity during the
time of outbreak decreased a significantly larger degree (by 16%)
than in the outbreak localities (by 1%).
      Consequently, the increase of production of the grass layer as
a result of the outbreak of leaf rollers compensates not only for
the loss of growth of trees, but also almost completely for the
decrease of total production of the entire community, due to the
impact of unfavorable dry conditions for the growth of forests
during recent years. Thus, we consider the outbreak of the oak
leaf roller as a peculiar mechanism in the function of forest ecosystems, which is important during periods of sharp changes of
external environment for limiting loss of primary production, and
also for preservation of total community production on a relatively
constant level.

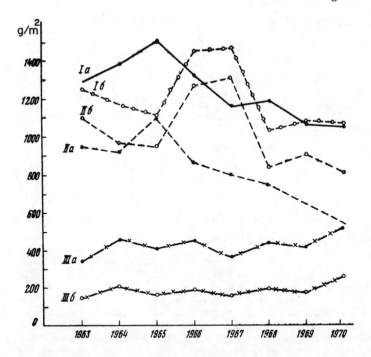

Figure 7
Dynamics of primary productin of organic material during period
of outbreak of leaf rollers (dry weight). 1-total primary production; 2-phytomass production of woody layer; 3-same of grass
layer: a-phytomass production in outbreak localities; b-on undamaged sections. Indicators of production in outbreak centers
of leaf roller include tree dessication.

IMPACT OF OAK LEAF ROLLERS ON THE RATE OF BIOLOGICAL CYCLING

Diverse changes of the environment, observed during years of
outbreak of the oak leaf roller, influence the path and rate of many
biogeocoenotic processes, thus determining the type of biological
cycling. One basic indicator of biological turnover is the rate of
decomposition of dead organic remains.

In the oak groves of the European forest-steppe reserves of
dead organic material accumulate chiefly on the surface of the soil
as forest litter. Comparison of our data on dynamics of leaf litterfall and general reserve of litter during the time of outbreak of
oak leaf rollers with data of V. V. Gertzik (1959), from the same
section of a watershed oak forest in 1955-1957, allows us to characterize the difference in conditions and rate of decomposition
processes during these periods. Watershed oak forests of the
Central Chernozem Reserve differ by significant accumulation of
litter. Before the outbreak the thickness of this layer reached 10
cm in places (on the average approximately 5 cm), and an average
reserve of approximately 12 tons/ha. The structure of the reserve
of dead remains is illustrated by Table 31.

Table 31. Composition of aboveground dead remains of phytomass, %[a].

Index of reserve	Leaves of oak	Semidecomposed remains of leaves and branches	Branches	Fruit	Remains of grasses
Maximum	61	90	20	3	3
Minimum	6	25	2	--	<1
Average	33	54	11	1	<1

[a] According to the data of V. V. Gertzik (1959).

Since usually about 90% of the dead reserve on the surface of the soil is composed of oak leaves we gave particular attention to the dynamics of the decomposition of leaf litter. The litter layer as a rule is morphologically sharply divided into two horizons: Uppermost, formed by a fresh leaf litter fall, and lower, consisting of semi-decomposed parts of leaves, which have accumulated for several years. It is the latter horizon which often is strictly called litter. We will also call it "litter," and the upper horizon we will designate as "litterfall."

The weight relationship of these fractions of the dead phytomass can serve as an indication of the rate of decomposition of organic material (Rodin and Bazilevich 1965). Before the outbreak of oak leaf rollers, and also on the control sections during the period of outbreak, the total autumn reserve of the surface plant remains exceeded by 2.83.2 times the magnitude of the annual litterfall of oak leaves. Almost the same magnitude of difference remained in the spring (in the middle of May), when the biomass of litter was greater than the quantity of litter fall by 2.2 to 2.6 times. Consequently, during the years preceding the outbreak and also on the undamaged section the rate of accumulation of organic material was greater than its rate of mineralization. As a result there was an accumulation of litter fall and a relatively thick litter layer.

In the outbreak localities relationship between these fractions is the opposite. Yearly production of leaves entering the litterfall in the autumn is three times greater and in the spring 2 times greater than the total reserve of the dead phytomass. This indicates predominance of mineralization over litter fall accumulation. A sharp decrease of reserve of litter in the outbreak centers occurred not at the expense of decrease of leaf production, but chiefly as a result of intensification of processes of decomposition (Table 32).

In fact, litterfall of oak leaves during the outbreak decreased by 1.4 times, and the total reserve of the dead soil surface remains was more than 4 times greater. During the vegetative period before

Table 32. Reserve of leaf litter-fall and litter in watershed oak forest (g/m² air-dry weight)[a].

| Indicator | Before outbreak[b] | | During period of outbreak | | | |
| | | | Control section 1966 | | Center 1964–1970 | |
	Spring	Fall	Spring	Fall	Spring	Fall
Leaf litterfall	$\frac{420}{388-453}$	$\frac{180}{50-316}$	358	Not separated	$\frac{200}{132-180}$	Not separated
Litter	$\frac{940}{610-1267}$	$\frac{790}{570-906}$	932	Not separated	$\frac{106}{62-148}$	Not separated
Total	$\frac{1360}{998-1720}$	$\frac{970}{720-1222}$	1290	920	$\frac{306}{194-428}$	$\frac{74}{50-113}$
Average litter fall for the year	350		234		258	

[a] In the numerator—average size, in the denominator—the range.

[b] The data of V. V. Gertzik (1959).

the outbreak 28% of the total reserve of leaf litter and litterfall
decomposed on the average. In the same time during the outbreak of
leaf rollers the reduction of this reserve in weight was on the
average 75%. Thus in the outbreak centers decomposition of dead
plant remains was almost 3 times faster. As a result in the autumn
the general quantity of leaf litter and litterfall in the outbreak
centers was 12 times less than in the undamaged forests and, in
comparison with the period before the outbreak, 13 times less.

In order to determine the rate of decomposition of oak litterfall during the years of outbreak of leaf-eating insects special
experiments were conducted in 1967 and repeated in 1969 and 1970.[14]
They showed that during the vegetative period in the undamaged
forests litterfall of oak loses 33 to 35% of the original weight.
The collective data are close to the results of V. N. Mina (1954),
V. V. Gertzik (1959) and G. F. Kurcheva (1965), who determined that
in the forest-steppe groves during the warm season about 1/3 of the
yearly litterfall of oak is mineralized. According to observations
of T. R. Kokovinoe (1967), who conducted her own investigations in
the Central Chernozem Reserve during several years before the beginning of the outbreak, in one year (from one fall to the fall of
the following year) 35-51% of the oak litterfall decomposed.

In the outbreak centers of oak leaf rollers decomposition of
litter-fall is much more rapid. In one variant of the experiment
excrement of the leaf roller was added to the litterfall in a
quantity equal to average input during the period of larval development. In this instance, from spring until fall, 53% of the litter
fall decomposed. The excrements themselves, whose weight constituted 60% of the weight of litterfall, completely disappeared during
the second month of the experiment. Of the total organic material
(litterfall and excrement) during the indicated period, 85% decomposed.

The combined results allow us to conclude that complete mineralization of litterfall of oak leaves ordinarily requires not less
than 2-3 years. Apparently a similar time span is required for
complete renewal of litter which, as was shown above, decomposes a
little slower than litterfall. During years of outbreak of oak leaf
rollers the process of mineralization of plant litterfall flow
approximately 2 times faster, which prevents accumulation of litter.

The accelerated decomposition of litter and litterfall during
the period of outbreak depends on several factors. One is enhance-
ment of abiotic mineralization as a result of a significant quantity
of solar radiation which penetrates the canopy. In addition, high
solar radiation changes the hydrothermic regime in the litter layer,
increasing its temperature and humidity as a result of the increased
evaporation from the surface of the soil and regular deposition of
dew, further facilitating the loss of organic and chemical compounds.

A relatively high temperature, along with preservation of
significant humidity in the layer of dead plant remains, creates
favorable conditions for sapropytic organisms--invertebrates and
microflora. Their activity is increased and, as a result, there is
increased utilization of organic remains.

Of particular significance, as the experiments showed, is the
input of zoogenic litterfall excrements of leaf insects, their

[14]Methods of the experiments are described in the section on
  saprophages.

bodies and exuviae, and also leaf debris which, as already noted, is high in nitrogen and other nutrients.

Production of excrement by leaf rollers during the period of larvae development reaches 60 g/m^2, and on the average constitutes 30 g/m^2 (air-dry weight). The excrements are water-stable aggregates and in comparison with a similar mass of leaf litterfall have approximately 50 times more surface, which serves as a sphere of active development of saprophytic microorganisms.

A particular chemical composition of excrements of leaf rollers, especially a narrow ratio of carbon to nitrogen, also increases the activity of microbes. This ratio is 20 in excrement and in the litter it is 42. In the chewed remains of green leaves which fall to the surface the ratio of carbon to nitrogen is only 11. It is known that the most favorable organic compounds for development of microorganisms are those with C:N ratio that does not exceed 20 (Aristovskaya 1965).

In excrement the content of tannin decreases. It is accumulated in the larvae of the oak leaf roller in the form of crystals in epithelial cells of the middle gut (Fredericks 1932). The tannins are bacteriacidal compounds, which have a toxic effect on some groups of soil microflora.

Above it was shown, that the input of excrement to the surface of the litter and litterfall stimulated microbiological processes. Along with this, it is well known that invertebrate saprophages prefer litterfall modified by microbiological decomposition and readily use the excrement of the leaf-eating insects (Kurcheva 1971). Accordingly, accelerated decomposition of litterfall and litter in the outbreak centers of oak leaf rollers becomes understandable.

In this way, outbreaks of leafeating insects stimulate the processes of mineralization of plant litterfall and facilitate biological cycling as a result of rapid liberation of significant. quantities of material and energy accumulated in forest litter.

Outbreaks of oak leaf rollers also facilitate increased magnitude of biological cycling. Using data on chemical composition of various fractions of forest phytomass, given in Table 33, we calculated the quantity of some nutrients in the annual increment of organic material in the outbreak centers of leaf rollers and on the control section (Table 34).[15] During comparison of damaged and control sections great attention is given to the difference in total quantity of nutrients important to production of organic material. Damaged forests accumulate annually approximately 1.5 times more nitrogen, phosphorus and potassium than undamaged forests. This difference depends chiefly on the different production of the grass stand and its proportion of total production: on the control section the grass layer constitutes about 13% and in the outbreak centers 35% of total production. In this case the proportion of nutrients contained in annual growth of the grass layer is 45% to 60% of the nitrogen, 66% to 87% of the phosphorous, and 87% to 95% of the potassium in the total phytomass. Consequently, annual production of phytomass in damaged forest utilizes 30% to 50% more

[15]It was assumed that the ash content of tree roots was similar to ash content of sapwood, and that of the roots of grasses corresponds to the ash content in green aboveground parts.

Table 33.   Content of nutrients in organic material of
            phytomass and zoomass (% of absolute dry
            material).

Index	N	P_2O_5	K_2O
Grass stand[a]			
Goutweed	2.3	0.43	7.0
Herbage	2.2	0.23	3.8
Monocots	2.1	0.10	2.0
Tree stand[a]			
Sapwood	0.6	0.03	0.2
Branches	1.0	0.04	0.2
Autumn leaf litter-fall of oak	1.2	0.58	1.1
Litter	1.4	0.30	0.8
Zoogenic litter-fall			
Excrement of leaf roller	2.1	1.46	2.0
Bodies, exuviae	11.1	no data	
Green gnawed remains of leaves	4.2	1.72	2.1

[a] Data from T. P. Kokovina (1967).

nutrients. From the nutrients used annually in the biological cycle
all of the nitrogen and phosphorus and 60% of the potassium comes
from forest litter which decomposes during the period of outbreak.
In the centers of outbreak of oak leaf rollers about 9 kg of nitrogen, 2 kg of phosphorus and 6 kg of potassium per ha is introduced
into the cycle from decomposition of litter. The quantities of
mineral elements utilized by the forest ecosystem for annual production and the quantities going into the soil from the decomposed
plant remains are similar (Table 35).
     The difference in content of N, P, and K coming from the litter
fall and included in the growth of phytomass can be explained by the
following: reutilization of mineral compounds by grasses at the end
of the vegetative period by introduction of biogenic elements with
precipitation which penetrates through the crowns of trees and the
grass layer; leaching through the soil profile by the precipitation
and by uptake by the zoomass and microbial organisms. The avail-
ability for biological cycling that is, the quantity of biogenic
elements which return annually with plant litterfall and participate
in new production, is 1.4 to 1.7 times greater in the outbreak
centers of the oak leaf roller than in the undamaged sections.
The grass layer supplies most of the nitrogen and phosphorus in the
outbreak centers, and on the undamaged section the oak litterfall

Table 34. Content of nutrients in the annual growth of organic material of phytomass (g/m^2).

Indicators	N		P$_2$O$_5$		K$_2$O	
	Control section	Outbreak locality	Control section	Outbreak locality	Control section	Outbreak locality
Tree stand	5.40	3.36	0.24	0.17	1.54	1.08
Wood of trunk and roots	3.51	2.34	0.17	0.11	1.17	0.78
Branches	1.89	1.02	0.07	0.06	0.37	0.30
Grass stand	4.27	9.63	0.70	1.36	11.70	22.27
Goutweed	3.50	4.90	0.65	0.92	10.64	14.91
Herbage	0.41	3.81	0.03	0.40	0.72	6.48
Others	0.36	0.92	0.02	0.04	0.34	0.88
Total	9.67	13.49	0.94	1.53	13.24	23.35
Content of nutrients in the grass stand (%)	45.0	60.0	66.0	87.0	87.0	95.0

Table 35. Quantity of nutrients entering the biological cycle from different fractions of litterfall (g/m^2).

Fraction of litter-fall	N		P$_2$O$_5$		K$_2$O	
	Control section	Outbreak locality	Control section	Outbreak locality	Control section	Outbreak locality
Leaf litter-fall and litter	4.42	3.38	1.70	1.30	3.40	2.60
Zoogenic litter-fall	--	1.04	--	0.55	--	0.72
Excrement	--	0.59	--	0.41	--	0.56
Gnawed remains of leaves	--	0.34	--	0.14	--	0.16
Animal litter-fall	--	0.11	no data		no data	
Woody roots	0.15	0.10	0.01	0.005	0.05	0.03
Grass stand	4.27	9.63	0.70	1.36	11.70	22.27
Total	8.84	14.15	2.41	3.22	15.15	25.62
Proportion of elements released from the litter-fall of grass (%)	48	61	28	40	70	87

and litter supply most of it; respectively 61 and 40%, 50 and 70%. The potassium on both sections comes primarily from litterfall of grasses. For this reason 87% is available from decomposition of the grass layer in the outbreak centers while on the control section 79% was available.

Thus, in the years of outbreak of oak leaf roller there is acceleration of processes of biological cycling which is a reflected in the accelerated decomposition of plant litterfall, with continuous passing through a state of litter, and this in turn enriching the soil by addition of nutrients and facilitating increased primary production.

Everything stated above testifies to coevolution of forest-steppe oak groves and the complex of leaf-eating insects resulting in autoregulation of the community, which leads to a balance between various structural elements of the ecosystem.

II–2

Herbivores

The contribution of herbivorous animals to primary production and biological cycling of meadow–steppe in the mid-Russian uplands was evaluated from the group of plant-eating rodents, including the common vole (*Microtus arvalis*) the steppe microtine (*Lagurus lagurus*) and the spotted ground squirrel (*Citellus suslicus*). Of these the common vole is the most numerous species and by number and biomass is the principal vertebrate of the meadow steppe.

Analysis of the index of relative numbers of the common vole in the steppe of the Central Chernozem Reserve for a 40 year period, conducted by V. I. Eliceeva (1965), allowed classification according to three grades of abundance. They correspond to the grades of I. L. Kulik (1963) for forest and forest-steppe zones of the European part of the USSR (Table 36). During the period from 1954 through 1968 on the Central Chernozem Reserve there were two years in which numbers of common voles were graded high, five years with low numbers, and in the remaining years numbers were average (Table 37).

Our investigations of the contribution of voles to biological cycling took place during years of decreasing numbers (1967 and 1968), which was preceded by a two year period of average numbers. Thus, the conditions were fairly typical for meadow-steppe. On watershed sections of the steppe in 1967 and 1968 there were on the average 10 colonies of the common vole per ha and the average population in the colonies was three animals. Thus there were 30 common voles or 750 g of zoomass per ha. The whole area occupied by colonies of voles constituted 6 to 7% of the total meadow-steppe of the Reserve.[1] On the ravine slopes their population density is higher than on the flat portions, especially in dry years (average 27 colonies per ha) and altogether they occupy 17% of the area. Obviously the influence of the small mammals on productivity of plant cover is greater on the ravine slopes than on the flat areas.

[1]On the unmowed section the density of colonies was 15 per ha, and when including recently abandoned colonies, 50. From this one can conclude that during the years of high density of voles there are 50 colonies per ha and the number is between 150-200. This estimate of numbers was confirmed by excavation of holes on one of the unmowed sections during the year of high density of voles.

Table 36.   Grades of abundance of common voles (number of animals per
            100 trap-days).

Grading	Meadow-steppe of the Central Chernozem Reserve		Forest and forest-steppe zones of the European part of the USSR[a] (according to I. L. Koolik 1963)
	Spring	Fall	
Low	<2	<5	0–5 / 0–9
Average	4–10	6–14	6–15 / 10–99
High	16–18	19–20	16–30 / 100–500
Very high	--	--	<30 / <500

[a] In the denominator is shown the number of holes per ha.

The number of species of plants used by voles as forage is very
great. In the steppe they prefer mesophytic wide-leaf grasses
(quack grass, brome grass), sedges, legumes and some species of
composites. Voles eat chiefly the shoots. The quantity of forage
eaten daily by *Microtus* is equal on the average to 50 to 70% of
the animal's live weight. For the adult animals this is 14 to 15 g
of fresh grass during a 24-hr period (dry weight 4 to 5 g). The 24-
hr quantity of excrement by one adult animal reaches 1.5 g (0.8 g
dry wt), that is, they assimilate approximately 80% of the green
forage consumed (Bashenina 1962, Kucheruk 1963, Petrusewicz and
Macfayden 1970).

Consequently, with an average of 30 individuals per hectare the
voles eat 54 to 72 kg/ha of grass during a year on the flat sections
of the steppe watersheds and the quantity of excrement is 9 to 12
kg/ha (dry wt). The figures show that in meadow-steppe the role of
the vole in utilization of primary production is very small. They
consume only 2–4% of the harvest, and part of the material which is
returned by them in the form of excrement constitutes less than 0.5%
of the plant litterfall.

However, voles have strong influence on the structure of plant
cover, on the growth of grass and on the quantity of photosynthesizing
surface since, while eating the young growing parts of plants,
the number of damaged specimens is great.

Observations on the impact of voles and other herbivorous
mammals on the productivity of grass cover were conducted in mowed
steppe on four sections populated by voles, and simultaneously on
two control isolated areas 10 × 10 m, fenced by a metal wire with a
mesh size of 1 cm^2 (the height of the fence was 50 cm). We studied
the influence of vole activity on transformation of the aboveground

Table 37. Perennial dynamics of numbers of the common
vole in meadow-steppe (number of animals
per 100 trap-days)[a].

Year	Spring	Fall	Grade of number
1954	16.2	19.6	High
1955	0.5	1.2	Low
1956	9.6	14.0	Average
1957	1.6	0.6	Low
1958	1.2	4.0	Low
1959	0.4	13.2	Low-Average
1960	8.0	6.6	Average
1961	5.6	no data	Average
1963	18.5	no data	High
1964	0.3	3.3	Low
1965	8.1	14.6	Average
1966	8.0	8.0	Average
1967	4.0	1.0	Average-Low
1968	0.4	0.5	Low

[a] Data for 1954-1964 from V. I. Eliseeva (1965), for
1965-1968 from V. I. Eliseeva and K. S. Khodashova.

phytomass, on the structure of the plant cover, on illumination in
various layers of grass canopy, on hydrothermic regime of the soil,
on litter and ground layer of air, on the seasonal dynamics of
phytomass growth and the area of leaf surface of grass canopy and on
the decomposition processes.

INFLUENCE ON THE STRUCTURE OF PLANT COVER

The aboveground phytomass and the area of leaf surface were
determined monthly during the entire growing season. Samples were
taken from areas of 25 × 25 cm with 16 replicates. The phytomass

was separated by fractions (green and dead), and grasses by species.
Wet and dry weights were determined. Determination of leaf area
index was by the weight method (weight per unit area). At the end
of the growing season mass of roots and their distribution in the
soil profile of a layer 0 to 40 cm was determined. Soil monoliths
of 10 × 10 cm were taken with two replicates and from these, layer
by layer (every 5 cm in a layer of 0-20 cm, then every 10 cm), roots
were washed on soil sieves with various mesh sizes.

On the section of the steppe damaged by voles phytomass and
leaf surface area of the grass stand is less than in the control
areas, where the difference in leaf surface and in aboveground
phytomass is significantly greater than the difference belowground.
Thus, during the growing season the quantity of the belowground (in
the layer of 0-40 cm) phytomass on the control sections was 19%
greater than on the animal colonies (respectively 4168 and 3890
g/m^2), and the difference between quantities of aboveground phytomass was 50% (250 and 126 g/m^2),[2] and the area of leaf surface
on the control sections was greater by 52% (2.3 and 1.1 m^2/m^2).

Various species of plants react differently to consumption by
the voles, and their development on the damaged and control sections
proceeds differently. For this reason even the harvest of the
separate groups of plants decreases to different degrees.

The greatest losses are of legumes (by 67%), then various herbs,
sedges and broad-leafed grasses (by 58, 50 and 45%) and least of all
the narrow-leaf sheep's fescue and feather grass (by 38%). The
proportion of economic groups of plants on the damaged and control
sections differed little. On isolated areas the proportion of
grasses in aboveground phytomass was 28%, on the damaged sections--
30%; the sedges--6% and 6% respectively, herbs--29 and 31%. A
significant difference was observed only in the proportions of
legumes: on the vole colonies the proportion was 7% less (19% and
12%). However, the specific composition of various herbs on the
section populated by voles changed somewhat. Among the species
forming more than 70% of the phytomass, spirea, sandwort, and
plantain predominate; there is relatively more *Potentilla* and at the
same time less meadow clary, bedstraw and especially knapweed and
mullein.

The area of leaf surface of grass stand in the vole colonies
decreased greatly toward the end of the vegetative period which,
obviously, is associated with the poorest conditions for growth and
development of the numerous damaged plants (Table 38). Table 38
shows that during the period of most intensive photosynthesis and
development of phytomass (May-June) the area of leaves on the sections populated by voles increased 25% (the leaf index 0.8 and 1
m^2/m^2) while on the damaged sections it increased almost 70% (from
1.6 to 2.3 m^2/m^2). In June the leaf area index of legumes on sections populated by voles was 6 times less, and herbs by 2-3 times
less, than on the control section. A varied degree of reduction of
growth rate in the various groups of damaged plants caused the
change not only of leaf area index, but also of height and vertical
structure of the grass stand. It is especially noticeable on the
species having a large mass of leaves in the upper layer: mainly
legumes (vetch, lucerne, sainfoil) and some species of herbs.

[2]Here and further in the text all determinations of phytomass are
 given in dry weight.

Table 38.   Seasonal dynamics of leaf area index of basic
groups of grass stratum (m^2/m^2).

Groups	May		End of June	
	Control section	Vole colonies	Control section	Vole colonies
Grasses				
Wide-leafed	0.4	0.2	0.5	0.3
Narrow-leafed	0.1	0.1	0.26	0.23
Sedges	0.08	0.05	0.1	0.1
Legumes	0.2	0.03	0.3	0.05
Herbs	0.8	0.4	1.0	0.3

On fields populated by voles the average height of the major
species of the community, with the exception of feather grass,
does not exceed 12-15 cm at the peak of the growing season. The
wide-leaf grasses show strong decrease (72%) in growth, least is
shown by bedstraw and narrow leaf grasses--by 10 to 25%, the remaining species show approximately 40% decrease (Table 39).

The grass stand of the mowed sections of steppe, not damaged by
voles, can be divided into two distinct layers. In the lower layer
(0-15 cm) is concentrated mainly the leaves of herbs, in the upper
(higher than 15 cm)--of legumes. In the lower layer there is 40% of
the assimilating surface, in the upper--60% (at the time when
phytomass of these layers is almost the same--47% and 53% of the
total). On the vole colonies the grass cover is practically one-
layered; more than 90% of the green mass and assimilating surface of
the leaves is concentrated in the lower layer. In the upper layer
there are only a few generative shoots of grasses, vetch and some
types of grass. Therefore, during the period of most intensive
photosynthesis the difference in total leaf area index on the control sections and colonies was 96% in the upper layer and 69% in the
lower; in the wide-leaf grasses, 90% and 72% respectively; in the
narrow-leafed, 90% and 38%; and in the herbs 95% and 63% (Table 40).

CHANGE OF MICROCLIMATE

Thinning and change in vertical structure of the grass stand of
damaged areas influence illumination of the various layers and
other aspects of the microclimate.

Illumination. The intensity of illumination above the grass
stand, at its lower layer, and on the soil permit comparison of the
incoming radiation and its absorption by the various layers of the

Table 39. Differences in height of major species of plants.

Species	Height of shoots (cm)		Reduction of height on vole colonies	
	Control section	Vole colonies	cm	%
Bromegrass	31.6	8.7	22.9	72
Feathergrass	46.7	35.4	11.3	24
Sheep's Fescue	13.8	11.7	2.1	16
Sedge	13.6	8.7	4.9	36
Vetch	35.1	19.9	15.2	43
Clover	18.8	11.8	7.0	40
Meadow clary	15.8	9.1	6.7	42
Spirea	16.1	9.7	6.4	40
Bedstraw	16.8	15.0	1.8	11

grass stand.[3] The 24 hour course of illumination in various layers
of grass stand shows direct dependence on the size of leaf surface
of the layers above, the dependence increasing with height of the
sun's position. The greatest relationship between these indicators
is noted in the daytime hours (from 10 to 4:00) and it decreases in
the morning and especially in the evening hours (Fig. 8, Table 41).

The difference in intensity of illumination of the soil surface of the sections populated by the voles and the isolated areas
depends on the leaf area index of the entire grass stand. On the
vole colonies total leaf area index is 4 to 5 times less and illumination of the surface of the soil is 3 to 3½ times greater. It is
40% to 60% of total illumination (on the undamaged sections it is
10% to 20%). On the unharmed sections decreased illumination with
increasing depth in the grass stand occurs gradually: each layer
passes approximately 50% of the incoming radiation. On the colonies
the major flux of radiation reaches the lower layer.

As is known, in light-loving plants the light absorption fluc-
tuates between 12 and 17 to 25 and 35 thousand lux and in typical
steppe grasses it advances still more by 10 to 20 thousand lux

[3]Illumination was determined by Deluxe Light Meter "U-16": the
indices characterizing the total intensity of the light are not
precise measures and serve only for comparison of light intensity
of damaged and undamaged sections of grass stand.

Table 40.   Vertical structure of herbage during the period of full development of vegetation[a/].

Layer of grass stand	Grasses		Sedges	Legumes	Herbs	Weight of grass stand
	wide-leaf	narrow-leaf				
Control section						
Upper	$\dfrac{0.40}{43}$	$\dfrac{0.09}{36}$	$\dfrac{0.01}{3}$	$\dfrac{0.63}{72}$	$\dfrac{0.19}{18}$	$\dfrac{1.31}{40}$
Lower	$\dfrac{0.53}{57}$	$\dfrac{0.16}{64}$	$\dfrac{0.15}{97}$	$\dfrac{0.24}{28}$	$\dfrac{0.87}{82}$	$\dfrac{1.95}{60}$
Vole colonies						
Upper	$\dfrac{0.04}{27}$	$\dfrac{0.01}{3}$	No data		$\dfrac{0.01}{3}$	$\dfrac{0.05}{8}$
Lower	$\dfrac{0.15}{73}$	$\dfrac{0.10}{97}$	$\dfrac{0.01}{\text{No data}}$	0.02	$\dfrac{0.32}{97}$	$\dfrac{0.60}{92}$

[a/] In numerator--leaf area indices in m^2/m^2--in denominator, relationship by layers of grass stand in %.

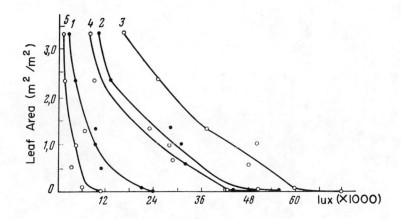

Figure 8
Relationship of size of leaf surface and illumination under cover of grassland at end of June and beginning of July.
1-at 0700 hours; 2-at 1000 hours; 3-at 1300 hours; 4-at 1600 hours; 5-at 1900 hours.

Table 41. Illumination of various layers of grass stand and soil at the end of May and beginning of June (Lux x 1000).

Hours (x100)	First layer	Second layer Control sections	Second layer Vole colonies	Soil surface Control sections	Soil surface Vole colonies
7	23.0 ± 0.2	10.2 ± 0.5	20.0 ± 0.4	2.2 ± 0.2	10.8 ± 1.6
10	50.0 ± 0.0	27.8 ± 1.8	44.0 ± 0.8	8.8 ± 0.5	32.4 ± 1.2
13	71.8 ± 0.2	36.8 ± 2.5	60.4 ± 1.2	15.6 ± 1.3	48.4 ± 1.4
16	55.6 ± 0.5	23.2 ± 1.1	43.2 ± 0.8	8.0 ± 0.5	28.8 ± 1.0
19	9.0 ± 0.04	5.2 ± 0.02	6.0 ± 0.1	1.6 ± 0.08	3.2 ± 0.1
Leaf area index (m^2/m^2) [a]	--	1.31	0.05	3.26	0.65

[a] Indices are for layers situated higher than the one in which illumination is determined.

(Zalenski, Shtanko and Ponomareva 1961, Alexeenko 1967). On virgin sections of meadow-steppe illumination of the surface of both the upper and lower layers of grass canopy exceeds the light absorption capacity during most of the day, or is at its upper limit. Consequently, the increase of illumination on the sections populated by voles cannot facilitate increased photosynthesis of the herbage: it has an effect only on the development of plants at ground level.

On the soil surface of virgin sections intensity of illumination in the middle of the day only corresponds to light absorption. At other times it is somewhat lower, and in the morning and evening it is at or below the compensation point. Consequently, part of the day the plants of this layer do not photosynthesize. On the vole colonies illumination of the surface of the soil during a large part of the day significantly exceeds light absorption. Only in the morning does it attain the lower limit, and in the evening, even less. However, in the morning and evening it is higher than the compensation point. In this way, photosynthesis on damaged sections exceeds respiration during the entire daylight period.

The difference in the daily course of light intensity at the soil surface probably has an effect on growth of shoots and second growth of plants eaten by animals (rodents and insects). According to our observations, at the end of the growing season the shoots and second growth grew more slowly on the virgin sections than on the vole colonies because, in addition to less illumination of the soil layer, there was less moisture and this became worse with its removal by more plants.

The Regime of Temperature and Humidity. Thinning of grass stands on sections populated by voles and the related increased illumination resulted in changes of temperature and humidity of the ground layer of air, litter and soil. The daily course of temperature and humidity and their maximum amplitude influence the intensity of many biological processes.

Temperature and humidity on the surface of the soil was determined by mercury thermometers and psychrometers every three hours. Simultaneously, soil thermometers measured temperature at depths of 5, 10, 15, and 20 cm. The 24 hour amplitude of temperature at the soil surface was determined by maximum and minimum thermometers. The 24 hour amplitude of temperature at soil surface was determined by maximum and minimum thermometers. The 24 hour course of temperature and humidity of the ground layer of air (at a height of 1 m and in the grass canopy) were registered by automatic thermographs and hygrographs.

Temperature in the thin grass canopy of vole colonies was generally higher than in the thick grass stand of the virgin sections. In the day time the difference was 1.5 to 2.0°C, at night it was 0.5 to 1.0°C (Fig. 9). The difference in thermal regime on the soil surface was significantly greater. Poorly shaded soil on sections populated by voles is strongly heated in the day time. In the morning hours it is warmer by 3 to 4°C than the shaded soil of the control sections. In the daytime the difference constitutes on the average 8 to 8.5°C, and on the hottest days 15 to 16°C. With the setting of the sun the picture changes. The thin grass stand allows escape of a large part of the long wave radiation from the soil, for this reason in the colonies the surface of the soil quickly cools and at night temperature is lower by 1.7°C (Fig. 10). As a result, the amplitude of 24 hour fluctuations of soil surface

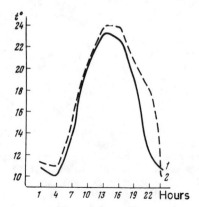

Figure 9
24 hour temperature course of the ground layer (end of June, beginning of July). 1-control sections; 2-vole colonies.

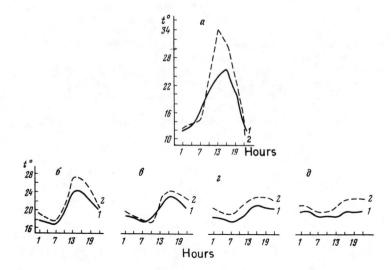

Figure 10
24 hour temperature course on soil surface and at various depths (end of June, beginning of July). 1-control sections; 2-vole colonies: a-on the surface, at depth; b-5 cm; c-10 cm; d-15 cm; e-20 cm.

temperature of the colonies increases by 11.4°C and is 2 times greater than on the virgin sections of the steppe.

Strong heating of the soil in the day and sharp 24-hour gradient of temperature affect the humidity of the ground layer of air. On the sections damaged by small mammals daytime temperature is lower than on the virgin lands (Fig. 11), especially in the hot

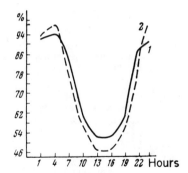

Figure 11
24 hour moisture course of the ground layer (end of June, beginning
of July). 1-control sections; 2-vole colonies.

afternoon hours (by 3 to 5%). Toward evening the difference gradually levels out. At night and early in the morning (from midnight
to 0500) on the colonies the humidity is greater by 2 to 8% (associated, obviously, with a stronger night cooling of the open soil
and condensation of moisture). With the sunrise and increased
temperature it again sharply falls until noon, decreasing synchronously with changes of humidity on the undamaged sections, remaining
1 to 3% lower.

In this way, in the summer the hydrothermic regime of the soil
surface and the ground layer of air on the sections damaged by voles
differs by having a higher temperature and a lower humidity in the
daytime, and a higher humidity at night, and with greater 24-hour
amplitude of these indicators. Obviously, this must be reflected
in the intensity of biological and physical processes of the soil
surface and in the grass canopy.

For example, transpiration is related to the hydrothermic
regime of the ground layer of air (Ivanov, Silina et al. 1951). In
many species of plants the relationship is so close that transpiration can be estimated from temperature, without direct measurement. It is also established that temperature changes of 1 to 3°C
and humidity changes of 5 to 8% cause changes in transpiration of
various species of plants by 10% or more (Gordeeva 1952, Kleshnin
and Shulgin 1963, Evdokimova 1963, Fundamentals of Forest Biocoenology
1964).

On sections populated by small mammals the thermal regime of
the upper 20 cm layer of the soil also changes. As is seen in Fig.
11, in this layer the temperature is higher than on the control
areas.

On the soil surface of the undamaged sections the amplitude of
24-hour fluctuation of temperature is 12.2°C, and on the damaged
sections 23.6°C. This occurs chiefly at the expense of 24-hour
maxima, the difference on these sections being 8.1°C (on virgin
sections the 24-hour maximum is 25.5°C, on the sections populated by
voles it is 33.6°C). With depth the differences in temperature
regime decrease (chiefly at the expense of lower diurnal temperature
and nocturnal cooling of the soil in the colonies). At a depth of

5 cm maximum 24-hour temperature of the soil on damaged sections decreases (in comparison with the surface) by 7.3°C, and on the undamaged by 1.1°C. Minimum temperatures increase by 6.8 and 4.9°C, respectively. The 24 hour amplitude of temperature on the colonies varies by a factor of 3 (by 8.7°C), and on the control sections by a factor of 2 (by 6.8°C).

At a depth of 10 cm the 24-hour amplitude of soil temperature on damaged and undamaged sections differs by 1.7°C (7.4 and 5.7°C). Heating of the soil occurs slowly. The 24-hour maximum, independent of the temperature of the soil surface, shifts to late afternoon hours and is lower by 1 to 1.3°C. At a depth of 15 cm the temperature regime of the soil on both sections is still closer. The 24-hour amplitude of temperature decreases by 1½ times and on the areas populated by small mammals by 0.2 to 1.5° more than on the isolated areas. During 24-hour periods the temperature changes synchronously but on the colonies it is approximately 1.5 to 2.0°C higher than on the isolated areas (19.1 to 23°C and 17.5 to 21°C).

In this way, the changes of thermal conditions of the soil, caused by activity of voles, manifest themselves only near the surface. Even in the uppermost horizons of the soil they are smoothed and at a depth of 10-20 cm almost disappear. Consequently, the voles have an effect only on the processes at the surface (including litter) and in the upper 10 cm layer of the soil.

Soil Moisture. Observations of moisture in the soil showed differences in seasonal changes on damaged and control areas. In spring, after the disappearance of snow but before the beginning of the growing season, the moisture supply of the upper meter of soil is similar on all the sections (the difference did not exceed 1% with 1% reliability). As water utilization increases soil moisture on the damaged and undamaged sections begins to differ. This was observed in 1967, when May and the beginning of June were very dry, and the reserve of moisture was not replenished by rain. Toward the end of the first 10 day period of June the upper meter of soil in the steppe was rather uniformly dry with a moisture content of 15 to 17%. On the sections populated by voles strong drying was noted only in the upper 20 cm layer.

After heavy rains, which occurred in the 2nd and 3rd 10 day period of June, soil moisture increased, while on the damaged section the moisture was 2 to 11% higher in the entire meter thickness of the soil (with the exception of the upper 10 cm) than on the control. In the beginning of July the rain ceased and the moisture began to evaporate, especially on the colonies, where the soil was heated more strongly. Because of this the difference in moisture of the upper layer of soil on the damaged and control section decreased 1 to 4%. From the 6th through the 17th of July it was dry and hot, on the surface of the soil a dense crust formed which reduced physical evaporation, and the soil moisture was lost almost exclusively by transpiration. Toward the end of the vegetative period humidity of the upper layer of the soil (5 to 10 cm) on the colonies was 2% lower and in the remaining part of the profile 4 to 5% higher. At this time the reserve of moisture on the damaged sections exceeded the wilting coefficient while on the control areas in the 0-40 cm layer it was less than the wilting coefficient (Table 42, Fig. 12).

Table 42. Seasonal dynamics of soil moisture (% of dry weight).

Depth (cm)	Control sections						Vole colonies					
	April	June			July		April	June			July	
	21-30	1-10	11-20	21-30	1-10	11-20	21-30	1-10	11-20	21-30	1-10	11-20
0-5	32.8	16.3	36.4	48.8	25.3	17.0	34.0	14.5	34.6	42.1	22.5	14.7
5-10	31.3	16.1	23.0	38.8	24.2	18.5	31.7	15.7	19.0	39.3	23.6	15.4
10-15	30.0	15.4	17.0	33.4	24.9	14.9	31.1	16.4	18.0	36.0	26.6	17.3
15-20	29.8	15.5	15.9	15.0	22.7	15.6	30.5	17.3	18.6	25.9	24.9	18.4
20-30	28.5	16.1	16.1	18.3	21.0	15.2	28.5	18.9	19.9	21.4	23.3	19.3
30-40	26.7	17.4	15.9	20.3	18.6	15.1	29.8	20.8	21.5	26.4	22.6	18.5
40-50	25.7	16.9	16.5	19.1	18.5	15.0	28.0	21.6	21.7	24.1	19.4	18.7
50-60	25.5	15.1	16.4	20.8	18.4	14.9	26.8	22.0	22.0	25.9	19.9	19.4
60-70	25.5	15.8	16.0	19.5	15.6	15.8	25.9	21.5	22.1	24.8	18.3	18.9
70-80	24.6	16.1	16.3	19.9	15.4	14.3	25.2	20.2	21.4	23.1	19.2	19.3
80-90	24.0	15.9	15.1	19.8	16.6	14.8	24.9	20.1	19.5	23.0	19.6	19.4
90-100	25.4	16.2	15.4	21.2	18.6	15.6	24.9	21.3	20.4	24.7	19.7	20.0

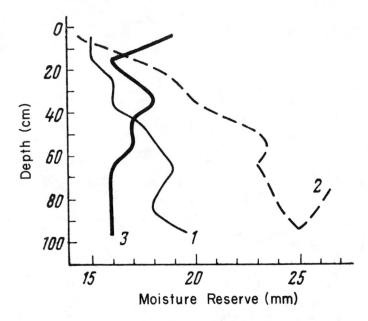

Figure 12
Moisture reserve in humus horizon of the steppe chernozem soil
during peak vegetation development of grass canopy (second 10
day period of July). 1-control sections; 2-vole colonies; 3-
wilting moisture level.

     The differences in water regime of the colonies' soil and of
the unpopulated steppe sections may be explained chiefly by differing amounts of evaporating leaf surface of the grass canopy. For
this reason in the spring before the beginning of vegetation growth,
when soil moisture is used chiefly on physical evaporation, its
reserve on damaged and control sections is almost the same. In
direct relation to development of vegetation physiological evaporation begins to predominate over the physical and utilization of
moisture depends more and more on the size of the transpiring surface and the mass of absorbing roots.
     In meadow steppe the majority of roots (80%) are concentrated
in the upper 40-50 cm layer of the soil, including 60% in the layer
of 0-10 cm (Gertzik 1955, Afanaseeva 1966). This regular distribution of roots is characteristic also for those sections damaged by
the voles (in g/m^2 dry weight):

Depth (cm)	Control Section	Vole Colonies
0-5	1990	1970
5-10	760	515
10-15	443	260
15-20	295	150
20-30	385	310
30-40	295	185
0-40	4168	3390

The root biomass on the vole colonies is 19% less than on the control section, and in the main part of the root layer (0-10 cm) there is still less (only 9 to 10% of the control). In addition, the leaf area index of the grass canopy in the colonies is lower by a factor of 4.5 than that of the undamaged sections. Consequently, utilization of moisture by transpiration on the sections populated by voles should be less. By eating the plants the voles disturb the natural utilization of moisture from the soil profile. For example, they damage mainly species with surface roots, and then the utilization of moisture from the upper horizons of the soil will be less than from the lower.

For verification of this hypothesis we compared the distribution of moisture in the soil profile on damaged and control sections with corresponding leaf area indices and root mass distributions for a given horizon. This gives a picture of the utilization of moisture by transpiration from various horizons of the soil. The leaf area index, corresponding to the mass of roots in a given horizon, is determined by the formula:

$$S_n = S_\Sigma - (S^- - S^+)$$

where S_n is the leaf area index corresponding to the amount of roots at a given depth (n in cm), S_Σ is the average total leaf area index of the entire grass stand, S^+ is the leaf area index for those species rooted primarily in depth interval n, and S^- is the leaf area index for those species rooted primarily in depth zones other than n.[4] Results indicate that on the sections populated by voles on control areas, the leaf area index of the species with the majority of roots in the layer of 0-50 cm was twice as great as the species whose roots are located in the 50-100 cm layer (Table 43 and 44). Between the reserve of moisture in various horizons and the area of transpiring leaf surface, there is a strong inverse relationship. The degree of relationship on the damaged and undamaged sections is not the same and changes seasonally (Fig. 13). In the vole colonies leaf surface increases more slowly over a longer time period. In those species with roots primarily in the 0 to 50 cm horizon the total leaf surface area is maximum toward the end of July. On the control sections it is maximum toward the end of June. Moreover, its growth rate on the isolated sections was 42% in June and 2% in July. On the sections populated by voles in June and

[4]Calculations are from the data and method of V. I. Golubev (1962) on the system of herbaceous plants of the Central Chernozem Reserve.

Table 43.   Example of calculation of leaf area index corresponding to the root mass in various soil layers ($S_\Sigma = 2.27$).

Depth (cm)	S^-	S^+	$S^- - S^+$	S horizon = $= S_\Sigma - (S^- - S^+)$
0–10	0.34	--	-0.34	1.93
10–20	0.60	0.17	-0.43	1.84
20–30	0.64	0.21	-0.43	1.84
30–40	0.66	0.23	-0.43	1.84
40–50	0.67	0.23	-0.44	1.83
50–60	1.50	0.31	-0.19	1.08
60–70	1.50	0.24	-1.26	0.01
70–80	1.62	0.10	-1.50	0.77
80–90	1.77	0.07	-1.70	0.57
90–100	1.77	0.07	-1.70	0.57

July the value was 25% (change of leaf area is indicated in relation to the previous month). In the plant species with deep distribution of roots total leaf surface increases more slowly. On isolated sections it increases very slowly during the entire vegetative period, and on the colonies it grows quite sharply at the end of this period. The seasonal course of moisture reserve in various horizons reflects seasonal changes of the leaf area index of that part of the grass stand whose roots are located in the corresponding horizon (Fig. 13).

A tentative picture about the degree of influence of voles on the moisture reserve in the humus layer of thick chernozem soil indicates differences between control sections and the sections occupied by small mammals in the utilization of moisture by transpiration and the reserve of water in the soil. During the growing season the average transpiration rate of steppe grasses is 0.2 to 0.7 g of water per 1 g of raw weight per hour (Gordeeva 1952, Redulesku-Ivan 1965). The average 24 hour duration of the strongest transpiration is 12–15 hours (Bejdeman, Bespalova and Rakhmanina 1962). Proceeding from this, the 24 hour use of moisture by transpiration in meadow–steppe tentatively can be considered as 4 g per gram of raw weight of plants. Using this value and knowing the phytomass of the grass stand, we calculated an approximate use of moisture during 12 days at the end of the growing season (6 to 17 of

Table 44. Leaf area index corresponding to the mass of roots in various soil layers (m^2/m^2).

Depth (cm)	Control sections					Vole colonies				
	1967			1968		1967			1968	
	21 May	24 June	17 July	12 May	13 June	21 May	24 June	17 July	12 May	13 June
0–10	1.43	1.93	2.01	1.25	2.04	0.69	0.85	1.06	0.39	0.53
10–20	1.36	1.85	1.87	1.09	1.66	0.71	0.83	1.12	0.40	0.66
20–30	1.42	1.84	1.79	1.04	2.15	0.71	0.75	1.06	0.39	0.63
30–40	1.43	1.85	1.77	1.01	2.44	0.66	0.83	1.05	0.37	0.62
40–50	1.42	1.83	1.75	1.36	1.55	0.66	0.83	0.04	0.37	0.61
50–60	0.96	0.99	1.06	0.85	1.32	0.45	0.42	0.67	0.33	0.55
60–70	0.91	1.01	.090	0.63	1.02	0.40	0.37	0.57	0.30	0.43
70–80	0.79	0.77	0.72	0.35	0.83	0.33	0.30	0.46	0.27	0.25
80–90	0.69	0.58	0.70	0.42	0.74	0.30	0.28	0.48	0.27	0.22
90–100	0.69	0.58	0.70	0.42	0.74	0.30	0.28	0.48	0.27	0.22

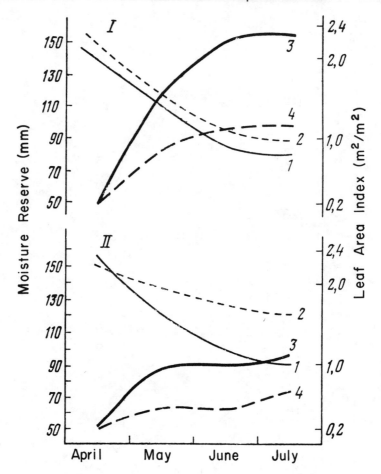

Figure 13
Seasonal changes of soil moisture reserve and size of leaf surface
of grass stand with majority of roots at layer of 0–50 (I) and
50–100 cm (II). 1–moisture reserve in soil of control sections;
2–same, of colonies; 3–leaf surface of grass stand of control
sections; 4–same, of colonies.

July) on the damaged sections and on the isolated areas. Since, as
was indicated above, there was a crust on the soil, moisture was
expended chiefly by transpiration, then the comparison of soil
moisture in the beginning and the end of the time by segments serves
as an indicator of moisture use by transpiration.
     On the control sections the reserve of moisture in the 100 cm
layer of the soil on the 6th of July was 213 mm, on the 17th of July
171 mm, the calculated cost of transpiration during this segment of
time was 34 mm. On the vole colonies these indicators were of the

following sizes: 240, 215, and 21 mm. Thus, during this period the
moisture utilization by transpiration was 38% lower on the sections
occupied by small mammals, which corresponds to the measured difference in the reserve of soil moisture during this same time (40%),
established on the basis of field determination of soil moisture.

The general reserve of moisture on the sections populated by
voles was 26% greater at the end of the vegetative period than on
the control sections. As a result of activity of the voles in the
humus horizon 440 cubic meters of water per hectare was conserved
(of this 150 cubic meters per hectare was in the layer 0 to 50 cm).
For comparison, the difference in the reserve of moisture at the 100
cm layer of soil of the mowed and unmowed sections of the steppe
reaches 8%, according to the data of V. V. Gertzik (1955), and on
the absolute reserve and mowed section a total of 2% (according to
observations of V. V. Gertzik and I. P. Kokorino at the end of July
1967).

INFLUENCE ON THE PROCESSES OF ACCUMULATION OF PHYTOMASS

Reduction of total transpiration by the grass canopy on the
vole colonies, leading to decreased expenditure of soil moisture and
a longer preservation of the reserve of moisture in the upper root
layers of the soil, affected the seasonal dynamics of moisture of
plants and the duration of the vegetative period and growth of the
phytomass.

On the section populated by voles the moisture content of many
species of herbs and legumes (and also of these groups in general)
is higher than on the undamaged sections. For a large part of the
vegetative period this difference is greatest in the herbs, and at
the end of the vegetative period, in the legumes (Table 45).

At the end of summer the species showing differences in moisture content are mostly those species with deeper roots, which
find particularly favorable conditions on the sections populated by

Table 45. Seasonal dynamics of plant moisture, 1967 (% of dry weight).[a]

Group	May		June		July	
	Control sections	Vole colonies	Control sections	Vole colonies	Control sections	Vole colonies
Grasses and sedges	133	107	136	112	75	69
Legumes	236	219	168	219	94	141
Herbs	209	335	216	365	130	129

[a] Plant moisture content (%) = $\dfrac{\text{fresh weight} - \text{dry weight}}{\text{dry weight}} \times 100.$

voles. It should be noted, however, that in very hot dry years (for example, 1968), when the weakly shaded soils of the colonies is strongly heated increasing physical and physiological evaporation, the picture changes. In those years the spring moisture of the plants is the same everywhere, but toward the middle of June on the sections populated by the voles it is lower, especially in the mesophytic types. Thus, if in the normal moisture year 1967 the moisture of the grasses and sedges was lower by 18% on the colony areas during the period of complete development of phytomass in comparison with their moisture on the isolated areas, and herbs and legumes were higher by 69 and 42%. In the dry 1968 year it was lower in all of these groups of plants by 11, 25, and 37%.

The development of separate species and groups of plants, and consequently the growth of green mass on populated and unpopulated sections, is not the same. This is observed particularly in comparison of intensity of growth of damaged plants on colony sections and on isolated quadrats. During the period of most active growth conditions of development of plants on the colonies are worse, especially in the soil surface layer. The number of sprouts there is 3 to 10 times fewer and the second growth is 1.5 to 6.0 times less (it is especially slowed in the legumes). At this time illumination of the soil and the lower layer of grasses on the damaged and unharmed sections differs comparatively little. At this time the upper layers of the soil on the colonies are strongly heated and dry quickly. The height of the shoots of the major species of the community of plants is 1.3 to 1.9 times less in the middle of June on the damaged section (especially slow is the growth of legumes, herbs and bromegrass). Toward the end of the vegetative period the situation changes. At this time the plants of the lower layer on the sections with colonies grow noticeably. This is connected with the fact that there are more favorable conditions of soil moisture and illumination in the lower layer of the grass canopy and on the soil surface (Table 46). In accordance with growth of different major groups of plants total growth of the grass stand was found to be varying (Table 47-49).

During May and June the mass of the grass canopy increased by 80% on the isolated sections and by 35% on the sections populated by the voles. As a result of the decreased growth rate of plants on the vole colonies the difference in phytomass on these sections toward the end of June increased 15%. However, as already mentioned, many plants on the sections populated by voles grew by 23 weeks longer.[5] At this time the green phytomass increased by 22%, which somewhat compensated for the earlier loss of biomass. Average production of grass on the vole colonies constituted 50% of the harvest on the isolated quadrats.

The impact of voles on production of the grass stand becomes greater with unfavorable meteorological conditions even if the number of their density is lower. Thus, in 1968 despite the decrease of vole numbers, the loss of production of the colonies was greater especially on the production of the more mesophytic group-- legumes, wide-leaf grasses and herbs. The same was observed even on recently abandoned colonies of the voles.

[5]On the sections populated by other types of voles (for example, social) the plants also grew longer than on the virgin sections of the steppe (Voronov 1935, Kucheruk 1963).

Table 46. Growth rate of major species of plants (cm).

Index	Months	Bromegrass	Feathergrass	Sheeps fescue	Sedge	Clover	Vetch	Meadow clary	Spirea	Bedstraw
Height of shoots of undamaged plants										
Control sections	Mid-June	31.3	46.7	13.8	13.6	18.8	35.1	15.8	16.1	16.8
Vole colonies	Same	16.3	35.4	11.7	8.7	11.8	19.9	9.1	9.7	15.0
Second growth during one month										
Control sections	May-June	9.3	8.4	5.7	5.1	5.6	7.6	1.8	1.7	4.1
Vole colonies	Same	5.2	5.6	3.4	2.9	2.6	1.2	1.1	0.0	2.5
Control sections	June-July	7.4	8.9	4.3	3.3	5.3	4.5	5.2	4.0	3.7
Vole colonies	Same	14.1	10.7	3.7	6.6	4.5	2.8	3.8	5.1	4.8

Table 47.   Changes of green phytomass and leaf surface area
of grass canopy on sections occupied by voles
(% of the grass canopy on control squares)[a].

Group of grass stand	1967			1968	
	May	June	July	May	June
Grassy vegetation	$\frac{55}{50}$	$\frac{41}{44}$	$\frac{50}{48}$	$\frac{37}{38}$	$\frac{29}{30}$
Grasses	$\frac{65}{68}$	$\frac{69}{70}$	$\frac{55}{57}$	$\frac{--}{62}$	$\frac{--}{42}$
Wide-leafed	$\frac{46}{47}$	$\frac{59}{60}$	$\frac{55}{54}$	$\frac{54}{60}$	$\frac{37}{35}$
Narrow-leafed	$\frac{125}{113}$	$\frac{88}{89}$	$\frac{62}{62}$	$\frac{52}{57}$	$\frac{62}{63}$
Sedges	$\frac{66}{60}$	$\frac{75}{90}$	$\frac{5}{5}$	$\frac{33}{34}$	$\frac{37}{38}$
Legumes	$\frac{20}{13}$	$\frac{16}{16}$	$\frac{43}{44}$	$\frac{8}{8}$	$\frac{4}{3}$
Herbs	$\frac{62}{48}$	$\frac{21}{39}$	$\frac{53}{49}$	$\frac{32}{32}$	$\frac{34}{38}$
Mosses	--	46	14	10	10

[a] In numerator--index of phytomass, in denominator--index of
leaf area.

     In the spring on the damaged sections better conditions are
created for development of xerophytic narrow-leafed grasses (at this
time their phytomass is 25% greater and the leaf area is 13% higher
than on the control areas) and at the end of the vegetative period--
for development of legumes and some types of herbs (plantain, strawberry, woodruff, *Potentilla*) resulting in a supplementary growth
of phytomass.
     For estimation of participation of animals in biological cycling,
their influence on the growth of not only the green but also the
belowground part of phytomass must be considered. As is known, one
of the basic factors determining intensity of photosynthesis is the
content of CO_2 in the ground layer of air. Moreover, about 30% of
the total CO_2 flowing into the atmosphere from the soil and litter
is given off by the roots.
     We did not have the opportunity to examine the seasonal dynamics
of the root growth and had only data on the relationship of the
aboveground and belowground phytomass at the end of the growing

Table 48. Seasonal and yearly dynamics of green phytomass
(g/m^2)[a/] .

Group	1967			1968	
	May	June	July	May	June
Grass stand	$\frac{139}{76}$	$\frac{250}{103}$	$\frac{249}{126}$	$\frac{143}{53}$	$\frac{275}{79}$
Grasses	$\frac{61}{40}$	$\frac{89}{69}$	$\frac{115}{65}$	$\frac{52}{28}$	$\frac{87}{37}$
Sedges	$\frac{--}{--}$	$\frac{8}{--}$	$\frac{14}{0.07}$	$\frac{4}{1}$	$\frac{7}{3}$
Legumes	$\frac{27}{5}$	$\frac{47}{7}$	$\frac{36}{15}$	$\frac{15}{1}$	$\frac{77}{3}$
Herbs	$\frac{51}{31}$	$\frac{106}{27}$	$\frac{84}{45}$	$\frac{72}{23}$	$\frac{104}{36}$
Mosses	$\frac{--}{--}$	$\frac{63}{29}$	$\frac{56}{8}$	$\frac{49}{5}$	$\frac{75}{8}$

[a/] In numerator--on control sections, in denominator--on
vole colonies.

season. At this time on the sections populated by voles the green
phytomass aboveground was 50% less and of roots 19% less than on the
isolated quadrats. In summer the voles eat almost exclusively the
green parts of the plants, and the decrease of phytomass of roots in
the colonies is due only to the reduced growth of damaged plants.
In this case, it is possible to limit the growth of root mass,
determined by the damage to stems and leaves. This is partially
compensated by the increase of light on the damaged sections, stimulating translocation of products of assimilation from the leaves to
the roots and facilitating growth of belowground parts (Alexeenko
1967). Toward the end of the vegetative period the phytomass
relationship of green parts to roots (in the layer of 0-40 cm)
constituted 1:17 on the undamaged section and 1:27 on the damaged.
    The changes in the relationship of root mass which produces
CO_2, and the assimilating green mass, must have an effect on the
content of CO_2 in the ground layer of air on the sections damaged by
the voles. For verification of this hypothesis experiments were
designed to provide tentative indices of differences in CO_2 in the
ground layer of air (the quantity CO_2 evolved by the soil and litter,
absorbed by the grass stand, and their relationship) on damaged and
undamaged sections. The intensity of evolution of CO_2 was determined according to the method of Shtatnova (Makarov and Matzkevitch
1966). Our method is still very imperfect (particularly because of

Table 49.   Seasonal and yearly dynamics of leaf area index (m^2/m^2).

Group	1967			1968		
	May	June	July	May	Mid-June	End of June
Grasses	$\frac{0.49}{0.31}$	$\frac{0.78}{0.54}$	$\frac{1.00}{0.57}$	$\frac{0.45}{0.25}$	$\frac{0.76}{0.32}$	$\frac{1.18}{0.30}$
Sedges	$\frac{0.08}{0.05}$	$\frac{0.10}{0.09}$	$\frac{0.18}{0.01}$	$\frac{0.05}{0.02}$	$\frac{0.10}{0.03}$	$\frac{0.15}{0.01}$
Legumes	$\frac{0.20}{0.03}$	$\frac{0.33}{0.05}$	$\frac{0.27}{0.12}$	$\frac{0.11}{0.01}$	$\frac{0.57}{0.02}$	$\frac{0.87}{0.02}$
Herbs	$\frac{0.83}{0.40}$	$\frac{1.05}{0.31}$	$\frac{0.85}{0.40}$	$\frac{0.81}{0.26}$	$\frac{1.03}{0.38}$	$\frac{1.06}{0.33}$
Total	$\frac{1.60}{0.79}$	$\frac{2.26}{0.99}$	$\frac{2.30}{1.10}$	$\frac{1.42}{0.54}$	$\frac{2.46}{0.75}$	$\frac{3.26}{0.66}$

[a] In numerator--on control section, in denominator--on vole colonies.

little replication) for this reason the data cannot be considered
absolute indicators and can be used only for comparison of the CO_2
on damaged and undamaged sections, since errors of method in both
instances are the same.

The experiments were conducted in two variants: in one instance the grass canopy was cut, and in the other it was preserved.
The content of carbon in the ground layer of air toward the end of
the experiment in the first case corresponds to the amount from soil
and litter, and characterizes the intensity of their "breathing."
The difference between the content of carbon in the first and second
period corresponds to the quantity absorbed by the grass canopy.
Results of the experiments show that the quantity of carbon separated from the soil and litter on the colonies and isolated areas,
differs by a total of 4%. At the same time the quantity absorbed by
the grass canopy changes in proportion to the size of the leaf area
index; on the colonies the fixation of CO_2 is 2.2 times less (by
57%) than on the control sections (Table 50).

It should be underscored, that although these indicators are
highly sensitive, they demonstrate the possibility of applying
similar methods of determination of the gas regime and biological
activity of the soil to estimate the influence of phytophages on the
content of CO_2 in the ground layer of air.

THE ROLE OF VOLES IN DECOMPOSITION PROCESSES

The impact of voles on the accumulation and mineralization of
litterfall is manifested in various forms. They fertilize the soil

Table 50.   Change of CO_2 content in near ground layer.

Index	Control quadrats	Vole colonies
Leaf area index of grass canopy (m^2/m^2)	2.3	1.1
Mass of litter (g/m^2)	121.0	90.0
Mass of roots in layer of 0–40 cm (g/m^2)	4172.0	3390.0
Quantity of CO_2 released from soil and litter (mg for 1 m^2/hr)		
Variant without grass	414.0	397.0
Variant with grass	309.0	352.0
Quantity of CO_2 absorbed by grass stand (mg for 1 m^2/hr)	105.0	45.0

with their bodies and excretions, creating a favorable substratum for development of microorganisms. The remains of the grasses gnawed by the voles mineralize faster than the dry dead grass. The change of the microclimate caused by them exerts an influence on the rate of biological processes and the speed of abiogenic mineralization of litterfall.

The Mineralization of Excrements. A characteristic peculiarity of meadow-steppe and oak forests of the forest-steppe mid-Russian upland is the lack of accumulation of excrement of small animals on the surface of the soil. Even during the period of high numbers of voles a most careful examination of litter reveals very few of their droppings, indicating rapid decomposition.

For verification of this we established two series of experiments in the steppes and on the forest glades in the fall of 1966. In fine mesh Capron net bags, filled in one series with chernozem soil and in the other with white sand, were placed 25 g (dry wt) of excrement collected during the summer. The net bags were placed level with the surface of the soil and covered by litterfall and stalks of the growing grasses. Hydrothermic conditions, and also the possibility of penetration of soil and litter invertebrates, were the same as in natural conditions. The light substrate allowed us to judge whether the droppings disappeared as a result of very fast mineralization or by disintegrating into small pieces. In the dark substrate they are mixed with the pellets of chernozem and become difficult to distinguish. Experiments were conducted during four years. Annually in the fall the net bags were taken out and the droppings were removed (the soil together with the droppings was sieved through a set of soil sieves, and later each fraction was

separated by hand), weighed, and the fraction mineralized was determined.   The remaining part of the droppings was again placed into
the net bag for continuation of the experiment.

During the first year in the steppe 55% on the average had
mineralized, and in the forest 67% of the droppings had mineralized.
During the second year-correspondingly 20% and 22 to 23%, during the
third year 8 and 6%, during the fourth year 5 and 4%.   The majority
of the droppings mineralized during the first two years.   The rate
of decomposition of droppings on chernozem and on sand was the same.
However, before careful sieving through the complete set of soil
sieves and the successive manipulation of each fraction by hand,
it appeared that the droppings on the chernozem were preserved very
little, since, becoming smaller and drying out, they were almost
indistinguishable from the dry particles of the soil.   Thus, the
apparent lack of droppings in the natural litter and on the surface
of the soil is explained not only by the rapid mineralization but by
their indistinguishability from the soil.   The differences in rates
of mineralization of droppings in the steppe and in the forest
glades were noted only during the first year (Table 51).

The process of mineralization of plant litterfall proceeds
at approximately the same rate.   During the first year on the
average 60% of the plant litterfall had mineralized.   During the
second year, depending on meteorological conditions, 20 to 30%
(Afanaseeva 1964, Kurcheva 1965, Kokovina 1967).

Simultaneously with the experiments described in the steppe
observations were made of the speed of mineralization and the accumulation of fresh excrement on the sections occupied by voles.
At the beginning of summer two series of 16 squares (each 25 × 25
cm) were placed on these sections and droppings were collected
from these.   Afterwards, on the squares of one series, the accumulated droppings were collected every five days.   Such a time span
was used because daily observations on the permanent squares showed
that the major part of excrement gradually dries up and breaks down
during 8 to 10 days and only a small quantity was preserved for a
longer time.   On the squares of the second series the droppings were
collected only after three months.

The experiments showed that during the three summer months on
the soil of the colonies there is deposited on the average of 3.4
g/m^2 of fresh droppings (10 to 15 g/m^2 during the year, which is
equivalent to about 10% of the yearly quantity of plant litterfall).
Toward the end of the third month of the experiment the quantity of
accumulated droppings was 2 g/m^2.   Consequently, during July-August
approximately 42% of the fresh droppings had mineralized.

Animal excrement represents very favorable substrate for development of microorganisms and increasing the rate of processes of
mineralization of organic remains.   This is known for invertebrate
animals in the forest-steppe (Kurcheva 1971, Zlotin and Khodashova
1972).   Obviously, a similar role is played by the excrement of
herbivorous rodents, affirmed by the results of field experiments.
One series of the fine meshed net bags was filled with 20 g (here
and below referring to dry weight) of clean steppe litter, the
second series by the same quantity of litter with addition of 1.2 g
of vole droppings (the ratio of quantity of droppings to litter,
as in the colonies of voles, was 1:16.6).   During the first year 48%
of the clean litter had mineralized and 65% of the litter mixed with
droppings.

Table 51. The rate of mineralization of vole droppings.

Place of experiment	Initital quantity (g)	Remains (g)				Mineralized part[a]			
		1967	1968	1969	1970	1966–1967	1967–1968	1968–1969	1969–1970
Steppe									
Soil	25	11.8	6.6	3.5	3.0	$\frac{13.2}{53}$	$\frac{5.2}{20}$	$\frac{2.1}{10}$	$\frac{0.5}{2}$
Sand	25	10.5	5.3	3.7	1.3	$\frac{14.5}{56}$	$\frac{5.2}{21}$	$\frac{1.4}{6}$	$\frac{2.4}{10}$
Forest glade									
Soil	25	8.9	2.2	1.6	0.7	$\frac{16.1}{64}$	$\frac{6.7}{27}$	$\frac{1.2}{5}$	$\frac{0.9}{4}$
Sand	25	7.1	1.2	0.0	0.0	$\frac{17.9}{71}$	$\frac{5.9}{24}$	$\frac{1.2}{5}$	$\frac{0.0}{0.0}$

a/ In the numerator the indices are in grams, in the denominator they are in % of initital quantity.

103

Mineralization of Plant Litterfall. Seasonal dynamics of the aboveground phytomass, including dead plant remains, is quite different on sections damaged by the voles and on the isolated quadrats. This is because the voles influence not only the growth of phytomass but also the decomposition of litterfall. Thus, on the control sections, the mass of dead plant remains sharply increased from May to June, litter continued to grow insignificantly during the entire period of vegetation growth and decreased in the fall. This regularity was noted earlier for meadow steppe by A. M. Semenova-Tian-Shanskaya (1966) and by E. A. Afanaseeva (1966). On the damaged sections the quantity of dead plant remains at the beginning of summer increased only slightly and then began to decrease, sharply decreasing toward the end of September (Table 52).

Seasonal changes of the mass of parts on the isolated quadrats coincided with the seasonal dynamics of mass of litter-fall and of litter on the colonies (Fig. 14), indicating the intensity of processes of accumulation and mineralization of litterfall on these sections.

For explanation of the influence of voles on the contribution, accumulation, and mineralization of dead plant remains we made monthly calculations of the relationship of litterfall and litter on the isolated areas and on the colonies (Table 53). These calculations indicate the balance between accumulation and mineralization of plant litterfall in the summer to fall period. On the isolated sections in summer and fall the processes of mineralization flow very weakly and accumulation of dead remains predominate over mineralization. During the first half of the summer there is intensive accumulation of standing dead. The reserve increases by 3 to 4 times. The biomass of litter at the beginning of summer increases 26% (due to destruction of standing dead), and later it changes little. At the end of summer rapid decomposition of standing dead begins, accompanied by partial mineralization of litter. From the middle of July to the middle of September 80% of the standing dead that accumulated during the summer mineralizes, and in total 32% of the litter. As a result, by autumn the general biomass of dead remains increases 38% in comparison with spring. This coincides completely with the data of A. M. Semenova-Tian-Shanskaya (1966) according to whose observations on the mowed and unmowed steppe at the end of summer and in the fall accumulation of dead material always exceeds decomposition.

The activity of voles brings a sharp change in the balance of accumulation and mineralization of litterfall. On the colonies of these small mammals decomposition of dead material during the summer and fall predominates over accumulation. In the beginning of summer standing dead mineralizes faster than litter. In May biomass of standing dead decreases 69%; because of this the mass of litter increases 33%. But later the relationship changes. In June-July there occurs a significant accumulation of cellulose. Because of the shoots gnawed by small mammals, its biomass increases by 4 times. However, formation of standing dead occurs by intensive destruction of the dead parts. During the two following months (the middle of August to the middle of September) 80% of the cellulose mineralizes and almost 60% of the litter. As a result, toward fall the total biomass of dead aboveground parts was 50% less than in the spring (Table 54).

Table 52. Seasonal dynamics of the dead aboveground phytomass (g/m^2).

Index	Control sections				Vole colonies			
	May	June	July	September	May	June	July	September
Phytomass	104	182	203	203	132	164	137	64
Standing dead[a]	12	58	82	17	28	9	47	9
Litter	92	124	121	126	104	155	90	55

[a] Litter-fall of the aboveground parts in grassy steppe communities.

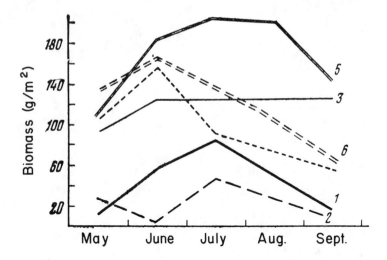

Figure 14
Seasonal dynamics of the biomass of aboveground dead vegetative
remains. 1-standing dead on control sections; 2-standing dead
on colonies; 3-litter on control sections; 4-litter on colonies;
5-average biomass of dead aboveground parts of plants on control
sections; 6-average biomass of dead aboveground parts of plants
on colonies.

In this way activity of the voles modifies the seasonal course
of mineralization of plant remains and significantly increases the
rate of this process during the summer. Obviously, this is due
primarily to changes of microclimatic conditions in damaged sections. In meadow-steppe the major factors controlling the rate of
decomposition processes are abiogenic factors, chiefly light and the
thermal environment of litterfall. Experiments showed that under
the influence of only these factors about 70% of the steppe litterfall mineralizes (Zlotin 1969a). As was pointed out above, on
sections damaged by voles the illumination and temperature of the
surface of the litter and soil was significantly higher than on the
undamaged sections. At the end of June and beginning of July,
during the period of most intensive decomposition of litterfall,
on the sections occupied by voles illumination of litter was 3 to 5
times greater and the temperature was higher by 4 to 10°C than on
the control sections (Fig. 15). The difference of illumination was
especially great (5.5 times) during the period of greatest intensity
of short wave radiation, the early morning hours.

The increased intensity of abiogenic decomposition of plant
remains on the colonies is facilitated by mechanical impact of small
mammals. The gnawed plants quickly dry out and break off; the
animals break up and crush the litterfall, accelerating its
mineralization.

The moisture regime in the soil of the colonies affects the
vertical distribution and activity of saprophagic soil animals. The
representatives of the microfauna (nematodes, Collembola and others)

Table 53. Calculation of accumulation and mineralization of litter-fall from
the aboveground phytomass during the growing season.

Phytomass (g/m^2)	Months	Control quadrats[a]	Vole colonies[a]
Standing dead	May	12	28
	June	58	9
	July	82	47
	September	17	9
Excess over accumulation of standing	May	0	19
dead which went into litter	June	0	0
	July–		
	September	65	38
Litter	May	92	104
	June	124	155
	July	121	90
	September	126	55
Potential quantity of litter[b]	May	92	123
	June	124	155
	July–		
	September	186	128
Mineralized part of litter[c]	May	0	0
	June	0	65
	July–		
	September	60	73
Balance of litterfall			
Standing dead	May	12	28
	September	17	9
	May– September	+5	–18
Litter	May	92	104
	September	126	55
	May– September	+30	–49
Total litterfall	May	104	132
	September	143	64
	May– September	+39	–68

[a] The plus sign (+) in this and the following table indicates the litter-fall
accumulation, the minus sign (–) indicates its mineralization.

[b] Total litter mass at the beginning of the given period ard part of standing
dead which was destroyed at the end of this period.

[c] Difference between potential and actual litter quantity.

leave the dry heated layer of soil and go to deeper layers. On the
virgin section in summer they concentrate in the 0 to 3 cm layer,
and on those sections with voles--in the layer of 5 to 20 cm.
Representatives of the mesofauna, especially dominant groups of
earthworms, are opposite, rising to the higher horizons (40 to 10
cm) where their numbers increase, and hence their distribution in
the soil profile becomes more uniform. In addition, on the vole

Table 54.   The balance of accumulation and mineralization of
            litterfall during the vegetative period (% of biomass
            at the beginning of the period).

Index	Months	Control quadrats	Vole colonies
Standing dead	May	+358	-69
	June	+41	+422
	July-September	-80	-81
Litter	May	+26	+33
	June	-2	-26
	July-September	-32	-58
Total litterfall	May-September	+38	-52
Standing dead	May-September	+42	-64
Litter	May-September	+33	-48

colonies they are active during the entire vegetation period and do
not have a summer diapause, as in the virgin steppe. All of this
changes the relative role of the various groups of invertebrates on
the vole colonies in mineralization of litterfall during the summer
months.

Finally, on the sections populated by the animals, conditions
favorable for various groups of saprophytic microorganisms are
created. This is connected with introduction into the litter of the
zoogenic litterfall (excrement and gnawed plants), serving as a
substrate for development of microorganisms. As special experiments
showed, a supplement of vole excrement and other phytophages accelerates mineralization of the plant litterfall (Zlotin and
Khodashova 1972). On the vole colonies the litter, mixed with
animal excretions, is permeated by the mycelia of microscopic fungi.
In addition, microbiological processes were favored by the hydro-
logic regime on the sections populated by voles. In hot and dry
periods, as a result of sharp fall of temperature and nightly condensation of moisture in these sections, there is abundant dew
which moistens the litter fall and litter (in the night and morning
hours the difference in moisture of the ground layer of air on the
colonies and on the control sections was as high as 8%). In rainy
periods the opposite occurred. A more dense layer of litter on the
isolated quadrats was impregnated with water and its moisture content reached 72%, significantly exceeding the moisture level
favorable for development of microorganisms (Bondarenko-Zozulina
1955). On the colonies the loose layer of litter and litterfall
quickly dried in the intervals between rain and its moisture decreased to 26%. We hypothesize that in the summer months on the
sections populated by voles microclimatic conditions are created

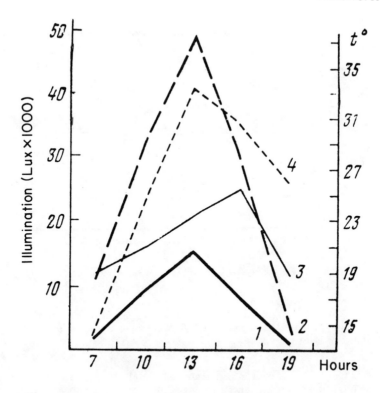

Figure 15
Illumination and temperature on the litter surface (average for
the period of last 1/3 of June, first 10 days of July). 1-
illumination on the control sections; 2-the same, on the colonies;
3-temperature on control sections; 4-the same, on the colonies.

which facilitate periodic activation of microbial organisms (particularly the sporophytic forms).

Consequently the voles, as other groups of phytophages, play an
important role in the decomposition processes, acting as catalysts,
increasing the intensity of the factors that promote mineralization
and abiogenic decomposition. In this case the significance for
cycling of biological materials is not only acceleration of mineralization of litterfall, but also a change of its seasonal course.

Intensive decomposition of litterfall during the growing season
due to activity of the voles results in a significant part of the
nitrogen and minerals entering the soil, to be absorbed again by
the plants, not carried out of the root inhabited layer, thus being
drawn into the annual biological cycle. Obviously, a soil supplement of nutrients (along with a larger reserve of moisture) is one
of the reasons for increased duration of the vegetation season of
the grass stand on the colonies. The period of supplementary growth
of the grass stand (the end of June to the middle of July) coincides
with the period of intensive mineralization of litterfall (Fig.
16). We used the data of E. A. Afanaceeva (1966) to calculate that
71% of nitrogen and 36% of the minerals entering the soil from the

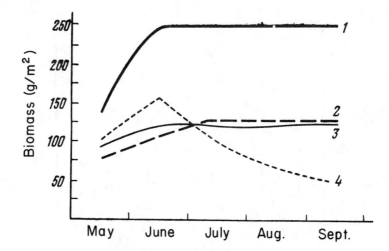

Figure 16
Seasonal dynamics of green biomass growth and destruction of
litter. 1-biomass of green parts on control sections; 2-the
same, on the colonies; 3-biomass of litter on control sections;
4-the same, on the colonies.

decomposed parts of litterfall were used in the supplementary growth
of green phytomass during the indicated period. The major biogenic
elements from decomposition--potassium, phosphorus, sulphur and
magnesium--were absorbed completely by the plants, and calcium was
50% absorbed (Table 55).

In some years toward the end of summer after lengthy warm rains
in the meadow steppe, there are brief periods of decomposition of
litterfall accompanied by an increase of organic materials in
drainage waters on sloping regions (Afanaceeva 1966). Analagous
processes occur on the colonies of the voles. But, if in the virgin
soil summer decomposition of litterfall occurs only after a lengthy
warm rain, short thunderstorms which moisten the litter and the
upper layers of the soil are sufficient on the colonies. During
the period of our investigations such rains fell in the second and
third 10 day period of June.

IMPACT ON PRODUCTIVITY OF MEADOW-STEPPE

We will now try to estimate the influence of voles on the
annual production of meadow-steppe and also their participation in
the biological cycling in this ecosystem.[6]

[6]The term "productivity" is used to indicate the general characteristic of plant communities (or ecosystems) to produce organic material, and the term "production" (or increment) is used to designate
specific values of productivity in grams or kilocalories per unit
area (Minimum Program for Determination of Biological Primary
Productivity 1967).

Table 55. Balance of nitrogen and ash elements on vole colonies in June–July.

Index	Biomass (kg/ha)	N	Ash	SiO_2	Al_2O_3	Fe_2O_3	CaO	MgO	MnO	K_2O	SO_2	P_2O_5
Entering the soil from decomposed litter (kg/ha)	652	5.8	47.4	36.2	1.3	0.6	5.8	1.3	3.2	3.2	1.9	1.3
Use in growth of green phytomass (kg/ha)	233	4.1	17.2	7.4	0.2	0.02	2.8	1.1	0.02	4.1	1.7	1.7
Use in growth of green phytomass (%)	36	71.0	36.0	20.0	15.0	3.0	48.0	85.0	0.6	128.0	90.0	131.0

The influence of herbivorous animals, including the vole, is chiefly on the aboveground phytomass, and their biogeocoenotic role is expressed primarily in changes of annual production. As a base line for estimation of the magnitude of impact of voles on productivity of meadow steppe we can use only the production data of completely isolated quadrats.

As was shown above, the influence of voles on production of the grass stand manifests itself in various forms. During the vegetative period the voles exert an important influence on growth, eating the growing parts and simultaneously changing their conditions of development. They also exert an impact on productivity of the ecosystem, and on the production of green phytomass. The remaining part of the year the animals use only the net production.

During the period of our observations the average area per colony was 66 m^2 and populations reached three voles per colony. An adult animal during 24 hours eats on the average 5 g of dry forage and excretes 0.8 g of excrement (Bashenina 1962, Kucheruk 1963). Consequently, the colony of voles will eat 6.8 g per month per m^2 of green phytomass, returning to the litterfall 1.1 g of the reworked plant material in the form of excrement.

Toward the end of the vegetative period the net production of green phytomass on the isolated quadrats was 250 g/m^2, and on the damaged sections 126 g/m^2. However, considering that the voles ate 20 g/m^2 of green mass net production on the colonies must be calculated as 146 g/m^2. The difference in the actual net production on the isolated quadrats and the colonies (104 g/m^2) is due to poorer development of plants on the damaged sections. During the remaining part of the year, from the end of summer until spring of the following year, the voles eat an additional 61 g/m^2 of the aboveground biomass. In this way, the overall losses of annual production on the colonies constitutes 185 g/m^2 (74% of production of undamaged sections). Of the reduced production 81 g/m^2 (32%) is used as food by the voles, and 104 g/m^2 (42%) constitutes loss due to the reduced rate of growth of the grass stand on the damaged sections. The part of the growth used by the animals as food constitutes less than half (44%) of the total loss of annual production of the grass stand[7] and characterizes the impact of animals on the net production of grass, and not on the productivity of the community. For this reason estimation of the influence of this group of animals on ecosystem productivity based on the quantity of forage consumed gives an error (underestimate) of 56%. It is also incorrect to explain all losses of growth of the grass stand by "destruction" due to the voles. The aboveground phytomass eaten by the voles is transformed in the following way. Its larger part, 68 g/m^2 (84% of the consumed or 27% of the growth) is used for the formation of zoomass and energetic costs of the animals, and 13 g/m^2 (16% of the consumed or 5% of the growth) is returned to litterfall in the form of excrement.

As is known, in grass communities practically all annual growth of aboveground phytomass returns as litterfall. On the damaged sections, where part of the growth is used by the animals as food, the amount of litterfall decreases. To litterfall is added a total

[7]During the growing period the part of net production used as food is 16% of the total zoogenic losses.

of 78 g/m^2 (53% of the major growth), of which 65 g/m^2 (45% of the growth) constitutes litterfall and 13 g/m^2 from the vole excrement, differing in chemical and biological composition from the green phytomass and plant litterfall.

Consequently, as a result of the vital activities of voles production of green phytomass on the damaged sections of meadow steppe decreases by 41%. Of the net production of green phytomass (the actual net production) 32% is transformed by heterotrophic activity, of which 27% is used for the growth of zoomass and energetic expense of the animals and 5% is returned in changed composition to the litterfall (Fig. 17). The mass of litterfall on the harmed sections in comparison with the isolated ones decreases by 69%. This testifies to the fact that the biogeocoenotic role of phytophagous vertebrates is very great. They exert an important impact not only on the magnitude of primary production, the characteristic productivity of the ecosystem, but also on biological cycling of nutrients[8] and on the balance of material and energy accumulated by the green phytomass and liberated by decomposition of litterfall. In addition, because part of the primary production used by animals is transformed into zoomass, the relationship of growth and litterfall of green phytomass changes from 1:1 to 1:2 on the colonies.

During the period of our observations biomass of voles on the damaged section was 0.2 g/m^2 (here and beyond stated as dry weight). To the formation and maintenance of this zoomass are devoted the above-mentioned losses of primary production, a total of 185 $g/m^2/yr$. In other words, for the existence of 1 g of zoomass it is necessary to have about 1000 g of phytomass annually.

Above we characterized the influence of voles on productivity of permanently damaged sections. The influence of this group of animals on productivity of meadow-steppe as a whole depends on which part of the steppe area is occupied by the population and on the number of small mammals. As was already pointed out density of the vole settlement was 10 colonies per hectare and the number of animals 30 individuals per hectare. The damaged sections occupied 660 square meters per hectare, or 6.6% of the meadow-steppe area of the Central Chernozem Reserve.

With these numbers, it is not difficult to estimate the significance of voles (during the period of our investigation) in the biological cycling of the whole meadow-steppe. For calculation we start with the following indices: (1) productivity of the steppe characterized by the production of the aboveground phytomass of the isolated quadrats; (2) the total area of the damaged sections; (3) general losses of net production of the damaged sections toward the end of the vegetative period, and also the relationship of losses during the period of growth, due to the use of part of growth as food and the decrease of productivity of the community (16% and 84%); (4) the quantity of forage eaten by the voles after the end of the growing season, proceeding from the number of animals and the daily requirement of 5 g of forage per animal; (5) the total losses

[8]The capacity of the biological cycle is determined chiefly by the amount of organic material and ash elements contained in the growth of the green parts of the plants (Rodin, Remezov and Bazilevich 1968, Bazilevich and Rodin 1969).

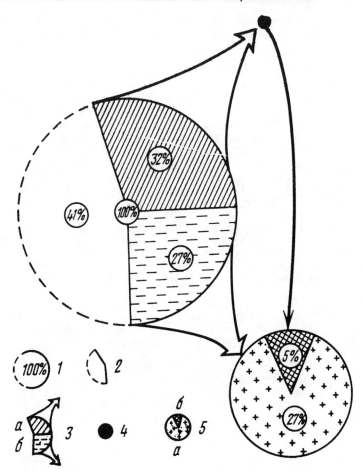

Figure 17
Formation of aboveground part of biological production on steppe
sections populated by field voles. 1-productivity of phytocenosis;
2-loss of productivity due to less growth of damaged plants; 3-
general production of phytomass: a-part of production used for
growth and energy expenditure of the zoomass and partial return
into litterfall; b-net production; 4-zoomass; 5-total aboveground
litterfall: a-vegetative; b-animal (excrement).

of annual production of the damaged sections, and also the relationship of losses due to utilization as food and the decrease of productivity of the community (44% and 56%); and (6) the portion of
grass growth used as food and that transformed into zoomass and
returned to the litterfall (84% and 16%). Calculations from these
data allow us to conclude that during the period of average vole
density their influence on productivity of meadow-steppe is relatively
small (Table 56). Total loss of annual production due to the vital
activity of this group of animals does not exceed 5%. Moreover,

Table 56.   Vole influence on productivity and biological cycling
of meadow-steppe.

Index	Biomass	
	g/m^2	Percent
Growth of green phytomass		
Potential[a/]	2.50	100
Actual	2.42	97
Harvest losses during vegetative period		
Lowering of productivity	0.067	2.7
Used as food	0.013	0.5
Harvest losses after vegetative period		
Used as food	0.04	1.6
General losses of annual productivity		
Lowering of productivity	0.067	2.7
Used as food	0.053	2.1
Consumed for growth of zoomass and energy of maintenance	0.044	1.8
Returned to litterfall with excrement	0.009	0.3
Actual litterfall of green parts		
Plant	2.38	95.2
Excrement	0.009	0.4
Relationship of actual litterfall and growth	$\frac{2.38}{2.42} = 0.099$	

[a/] Growth on isolated quadrats.

productivity of the steppe decreases approximately by 3%, and 2% of
the green phytomass is used as food. The capacity of biological
cycling is decreased approximately 3% and the relationship of organic
materials accumulated by the green phytomass and returned with its
litterfall is practically undisturbed (0.099 g/m^2). Based on information of fluctuation of numbers of voles in the meadow-steppe
of the Reserve, it is possible to hypothesize that in periods of
high density the overall losses of production of meadow-steppe
increase 2 to 4 times.

At the present time the voles prefer to settle on the areas of perennial grasses, adjoining sections of virgin steppe. On such areas their numbers are significantly higher and the influence on productivity is greater. Thus, on the clover area bordering steppe sections of the Central Chernozem Reserve, during the period of our observations, the sections damaged by voles constituted 16 to 19% of the total area. General losses of clover harvest on these sections reached 80 to 90%, and according to calculations for the total area of clover 14 to 15%.

Thus, high densities of herbivorous rodents not only use a definite part of the growth of phytomass, but more important they participate in the productive and destructive processes of the autotrophic portions of the biological cycle. It is important to point out the error of the widely used index "phytomass: zoomass" for characterizing the biogeocoenotic role of heterotrophs. This role can be determined only with regard to all forms of impact of animals on primary production. The most simple method of obtaining such an integral indicator is comparison of production of phytomass of sections with animals and isolated from them. It is appropriate also to mention that at the present time, the ecosystems of the virgin meadow-steppes of the central forest-steppe in the mid-Russian uplands, especially the animal populations, have been strongly changed by the multi-century impact of man. This refers also to the steppe sections of the Central Chernozem Reserve. In the preagri-cultural period in the steppe of the forest-steppe zone the biomass of phytophagous vertebrates was much greater, chiefly on account of the ungulates and large rodents such as marmots. Obviously, the impact exerted by this group of animals on natural ecosystems of the meadow-steppe was more significant in the past. This impact is possible to estimate from the influence of herbivorous mammals on productivity of pasture lands of virgin dry steppes (Formosov 1928, Formosov and Voronov 1939, Kucheruk 1963).

II-3

Consumers of Perennial Aboveground Parts of Plants

Study of the biogeocoenotic role of animals which are trophically connected with the perennial parts of plants was conducted by investigation of the ungulates (moose and roe deer) and hares. These are typical animals of the forest-steppe oak groves. Their influence on the woody-shrub layer of the ecosystem is very distinct and the ecological peculiarities make them a convenient object for study.

Moose and roe deer, sometimes numerous in the entire forest-steppe, were almost completely destroyed in the 19th century, and only recently have their numbers been restored. In the oak groves of the Central Chernozem Reserve the first moose were seen in the summer of 1953. From 1956 they began to appear regularly, but did not remain there. In the fall of 1959 small groups of moose appeared for the first time, and in the winter of 1960 and 1961 seven animals remained for the winter. Since that time moose live permanently in the oak groves of the Reserve and reproduce yearly. In the winter of 1961 and 1962 the number of moose on the Streletskaya section was 10, in 1962 and 1963 20 to 25 (counting transients), in 1963 and 1964 16, and in 1964 and 1965 10.[1] The roe deer began to come into the Reserve oak groves as transients during the winter of 1955 and 1956. In the summer of 1956 on the Streletsksya section a female roe deer with three fawns settled. In 1963 the number of roe deer on the Streletskaya section of the reserve increased to 7, in 1964 to 11, and in 1965 to 13.

Our investigations were conducted in 1964 and 1965 in the lands of Dubroshina and Soleviatnik. In the winter months average density of ungulates for 100 ha of forest area was 7 specimens (2 moose and 5 roe deer), of hares 7 to 10, and their zoomass (dry weight) 700, 150, and 35 to 50 kg, respectively.

The ungulates and hares feed in winter on the smallest twigs, which barely support their existence (Knorre 1959, Kaletski 1967, and others). Obviously, the food obtained by them is used completely for energetic maintenance. Moose and roe deer are rarely

---

[1]In 1962 and 1963 when the number of moose increased, they began to damage the oak groves. For this reason in the fall of 1963 10 of the animals were killed.

seen, and hares very rarely, in winter on the steppe sections surrounding small areas of oak groves. There are no large predators on
the Reserve. In these conditions the zoogenic cycle of transformation of material and energy, connected with the use of browse,
takes on a simple form and occurs on a limited area of the oak
groves.

Studying the biogeocoenotic role of consumers of perennial
aboveground parts of plants, we used the method of L. G. Dinesman
and V. I. Shmalgauzen (1961, 1967). We took a profile from each of
a series of trial areas of 100 m^2, which cut across all types of
forest. The number of quadrats in each type was in proportion to
the area. In the thinned oak grove 20 squares were placed, in the
complex oak groves 6, in the aspen 4, and in the forest cultures 12.
The quadrats were placed in a checker board pattern at approximately
equal distance from each other. On each quadrat were counted the
numbers of trees and shrubs, and in tall trees the number of lower
branches accessible to the animals. The number of trees and shrubs
eaten by the moose, roe deer and hares was noted also, and the
number of shoots eaten on each of these. The consumed parts were
counted in the beginning of May before the growth of leaves. The
diameters of twigs removed was also measured. This allowed us to
determine the average diameter of shoots for each woody species
eaten by the various types of animals (Table 57).

From each woody species we cut a hundred twigs whose diameter
in the place of cutting corresponded to the diameter in the place of
biting. The branches were dried in a drying oven and weighed, and
the weight of shoots consumed from each species per 100 square
meters of each type of forest was calculated.

On these trial quadrats we also counted the quantity of excrement left by the animals during the winter. The excrement was
counted in April, immediately after melting of the snow. At this
time it was lying on the surface of the consolidated litter-fall
and was distinguishable from the litter-fall remaining from the
preceding season. Piles of droppings of the moose and roe deer were
counted and collected on each trial quadrat. Excrement of hares was
collected on 5 squares of 1 m^2 each, placed at the corners and in
the center of each 100 meter square. Later the average dry weight
of one pile of droppings of moose and roe deer was determined and
the weight of excrement of the hare from 1 square meter. The collected piles of droppings of moose and roe deer were weighed and the
average weight of one pile was determined. From the collected
droppings an average specimen was taken (its weight corresponded to
the average weight of one pile) and dried in a drying oven. By the
same method we determined the weight of excrement of the hare from
one square meter. On the basis of data obtained we calculated the
weight of the droppings of each type on an average 100 square meter
area of forest.

Having treated the data obtained from all the trial squares, we
determined the average weight of plants eaten by the animals, and
the portion of the consumed food returned to the litterfall with
excrement during one fall-winter season on a unit of area of various
types of forest, and also of the entire forest area.

For estimating the role of ungulates and hares in the cycle of
nitrogen and ash elements contained in woody plants, chemical analysis
was conducted of the major forage of woody species and of excrement.

Table 57. Average diameter and weight of shoots eaten by the animals.

Forage species	Moose Diameter (mm)	Moose Weight (g)	Roe deer Diameter (mm)	Roe deer Weight (g)	Hare Diameter (mm)	Hare Weight (g)
	Consumed shoots					
English oak	3.0	0.70[a]	3.0	0.70	2.0	0.30
Tatarian maple	2.0	0.18	2.0	0.18	2.0	0.18
Aspen	3.0	0.88[a]	3.0	0.88	3.0	0.88
Willow	4.0	1.00	1.4	--	3.5	--
Crab apple	3.0	0.88	2.0	0.49	2.0	0.49
Pear	3.0	0.74	3.0	0.74	2.5	0.38
Rowan	3.6	1.00	3.6	1.00	3.6	1.00
European bird cherry	2.5	0.63	2.5	0.63	2.5	0.63
Hawthorn	1.4	0.18	2.2	0.42	2.4	0.42
Cherry	1.7	0.28	1.7	0.28	1.7	0.28
Blackthorn	2.0	0.39	2.0	0.39	2.0	0.39
Buckthorn	2.9	0.95	2.9	0.95	2.9	0.95
Vibernum	3.0	0.46	3.0	0.46	3.0	0.46
Raspberry	3.0	1.0	2.3	0.50	2.3	0.50
Dewberry	1.0	0.15	3.0	0.50	1.5	--
European prickwood	2.5	0.38	2.0	0.23	2.5	0.38
Warty prickwood	2.0	0.41	2.0	0.41	3.0	1.03

[a] According to data of Shafer (1963) the weight of one consumed red oak shoot is equal to 0.67 g, and weight of American aspen is equal to 0.81 g.

Samples for analysis were taken at the end of winter (an average specimen from 100 branches of each woody and shrub species and from excrement of each type of animal). Calculation of the quantity of chemical elements obtained and excreted by the animals per unit area was conducted on the basis of the relationship of biomass of the consumed forage (by species) and excrement. Productivity of the tree stands on both sections (in Dubroshina and Solviatnik) were established from sample trees, and the phytomass of the shoots consumed by the animals. In the sample trees we determined dry weight of the trunk, the branches and leaves of the first through fourth layers, and also the area of leaf surface. For determining phytomass we took average specimens of leaves, branches and trunks (the latter were cut into lengths of 10 cm) which were later dried in a drying oven. The area of the leaf surface was established by removing samples of 50 leaves of various sizes and thickness.

The influence of ungulates and hares on productivity of the tree stand was determined by comparing the productivity of two

sections of 40 year old oaks. One of them was fenced and suffered
almost no damage from animals, the other was systematically damaged
by them. On these sections in 1964 and 1965 the general height and
diameter of the trunk at the root neck and breast high, the length
and base diameter of upper branches were measured on 220 trees. We
also noted the number of damaged shoots. In each tree, as a rule,
there was only one terminal shoot. If it is eaten or broken, then
the following year the main shoot develops from the nearby lateral
bud, and the trunk at the place of biting is distorted. For this
reason traces of the consumption of upper shoots are preserved on
the young tree for a long time (at least 15 to 20 years) and it is
possible to judge from them during how many different years it was
damaged by the animals.

CONSUMPTION OF PHYTOMASS AND TRANSFORMATION OF CHEMICAL ELEMENTS

    The oak forest of 20 to 30 years age with thin undergrowth in
the regions of Dubroshina and Soloviatnik constitutes 55% of the
forested area, almost without undergrowth. 14% of the area is
occupied by mixed oak forest of the same age, but with a thick
undergrowth mainly of warty and European prickwood, blackthorn,
buckthorn and European bird cherry. In these oak groves 94% of the
species of the forest are oak with other important species being
pear, and rarely aspen, crab apple and rowan. Aspen forest occupies
3% of the forested area and is concentrated chiefly on the slopes of
the ravines; small sections with an abundance of aspen also occur in
the mixed oak forests. About 28% of the forest area is young forest
culture, young oak at an age of 5 to 30 years with an insignificant
mixture of the European prickwood, pear, tatarian maple, elm and
other species.
    Winter distribution of moose, roe deer and hare is not the same
in the oak forests of the Central Chernozem Reserve. This affects
their contribution to biological cycling. From November through
March the places of rest of roe deer and moose are confined to the
mixed oak forest. The roe deer feeds in the mixed complex oak
forests and in the oak cultures, and the moose chiefly in the
cultures. In the thin oak groves the moose and especially the roe
deer are very rare in the winter; they are seen chiefly when they
migrate from their place of rest to their place of feeding. The
hares in the first half of winter populate the oak forests uniformly
but beginning in February, if there is a lot of snow, they gather in
the forest cultures and on the edges of the oak forests where the
snow cover is more dense. They feed mainly in the little islands of
the mixed oak forest and aspen forest.
    Moose on the basic pastures (in the forest culture) eat about
120 kg of the browse per hectare during the winter, 68% composed of
shoots of oak and 26% of the European prickwood. In the mixed oak
forest the weight of the shoots consumed by moose is only 22 kg/ha.
In this case the proportion of European prickwood increases to 84%
(although the absolute weight decreases to 18.3 kg), 11 to 12% of
the consumed material is made up of shoots of blackthorn, European
bird cherry and pear, and the proportion contributed by oak shoots
does not exceed 1.6%. On small sections of aspen forest the weight
of consumed shoots is only 6 kg per ha (85% of consumption is of

aspen). In the thin oak groves the moose eat less than 1 kg of shoot per ha during winter.

In its preferred area (in the mixed oak forest) the roe deer eats on the average 17.5 kg of browse per ha during the winter. Of this, 66% is from warty prickwood and European bird cherry; about 17% from European prickwood, blackthorn and pear; 11% from oak, raspberry and aspen. In the forest cultures the roe deer feed less. The average weight of shoots consumed during the winter is approximately half as much (9.3 kg per ha), about 66% of it is from shoots of the oak and 33% from European prickwood. In the aspen forests the average quantity of forage eaten by the roe deer is only 2.5 kg per ha (70% from blackthorn and aspen and about 20% from European bird cherry and prickwood). In the thin oak grove this forage decreases to 0.9 kg per ha (chiefly used are the branches of raspberry, oak, pear, and the warty prickwood).

The main place for the hares feeding is the mixed oak forest where the weight of forage eaten during the winter exceeds 6 kg per ha, and in the aspen forests with thick undergrowth (3.8 kg per ha). They rarely feed in the forest cultures and in the thin oak grove, and the weight of consumed shoots decreases there to 0.24 to 0.38 kg per ha.

The general quantities of browse eaten by the animals during the winter reaches 128 kg per ha in the forest cultures, 45.6 in the mixed oak forest, 3.1 kg per ha in the thin oak grove. The quantity of droppings remaining is 22.6, 30.6, and 4.4 kg per ha, respectively. These numbers show that the animals accomplish the removal of organic material from the basic place of feeding into other sections of the forest.

On the whole, in the oak groves of the reserve 58% of the browse removed by moose during the winter comes from oak, about 33% from prickwood (25% European and 8% warty) and less than 8% from pear, European bird cherry, blackthorn, rowan, and raspberry. On the average for 1 ha of oak forest the moose eats 24.5 kg of oak shoots and prickwood and a total of 1.6 kg of the remaining forage species during the winter.

On the average, the roe deer eats in winter 5.1 kg of browse per ha, the major part of which is shoots of oak and warty prickwood (27% and 23%), a somewhat smaller part is from the European bird cherry and European prickwood (17% and 15%), and 15% from shoots of pear, raspberry, blackthorn, and aspen. It should be noted that although the overall phytomass of the browse processed by the roe deer is significantly less than that processed by the moose, their "load" on the basic species of undergrowth is the same (Table 58 and 59).

The hares on the whole forest eat during the winter a total of 1.3 kg of browse per ha, about 50% of which is from the shoots of blackthorn and buckthorn and about 24% from the European bird cherry and pear (Table 60).

The quantity of droppings accumulated during the winter on an average ha of forest includes 10.4 kg from moose, 1.3 kg from the roe deer and 0.5 kg from the hares. In relation to the weight of the browse eaten, the quantity of the organic material returned to the litterfall with the excrement is about 38% in the moose and hare and 25.5% in the roe deer (Table 61). The larger assimilation of forage by the roe deer is due by the fact that they eat the more delicate twigs which contain less cellulose.

Table 58.   Phytomass of browse eaten by moose during the fall-
winter period (kg/ha dry weight)[a].

Major woody and brush forage species[b]	Average	Oak grove		Aspen forest	Forest cultures
		Thinned	Mixed		
All branch forage	27.40	1.97	22.00	6.00	118.50
Oak	15.60	0.86	0.35	0.03	80.40
European prickwood	6.80	0.09	5.30	0.70	31.50
Warty prickwood	2.10	0.01	13.00	0.0	--
Pear	0.70	0.10	0.08	--	2.70
European bird cherry	0.21	0.01	0.86	0.06	--
Blackthorn	0.16	0.03	0.90	0.0	--
Rowan	0.15	0.24	0.0	--	--
Raspberry	0.15	0.21	0.10	0.05	--
Crab apple	0.14	0.22	0.0	--	--
Aspen	0.10	0.0	0.10	5.10	--

[a] In this table and also in tables 59 and 60 the dash indicates the absence of a given forage species.

[b] The species enumerated account for 88% to 90% of the forage eaten.

The entire group of browse consuming vertebrates in the forest eat and process on the average during one fall-winter season 33.8 kg of plant mass per ha of which they return 12.2 kg (36%) to the litterfall. The remaining part is assimilated by the organisms. The greatest quantity of phytomass processed is from oaks and European prickwood (approximately 17 and 7.5 kg per ha), signif- icantly less from the warty prickwood, pear, and European bird cherry, and still less from blackthorn and very little of the buckthorn.

The major role in processing of plant mass belongs to the moose. The relationship of weight of the shoots eaten by the moose, roe deer and hares is 21:4:1, and the weight of the dropping, re- turned by them to the litterfall is 21:3:1. For this reason, the impact of this group of animals on the various woody and brush species, and also their role in biological cycling, is determined chiefly by peculiarities of feeding by moose.

Table 59.   Phytomass of browse eaten by roe deer during the fall-
winter period (kg/ha dry weight).

| Major woody and brush forage species[a] | Average | Oak grove | | Aspen forest | Forest cultures |
		Thinned	Mixed		
All branch forage	5.10	0.90	17.50	2.50	9.26
Oak	1.37	0.17	0.65	0.03	6.20
Warty prickwood	1.16	0.10	6.50	0.0	--
European bird cherry	0.85	0.08	4.97	0.28	--
European prickwood	0.76	0.03	1.27	0.28	2.83
Pear	0.25	0.10	0.90	--	0.23
Raspberry	0.24	0.22	0.65	0.01	--
Blackthorn	0.17	0.01	0.90	0.82	--
Aspen	0.10	0.01	0.60	0.82	--

[a] The species enumerated account for 79% to 94% of the forage eaten.

     Chemical analyses of the woody forage and excrement of animals
permits estimation of the role of ungulates and hares in cycling of
separate elements. Based on the results of these analyses, calculations show that in the fall and winter season there is significant
accumulation of potassium, magnesium, and to a lesser degree, of
phosphrous by ungulates and hares.
     The balance of ash elements in organisms of various types
depends not only on the physiological peculiarities of the animal,
but also on the chemical composition of the major forage. Accumulation of potassium and magnesium are most characteristic of moose,
the larger part of whose winter forage is composed by shoots of oak
and European prickwood, which are rich in these elements (especially
rich in potassium is European prickwood). Besides this, in the
winter months the moose accumulate aluminum, which is also high
in the European prickwood. The relationship of these elements in
the forage of the moose and in the excrement is 15:1 for potassium,
9:1 for magnesium, and 2:1 for aluminum. In roe deer and hares the
relationship of the minerals in the forage and returned with the
excrement is for potassium 8:1 and 7:1, respectively, and for
magnesium 3:1 and 6:1. Obviously, the larger accumulation of magnesium by the hares is connected with the fact that buckthorn and
blackthorn, the basic winter forage of these animals, is rich in it.
In the same way may be explained the larger (in comparison with the
ungulates) accumulation of phosphorus, in which buckthorn, blackthorn

Table 60.   Phytomass of browse eaten by hares during the fall-winter
            period (kg/ha dry weight).

| Major woody and brush forage species[a] | Average | Oak groves | | Aspen forest | Forest cultures |
		Thinned	Mixed		
All branch forage	1.30	0.24	6.15	3.80	0.38
Buckthorn	0.33	0.02	1.85	0.97	--
Blackthorn	0.32	0.04	1.70	1.40	--
European bird cherry	0.16	0.01	0.97	0.16	--
Pear	0.16	0.08	0.55	--	0.14
Raspberry	0.04	0.04	0.12	0.06	--
Warty prickwood	0.02	0.0	0.0	0.95	--
Oak	0.02	0.01	0.03	0.0	0.8
Tartarian maple	0.02	0.0	0.02	0.0	0.08

[a] The species enumerated account for 79% to 100% of the forage eaten.

and especially in the European bird cherry are rich. The relationship of phosophrous in the forage and in excrement of hares is 4:1,
and in the moose and roe deer 1.5:1.

On the whole, in the oak forests the ungulates and hares in the
fall-winter period return to the litter fall a total of 10% of the
potassium and magnesium contained in the browse they consume. The
relationship of the remaining elements, obtained with the forage and
returned with excrement, is close to 1 (Table 62 and 63).

The ungulates and hares participate in the transfer of chemical
elements between types of forest. This is due to their peculiarities
of winter distribution. The major role belongs to the moose. The
relationship of biomass of forage and of excrement in the forest
culture is 7:1, and in places of rest 1:1 to 1:2. It is natural
that the moose transfers chemical materials to natural oak groves,
obtained from the oak and the European prickwood growing in the
forest plantings. Special attention is earned by the distribution
of manganese by moose, whose content in the oak is 2 to 10 times
greater than in other forage species, and of aluminum, which is
high in the European prickwood (Table 62). The quantity of manganese, taken by the moose into the zoogenic cycle, consitutes 3% of
the total annually entering the soil of the oak forest from plant
litterfall (Rodin and Bazilevich 1965, Afanaceeva 1966). In the
mixed oak grove the quantity of manganese entering the litterfall with excrement of the moose exceeds the quantity removed in

Table 61. Relationship of forage eaten and excrement.

Index	Type of forest	Moose	Roe deer	Hare	All types
Forage (kg/ha)	Thin oak grove	2.0	0.9	0.2	3.1
	Mixed oak grove	22.0	17.5	6.1	45.6
	Forest cultures	118.5	9.3	0.3	128.1
	Average	27.4	5.1	1.3	33.8
Excrement (kg/ha)	Thin oak grove	3.8	0.5	0.1	4.4
	Mixed oak grove	27.3	1.5	1.8	30.6
	Forest cultures	18.4	3.7	0.5	22.6
	Average	10.4	1.3	0.5	12.2
Portion of the organic material returned to litterfall, percent of the forage eaten	Thin oak grove	190.0	55.0	50.0	141.9
	Mixed oak grove	124.0	8.6	29.0	67.1
	Forest cultures	15.0	40.0	166.6	17.6
	Average	38.0	25.5	0.38	36.0

Table 62.   Content of nitrogen and ash elements in twigs of major forage plants and excrement (% absolute dry material).

Major species of forage plants and excrement	N	Ca	K	Mg	P	Al	Si	S	Fe	Mg	Na
Oak (undergrowth)	1.20	1.64	0.43	0.16	0.12	0.07	0.08	0.04	0.01	0.03	Sl.
Oak (forest–culture)	1.30	0.86	0.42	0.21	0.12	0.05	0.07	0.04	0.01	0.02	Sl.
Pear	1.58	1.41	0.46	0.09	0.01	0.03	0.33	0.04	0.02	--	0.01
Crab apple	0.78	2.32	0.36	0.13	0.09	0.05	0.12	0.05	0.01	0.01	Sl.
Aspen	1.22	1.26	0.54	0.07	0.01	0.03	0.29	0.10	0.01	--	0.01
Rowan	0.98	1.04	0.23	0.11	0.07	0.04	0.11	0.03	0.01	--	Sl.
European prickwood	2.05	1.60	0.92	0.32	0.15	0.27	0.02	0.07	Het	0.01	Sl.
Warty prickwood	1.33	1.05	0.48	0.16	0.13	0.08	0.16	0.06	0.02	--	0.01
European bird cherry	1.35	1.02	0.44	0.14	0.22	0.05	0.24	0.05	0.02	0.01	Sl.
Blackthorn	1.48	1.21	0.50	0.14	0.16	0.05	0.19	0.07	0.02	Sl.	0.01
Buckthorn	0.92	1.77	0.62	0.31	0.21	0.08	0.10	0.06	0.01	0.01	0.01
Steppe cherry	1.23	0.77	0.48	0.15	0.16	0.12	0.09	0.03	0.02	0.01	0.01
Excrement of:											
Moose	1.22	2.21	0.08	0.10	0.18	0.13	0.23	0.12	0.03	0.02	0.01
Roe deer	1.46	2.78	0.18	0.19	0.32	0.15	0.56	0.17	0.03	0.03	0.01
Hare	1.38	2.23	0.30	0.08	0.15	0.18	0.13	0.06	0.05	0.02	0.02

Table 63. Content of nitrogen and ash elements in forage (g/ha) and excrement (% of the amount in the forage).

Index	N	Ca	K	Mg	P	Al	Si	S	Fe	Mn
Moose										
Forage	388.0	280.0	140.0	90.0	30.0	29.0	19.0	13.0	2.0	3.0
Excrement	32.7	82.1	6.4	11.1	66.6	48.3	126.3	100.0	150.2	66.6
Roe deer										
Forage	68.0	50.0	25.0	10.0	6.0	2.0	6.0	0.1	0.1	0.1
Excrement	28.0	80.0	12.0	30.0	66.6	100.0	116.6	2000.0	100.0	100.0
Hare										
Forage	13.0	16.0	7.0	3.0	2.0	1.0	5.0	1.0	1.0	0.1
Excrement	53.8	62.5	14.3	33.3	50.0	100.0	100.0	100.0	100.0	100.0
All types										
Forage	469.0	346.0	172.0	103.0	38.0	32.0	30.0	14.0	2.0	3.0
Excrement	32.9	81.4	7.5	12.6	63.1	53.1	120.0	17.1	150.0	66.6

forage by 520 times, of iron and sulphur, by 2.3 times, and of
phosphorous and aluminum, 1.5 to 2 times (Table 64).

It should be underscored that even with a high number of
animals, as observed during the period of our investigations, the
weight of shoots consumed by them during the winter and the weight
of their excrement both are in the range of 10 to 30 kg per ha. At
that time the biomass of annual increment of the aboveground parts
of plants and the biomass of the plant litterfall by the forest-
steppe oak is greater by several tons per ha (Rodin and Bazilevich
1965). In this way, the entire group of browse consumers draw into
the zoogenic cycle of the biological cycle a total of about 1% of
the organic material accumulated by vegetation during the growing
season. This indicates that the zoogenic cycle transforming material of the perennial parts of plants plays a relatively small
role in the general biological cycle. It is true both for the total
plant material and for the separate elements. The exception is some
of the micro-elements (for example manganese), whose gross content
in the phytomass of the tree stand is negligible, but they selec-
tively accumulate in separate types of forage plants and then are
transferred by the animals.

INFLUENCE ON THE PRODUCTIVITY OF OAK FORESTS

Ungulates and hares eat only a small part of the young shoots,
and for this reason the number of shoots and trees damaged is very
great. In natural oak groves the young trees and shrubs of the
undergrowth suffer more than anything else. Moose damage chiefly
the European and warty prickwood and the oak seedlings. In the
mixed oak grove all the shoots in 82 to 83% of the bushes of prickwood are eaten by them (including 70 to 80% of the shoots the moose
ate during one fall-winter season). The roe deer and especially the
hares damage a smaller number of trees, but they eat more of those
than does the moose. From the roe deer damage chiefly maple,
European bird cherry and the warty prickwood. However, the proportion of these species that are strongly damaged does not exceed
45%. Young trees suffer even less (with the exception of pear in
thin oak grove). The hares, in contrast to the ungulates, damage
primarily the seedlings of the trees, chiefly the accompanying
species (crab apple and pear) and to a smaller degree the oak. Among
the shrubs of the undergrowth blackthorn suffers more than anything
else (Table 65).

As is seen from the data given in Table 65, very great damage
is caused to the woody-brush layer of the forest-steppe oak groves
by the vertebrate consumers of browse. The leading role belongs to
the moose which does much damage to the major species, the oak and
prickwood. During the 6 to 7 year period since the time of moose
settlement in the Reserve oak forests, they almost completely destroyed the annual growth of prickwood each year. As a result, the
shruby layer where prickwood was dominant was very depressed and
thin, and in places of winter resting, almost completely destroyed.
Fruit bearing of the prickwood strongly decreases, and gradually
this species drops out of the phytocoenosis.[2]

[2]We could not measure the difference in fruit bearing of healthy and
damaged prickwood, since at the period of our observations practically

Table 64. Content of nitrogen and ash elements in forage (g/ha) and excrement (% of amount obtained with forage) in various types of forest.

Type of forest	Index	N	Ca	K	Mg	P	Al	Si	S	Fe	Mn
Moose											
Thin oakgrove	Forage	18.0	250.0	6.0	21.0	6.0	1.0	2.0	0.1	2.0	0.1
	Excrement	255.5	33.6	50.6	19.0	116.6	500.0	450.0	5000.0	50.0	100.0
Mixed oakgrove	Forage	361.0	180.0	675.0	41.0	28.0	25.0	23.0	13.0	3.0	0.1
	Excrement	92.2	33.3	3.4	63.4	178.6	144.0	26.1	230.8	233.3	52000.0
Forest cultures	Forage	1733.0	1193.0	630.0	180.0	144.0	122.0	70.0	50.0	10.0	16.0
	Excrement	12.9	34.1	2.4	10.0	2.0	19.7	61.4	40.0	50.0	18.8
Roe deer											
Thin oakgrove	Forage	7.0	7.0	2.0	1.0	0.5	0.3	1.0	0.1	0.1	0.1
	Excrement	100.0	200.0	50.0	100.0	400.0	333.3	30.0	1000.0	200.0	200.0
Mixed oakgrove	Forage	221.0	170.0	70.0	23.0	22.0	11.0	27.0	9.0	2.0	1.0
	Excrement	9.9	23.5	4.3	13.0	22.7	18.1	29.6	22.2	250.0	500.0
Forest cultures	Forage	142.0	98.0	53.0	22.0	5.0	12.0	5.0	5.0	1.0	1.0
	Excrement	38.0	105.1	15.1	31.8	240.0	50.0	420.0	120.0	600.0	100.0
Hare											
Thin oakgrove	Forage	2.0	2.0	1.0	0.3	0.2	0.1	0.3	0.1	0.1	0.1
	Excrement	50.0	100.0	30.0	33.3	50.0	200.0	333.3	100.0	100.0	100.0
Mixed oakgrove	Forage	65.0	70.0	50.0	20.0	13.0	5.0	10.0	6.0	1.5	0.2
	Excrement	38.4	57.1	10.0	10.0	15.4	80.0	200.0	33.3	66.0	200.0
Forest cultures	Forage	3.0	5.0	2.0	1.0	0.2	0.1	0.5	0.2	0.1	0.1
	Excrement	233.3	200.0	50.0	50.0	250.0	1000.0	1000.0	250.0	200.0	100.0

Table 65. Damage of major forest forming species and shrubs (%)[a].

Species	Thin oakgrove			Mixed oakgrove			Forest cultures		
	Moose	Roe deer	Hare	Moose	Roe deer	Hare	Moose	Roe deer	Hare
Oak[b]	21/25	12/28	14/60	33/61	8/19	28/100	82/40	29/4	5/<0.1
Pear[b]	7/22	70/72	100/45	14/90	7/30	7/?	58/57	0/0	6/1
Crab apple[b]	5/30	?/100	66/100	0/0	?/?	?/?	--	--	--
Rowan[b]	23/62	7/?	?/100	0/0	0/0	0/0	--	--	--
European prickwood	33/94	1/100	?/100	82/100	20/100	6/100	100/97	?/26	0/0
Warty prickwood	23/32	21/100	1/1	83/100	33/98	5/100	--	--	--
Tartarian maple	?	40/100	0/0	0/0	43/58	9/?	4/?	0/0	7/?
European bird cherry	27/2	45/100	?/100	40/51	18/72	2/70	--	--	--
Blackthorn	3/66	21/100	40/100	9/79	24/10	33/50	--	--	--
Buckthorn	0/0	7/100	28/100	0/0	?/4	31/?	--	--	--

[a] In the numerator it is the % of trees damaged, in the denominator it is the % of shoots damaged.

[b] Shoots and lower branches.

The oak cultures (up to 30 years age) suffer most from the ungulates, chiefly from moose, along with pear and prickwood. In these forests the moose completely ate the prickwood, ate more than 50% of the pear, and in 82% of the oak they damaged 40% of the shoots on the average. The roe deer damaged 29% of the oak, and the hares about 5%, but the degree of damaged to oak (the number of shoots eaten) was not large, not more than 4%.

The youngest (5-9 year old) trees suffer most. The moose forage in the oak plantings during the entire fall-winter season, eating chiefly the upper and rarely the lateral shoots. They do slightly less harm to the 10 to 14 year old oaks that are somewhat taller and for this reason less accessible. The moose, trying to reach the tops, often break the upper part of the trunk and, in addition, eat the bark.

---

[2] all the shrubs were eaten and almost none of them bore fruit.

In the groves of older age (more than 15 years) the damage to oaks was less, since at the time moose appeared in the Reserve the trees were already sufficiently high. The plantings, scattered in small sections among the oak forest, were damaged most of all. However, the nature of the damage to the forest culture of this age was particularly ruinous for the trees: the moose eat much bark, often girdling the trunk, leading to death of the trees. For this reason, although the percent of damaged oaks in the groves of older age was not great, mortality among them is greater than among the 5 to 9 year old age class. It is also important that the groves of the 16 to 30 year old trees occupy the major area of the forest culture (Table 66).

We will remember that for the estimation of animal influence on the productivity of the tree stands we studied growth and biomass of trees in isolated and control areas in one type of 14 year old oak grove. These groves (just as all others in the studied oak groves) were damaged mainly by moose. Traces of their feeding were noted on all the damaged oaks, while traces of feeding by roe deer appeared on 30%, and of hares on 7% of the trees. In this case the moose ate more than 40% of the shoots, the roe deer 4% and the hares less than 1%. For this reason all the data presented characterize chiefly the influence of moose on productivity of the tree stands.

Growth of young trees in height is decreased especially strongly because of damage to the main upper shoot (Dinesman 1961). This

Table 66.   Moose damage to the forest cultures of oak.

Index	Age of forest culture (years)		
	5-9	10-15	>15
Occupied area[a]	$\frac{22}{9}$	$\frac{55}{23}$	$\frac{162}{68}$
Average height (m)	<2.5	2.5	>4-5
Number of damaged trees	76-83	56-75	7-14
With upper shoots eaten	54-62	29-48	0
With lateral shoots eaten	13-19	29-48	0
With broken trunk top	0.3-2.7	27	0
With bark eaten	0	0	7-14[b]

[a] In the numerator it is in hectares, in the denominator in %.

[b] In 1.3 to 2.8% of the young oaks bark is eaten for 2/3 of the circumference or more.

criterion is accepted by us for estimation of degree of damage to oaks. By the quantity of stumps and distortion of the trunk one can judge approximately the number of years the animals had eaten the upper shoot.

On sections regularly damaged by moose, in the majority of oaks (59%) the upper shoots were eaten 3 or 4 times (that is they were eaten during 3 to 4 different years), in 27% one to two times and in 14% 5 times or more. Such distribution of damage coincides with varying numbers of moose in the Reserve oak groves in different time periods. As was already pointed out, in the oak groves of the Central Chernozem Reserve the moose appeared in 1959, and in 1961 through 1965 their numbers were high (especially in 1961-1963). Evidently, the majority of oaks were damaged during those years.[3]

This is confirmed by the fact that in a larger part of the trees, damaged one to four times, traces of eating upper shoots were found in the upper part of the trunk, and also by the relationship of number damaged in 1964 and 1965: in 1964 the upper branches were eaten in 85% of the oaks, and in 1965 a total of 19%.

Observations showed that repeated eating of the upper verticle shoots strongly slowed the annual growth of the main shoot. Even in oaks with one shoot eaten the growth in height decreased by 19%, with two shoots eaten growth decreased by 30%, with three and four shoots by 50%, and with damage of five shoots the growth in height of the trunk practically ceased. Slowing of the yearly growth of trunks for several years is reflected in the overall growth of the tree. Single eating of the upper shoot decreases the general height of 14 year old oaks by 3% on the average, when eaten twice by 8 to 10%, four times by 18%, five times and more by 34% (Fig. 18).

Eating of the upper shoots reduced not only trunk growth in height but also in diameter. In oaks damaged one to four times, the diameter of the trunk at the level of the root neck decreased by 15 to 20%, and at breast height by 20 to 30%; in oaks damaged five or more times, 20 and 70%, respectively.

We were interested in the effect on oak growth not only of the degree of damage to the upper shoots, but also of the time when damage occurred. In 14 year old oaks the shoots of the two most recent years were distinguishable from older ones. This allowed us to calculate the height of oaks at the age of 12 years.

It is evident that the degree of annual growth is closely associated with the degree of damage to the top in the current year (independent of damage in the preceding years). The effect of damage in the preceding years on the annual increase is gradually damped, and only in strongly damaged trees it is decreased by half. This may be explained by the fact that oaks at the age of 12 years suffered more from damage to the tops than did the 14 year old oaks; the first 1 or 2 times of damage lowered the height by 17%, 3 or more times by 30%. In 14 year old oaks decreases of height occurred only during the 4th and 5th times of damage (Table 67). In the years of high numbers of moose (1961 to 1963) the oaks were 10 to 12 years old, and strong damage during these years slowed their growth.

[3]We could not determine the exact time of damage of the upper part based on crooked growth of the trunk because it was not possible to cut the tree.

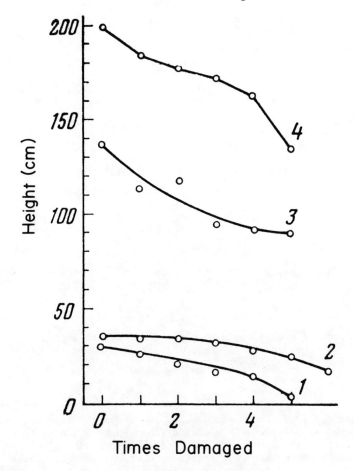

Figure 18
Dependence of annual growth in height and general height of various
ages of oak on the degree of damage caused by moose. 1–dependence
of yearly growth of 14–year old oak on the number of times of
damage to the upper shoot or whorl for the current winter; 2–
the same, for the entire period of growth (1951-1965); 3–dependence
of general height of 12–year old oak on the number of times of
damage to the upper shoot for the entire growth period (1951-
1963); 4–the same, of 14–year old oak trees (for 1951-1965).

In the two successive years the pressure from ungulates decreased
and the trees recovered.
Proceeding from the dependence of height and growth of 14 year
old oaks upon the degree of damage, four groups of trees can be
distinguished. Group 1, undamaged; Group 2, damaged one to three
times; Group 3, damaged four times; and Group 4, damaged five times
or more. The differences between height and growth of trees of the
different groups is significant (P < 0.05). For this reason, to

Table 67.   Influence of damage to the upper shoots on the height of oaks (cm).

Index	Number of times damaged[a/]					
	0	1	2	3	4	5 and more
12 year old trees						
Height	137	114	118	95	93	91
Reduction of height	--	23	19	42	44	46
Percent	--	17	17	30	30	31
14 year old trees						
Height	199	184	177	172	163	131
Reduction of height	--	15	22	27	36	68
Percent	--	3	8	10	18	34

[a/] For 12 year old oaks the number of times damaged during 1955-1963 is shown; for 14 year old oaks the number of times damaged during 1955-1965.

determine the productivity of damaged and undamaged tree stands, we selected sample trees from each of the separate groups (four per group). Productivity of the damaged tree stands was calculated on the basis of the number of trees in each of the various groups. In the damaged oaks the phytomass of the aboveground part (total and of separate parts of tree) decreased significantly more than height and growth. Damage of the top one to three times (Group 2) resulted in decrease of phytomass of the perennial parts of the tree by half. This is due to the changed form of the damaged trunk; it becomes tapered, since the increase in diameter of the part growing after consumption of the shoot is sharply decreased. Further increase in the number of times damaged has significantly less influence on the phytomass of the trunk and the branches, the difference in oaks of Groups 2 and 4 being a total of 10 to 12% (the diameter of the upper parts of the trunks of undamaged and weakly damaged trees differs more than between the weakly and strongly damaged trees, since the first damage was to 9 and 10 year old oaks with sufficiently thick trunks). Phytomass of leaves in the damaged trees decreases somewhat less. This is due to the formation of a large quantity of small leaves on the branches of the supplementary shoots. For this reason, in the oaks of Group 2 the area of leaf surface decreased a total of 28%, that is, approximately half of the decrease in phytomass of the perennial parts which showed 50% decrease. It is possible that a lesser reduction of the photosynthesizing surface compensates for the decrease of trunk growth and evens out the difference of phytomass growth between weakly and strongly damaged trees. But further increase of the degree of damage of shoots leads to a sharp decrease both of phytomass and of leaf surface (Table 68).

Knowing the number of trees on the area, the proportion in the various damage categories and the phytomass of the sample trees, it is not difficult to calculate the phytomass of the damaged and healthy tree stands (Table 69). During the period of high numbers of moose the phytomass of the damaged tree stands decreased by approximately one-half, especially the phytomass of branches. At this time the area of leaf surface was reduced 35% (due to the fact

Table 68. Phytomass and leaf surface of sample 14 year old oak trees (average for the group).

Index	Group			
	I	II	II	IV
Height of tree (cm)	209	183	162	132
Trunk diameter (cm)				
At the root neck	3.3	2.63.4	2.63.5	2.33.1
At breast high	1.3	0.8	0.8	0.5
Phytomass[a]				
Trunk	$\frac{0.52}{100}$	$\frac{0.25}{47}$	$\frac{0.27}{51}$	$\frac{0.20}{39}$
Branches	$\frac{0.16}{100}$	$\frac{0.07}{42}$	$\frac{0.07}{45}$	$\frac{0.05}{32}$
Leaves	$\frac{0.14}{100}$	$\frac{0.08}{59}$	$\frac{0.07}{51}$	$\frac{0.06}{47}$
Leaf surface				
(dm^2)	250	181	119	115
(%)	100	72	48	46
Number of trees per ha				
(%)	12	54	22	12

[a] In the numerator, kg (dry weight); in the denominator, %.

Table 69. Influence of ungulates and hares on phytomass and leaf area index of young oaks.

Index	Phytomass (tons/ha)			Leaf index (m^2/m^2)	Phytomass (%)			Leaf index (%)
	Trunks	Branches	Leaves		Trunks	Branches	Leaves	
Undamaged tree stands	3.6	1.1	0.9	1.7	100	100	100	100
Damaged tree stands	1.9	0.4	0.5	1.1	53	36	55	65
Reduction of phytomass and leaf area	1.7	0.7	0.4	0.6	47	64	45	35

that the majority of trees were in the second category of damage). Phytomass losses of oak result from the shoots eaten by animals in the fall-winter period and the decrease of growth rate of damaged trees.

The phytomass of the isolated undamaged sections of oak corresponds to the potential productivity of this type of forest. During the 4 to 5 year period of high numbers, the animals reduced by one-half the productivity of these tree stands (from 5600 to 2980 kg/ha). The major losses—39% (2170 kg/ha) were caused by the decreased rate of growth of the damaged trees and only 8% (450 kg/ha) constitutes the part used as food. Of this part 5% (290 kg/ha) was utilized in the energetic expenditures of the animals and 3% (160 kg/ha) was returned to the litterfall in the form of excrement (Fig. 19).

Analogous indicators of the influence of moose on gross productivity of 10 year old pines in a conifer-broadleaf forest were obtained by L. G. Dinesman and V. I. Shmalgauzen (1967). There too the gross phytomass of damaged tree stands decreased by 40%, of which about 35% constituted losses from reduction of tree growth. It is interesting to note that, although the numbers and zoomass of moose, and also the phytomass of tree stands, in the oaks of the Central Chernozem Reserve and the pine of the areas surrounding Moscow essentially differ[4] the degree of impact of moose on productivity of these biogeocoenoses and the relationship of losses of phytomass due to reduction of growth and transfer to other trophic levels appears to be the same.

The decrease of phytomass in the damaged tree stands brings with it a lowering of the quantity of nitrogen and ash elements drawn into the cycle by vegetation, and also a change of their balance in the "soil-vegetation" system. The biological cycling of minerals of woody structures occurs mainly at the expense of litterfall of leaves and dying of the roots. In damaged oaks production

[4]In the oak groves the number of moose reaches 2 specimens per km^2, the phytomass of the undamaged trees 5600 kg/ha, of the damaged 2980 kg/ha. In the pine forest the number of moose does not exceed 0.3 to 0.4 per km^2, the phytomass of the undamaged pine seedlings 181 kg per ha, of the damaged 109 kg per ha.

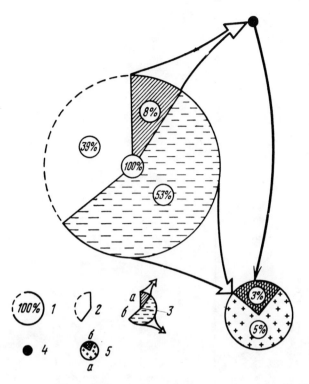

Figure 19
Participation of ungulates and hares on the formation of aboveground biological production of young oak trees. 1-productivity
of tree stand; 2-loss of productivity due to decreased growth of
damaged trees; 3-general production of tree stand: a-part of
production used for growth and energetic expenditure of zoomass
and partial return into the litterfall; b-net production; 4-
zoomass; 5-litterfall: a-leaf; b-animal (excrement).

of leaves is reduced by 403 kg/ha and their content of nitrogen and
calcium is reduced by 6 to 7 kg/ha each, of potassium and magnesium
by approximately 1 kg/ha, of phosphorus and sulphur by 0.5 kg/ha,
and of silicon by 0.23 kg/ha (Table 70).

Consequently, as a result of the activity of vertebrates consumers of browse forage, the quantity of organic material and basic
chemical elements drawn annually into the biological cycle through
the leaves in litterfall decreases by more than 40%. Thus, the
major role of the browse-eating animals in the biological cycle of
forest-steppe oak groves is not the affect on annual growth of woody
species, but on the changes of conditions for growth and development
of damaged plants. This involves a decreased productivity of the
tree stands and decreased rates of biological cycling. It should be
underscored that the forms of impact of this group of animals on
productivity of tree stands in various biogeocenoses are quite
similar.

Table 70. Influence of ungulates and hares on cycling of nitrogen and ash elements in young oak forest (kg/ha).

Index	Biomass of leaves (kg/ha)	N	Ca	K	Mg	P	S	Si
Undamaged tree stands	944	14.0	17.3	2.1	2.4	1.0	1.1	0.6
Damaged tree stands	541	8.0	9.9	1.2	1.4	0.6	0.6	0.3
Reduction of biomass	403	6.0	7.4	0.9	1.0	0.4	0.5	0.3

II-4

Root Eaters—Earth Movers

The participation of earth movers and root eaters in bio-coenotic processes was evaluated by utilizing the common mole-rat (*Spalax microphthalmus*), one of the most typical and numerous representatives of this trophic group populating the virgin meadow steppe and also the forest edge and steppe-like herb meadows of oak groves.

Spalax spends almost its entire life underground. Only during the period of dispersal do they apper for a short while on the surface. The burrows of the *Spalax* consist of a complicated system of foraging passages, concentrated in the upper layers of the soil, and nest chambers located at a depth of 2 to 3 m. The general length of the passages of one burrow is 150 to 350 m, and sometimes more (Dukelskaya 1932). Adult animals lead solitary lives, but their burrows are usually located close together and the foraging passages sometimes intertwine. This makes it difficult to determine the numbers of *Spalax*. Methods of absolute counting, based on exca-vation of the burrows and on capture of the animals, are very time-consuming, and their use for estimation of numbers on larger areas is practically impossible. For this reason, we used various relative indicators, which in combination allowed us to estimate the density of *Spalax* in the steppe and in the oak groves.

In thick chernozems of forest-steppe, the foraging passages of *Spalax* are located in the humus horizon, and the nest chambers in the deeper layers of cabonceous loam. For this reason, piles of earth (ejections) thrown out from the foraging and nest passages are well differentiated by color. This makes it possible to determine without excavation the number of animals by the distribution of their nest chambers and forage passages, and also to determine the borders of individual territories.

In the spring each year in the meadow-steppe and on the meadows in the oak groves on sample quadrats of 1 ha we marked with pegs and mapped all the fresh ejections. Every 10 to 15 days during the summer and fall locations of new ejections were added to the map. The distribution of ejections from the deep chambers of nest holes allowed us to judge the approximate number of animals living on the quadrats, and by the ejections from forage passages, which were grouped around each nest hole, the approximate size of foraging areas of individual animals.

Thus, in one of the steppe settlements of *Spalax* on an area of 1 ha in the spring we noted two nest areas (one of them with two nest chambers). Individual ranges of the animals occupied 0.1 to 0.2 ha, and the distance between the nest chambers was approximately 70 m (Fig. 20). At the end of May and the beginning of June dispersal of young began. At this time, not far from one of the nest

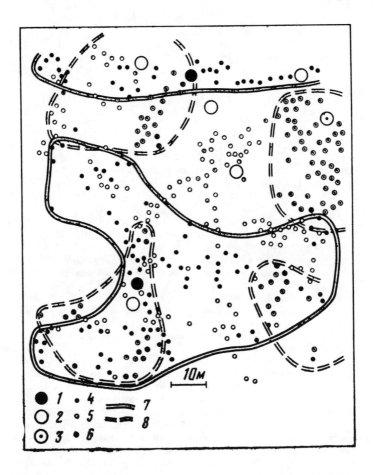

Figure 20
Steppe colony of mole-rats. 1-fresh ejections from nest chambers which appeared before dispersal of young; 2-the same, during the period of dispersal; 3-the same, after the period of dispersal; 4-fresh ejections from feeding tunnels which appeared before dispersal of young; 5-the same, during the period of dispersal; 6-the same, after dispersal; 7-borders of individual territories in the spring (May); 8-the same, after spread of young (July-October).

holes, appeared three groups of fresh nest hole ejections, each of them surround by ejections from foraging burrows. Evidently, the new holes belonged to the young animals. Judging by the distribution of fresh ejections, the foraging areas of individual animals at this time partially overlaped forming one large family area, an area a little larger than 1 ha on which lived 2 adults and 3 young animals.

At the end of June the mobility and the digging activity of *Spalax* sharply decreased, and the family section divided into four (one of the young animals probably died or went beyond the boundary of the area). On one of the individual areas ejections from the nest chamber were found beyond the boundaries of the mapped area. During July and September new ejections appeared only in the boundaries of these individual areas, the sizes of which fluctuated at this time from 0.08 to 0.12 ha, and the distance between them fluctuated from 30 to 50 m. On these areas the animals spent the winter and in the spring of 1965 there again appeared fresh ejections on these areas.

Observations on areas of constant size conducted during 7 years (1964-1970) showed that *Spalax* populated the same area during the entire time. During a larger part of the year the foraging areas of the separate animals in the boundaries of the settlement are isolated, and the distance between them exceeds 30 to 50 m. Only in the period of dispersal of young (the end of May and June) are the foraging areas of the family members essentially one area. The average diameter of an individual foraging area is 50 m, and of the family area 150 to 200 m.

Results of our observations of numbers and seasonal changes of size of foraging areas of *Spalax* coincide with the data of N. M. Dukelskoe (1932) and S. L. Ovchinnikova (1969), obtained by systematic capture of the animals and excavation of their burrows. This indicates the accuracy of the applied method which we used. Results of observations on the permanent areas showed that the numbers of *Spalax* can be determined by visual survey of their colonies and recording of activity in their foraging areas. It is best to conduct such studies in the spring, before dispersal of young, when the number of animals corresponds to the size of foraging areas. In summer the individual areas are mixed with family areas, and on each foraging area there are four to five animals (two adults and two to three young).

For examination of large areas we first crossed them in various directions on horse or by car and all colonies of the *Spalax* seen were added to the map. Later, in the boundaries of each settlement we conducted a visual survey of the foraging areas. In the tall grassy meadow-steppe it is best done before the beginning of vegetation growth. At this time in the watershed section, using binoculars, it is possible from one point to compose a map of distribution of groups of fresh dark ejections within a radius of nearly a kilometer. Density of the foraging areas was determined by walking transects at least 2 to 3 km in length, on which were noted all the fresh ejections from nest chambers and the foraging burrow systems. The width of the transect had to exceed the average diameter of the foraging area. During spring it was more than 50 m; during summer it was more than 200 m. The observations on transects were conducted by a chain of observers, walking from 10 to 20 m apart (depending on the height and degree of closure of the grass canopy).

For estimates of the number of *Spalax* in the oak forest we had to limit ourselves to walking transects on which were counted groups of fresh ejections. Observations of 1-ha study areas showed that the sizes of the forest glades were insufficient for a prolonged stay by this animal. Even on comparatively large glades (0.3 to 0.4 ha) *Spalax* do not live longer than 1.5 to 2.0 months. The glades, abandoned by *Spalax* in the middle of summer, are again populated by them, usually after a year, during the period of dispersal of young. This should be kept in mind during interpretation of results of the calculations of foraging areas on the transects.

The number of *Spalax* depends first of all upon the abundance and the quality of forage, roots of herbs, which is their major food. For this reason, in the meadow-steppe of the Central Chernozem Reserve the animals prefer the mowed sections where, according to the data of A. M. Semenova-Tian-Shanskaya (1966), the herbs and legumes compose 75% to 85% of the phytomass. On the unmowed sections of the steppe grasses predominate, and *Spalax* colonies are rarer. In the thin oak groves their colonies are confined to the herb glades or the steppe-meadow sections on the ravine slopes. On agricultural lands the animals settle mainly where perennial plants are cultivated and are very few in number where grain crops have been planted, on which they only rarely intrude from the neighboring virgin sections (Table 71).

Table 71.   Indices of *Spalax* abundance for 1 km^2 (average of several years for the summer period).

Location	Number of foraging areas	Number of specimens	Zoomass (kg)[a]
Steppe			
Mowed			
Watershed	19	95	23
Near ravine slopes	40–60	200–300	48–72
Gullies	60–90	300–450	72–100
Unmowed			
Watershed	5	25	6
Forest			
Waterhsed	9–12	45–60	11–14
Gullies	15	75	18
Fields			
Fields of perennial plants (clover)	30	150	36
Fields of grain (winter fields)	6	30	7

[a] The general zoomass of animals colonizing a section (two adults and two to three young) is 1.2–1.6 kg (live weight).

The numbers of *Spalax* and the distribution of their colonies in the steppe is relatively stable. In mowed steppe in 1964 the number of foraging areas per square kilometer was 19, in 1965 it was 23, in 1969 it was 20, and in 1970 it was 15. In the forest during these years numbers fluctuated from 5 to 14.

During the dry years in summer the animals dispersed from the watershed to the ravine slopes and the ravines, and in the spring they again colonized the watersheds. However, in the mid-Russian upland with its dissected relief and abundance of branched ravines with numerous channels, these seasonal dispersals are accomplished within the boundaries of one or several neighboring colonies, which stretch from the watershed to the ravine (usually along flat shallow drainages). In this case the animals apparently use the old burrows; in the early spring on the virgin sections of the steppe between two colonies about 100 m apart, one often can see from two to three single fresh ejections, traces of the animals dispersal movements by way of the old burrows.

VOLUME AND DYNAMICS OF BURROWING ACTIVITY

Study of the digging activity of *Spalax* was conducted on 1-ha sample areas in the steppe and in the forest where size was limited by the sizes of the glades, 0.3 to 0.4 ha. In the spring all the fresh ejections were marked by pegs and then every 10 days again all new ejections were noted. The method allowed us to estimate the yearly volume of digging activity of *Spalax*. Observation of sample areas was continued 4 years, which made it possible to trace a gradual "aging" of ejections—changes of their area and volume, of chemical and hydrothermic characteristics of the soil, disappearance and colonization by other animals, and determination of the speed of these processes.

Earth movers, including *Spalax*, bring to the surface only a part of the soil, and the remainder fills the old passages. The older the age of the colony and the more branches in the network of the old passages, the less soil is brought to the surface. This complicates determination of the yearly volume of digging activity of the animals, since, in the thick chernozem, distinguishing earth mounds formed in the current year from older mounds is usually impossible. For this reason we were forced to limit ourselves to determination of the volume of soil annually brought to the surface, conditionally calling it the volume of digging activity by *Spalax*. The true quantity of redistributed soil is significantly greater.

Observation of the seasonal dynamics of digging activity on the sample areas showed that during the vegetative period (from the middle of April to the middle of October) in the steppe colony there are on the average 371, and in the forest colonies 366 ejections per ha. At the end of May and June most ejections appear; in the steppe colony 40% of all the ejections, and in the forest colonies 72%. After dispersal of the young the intensity of digging activity by the animals decreases sharply (Table 72).

Knowing the average area, volume and weight per ejection (0.2 m^2, 0.02 m^3, and 6.1 kg dry weight), and also the number of ejections which appear during one year, it is not difficult to calculate the volume of digging activity of *Spalax* on the continuously colonized

Table 72.   Seasonal dynamics of *Spalax* digging activity
            (number of ejections appearing per ha)[a].

Dates	Number of new ejections per ha	
	Steppe	Forest glade
21–31 May	48	69
1–10 June	50	89
11–20 June	49	89
21–30 June	35	61
1–10 July	28	14
11–20 July	29	28
21–31 July	12	0
1–10 August	3	0
11–31 August 1–15 September	1	0

[a]At the beginning of the investigations on the steppe
area there were 22 ejections which appeared after the
disappearance of snow cover, that is, in approximately
a month and a half.

area, and also in the steppe and in the forest as a whole.   In the
steppe and forest colony it was the same.   Every year on 1 ha of a
colony about 7 m^3 of soil is brought out.   The weight of soil moved
constitutes 2.2 to 2.3 tons, which corresponds to 0.1% of the weight
(2120 tons per ha) of the upper 20 cm layer of the soil, in which a
majority of the passages are located.

However, considering the various densities of settlements,
the volume of the digging activity of *Spalax* on the whole in the
steppe is significantly greater than in the forest.

On the steppe watershed, where the number of foraging areas
reached 0.2 per ha, and the volume of thrown-out soil reached 1.4 m^3
per ha, the weight of the soil annually brought to the surface is
0.4 ton per ha (0.02% of the weight of the soil in the layer of 0 to
20 cm).   On the ravine slopes (0.4 to 0.6 of the foraging area,
the volume of the thrown-out soil is 3 to 4 m^3/ha) on the surface
during 1 year is brought up 0.9 to 1 ton per ha (0.04 to 0.02% of
the soil weight in the layer of 0 to 20 cm), and on the forest
watershed (0.09 to 0.12 of the foraging area, the volume of the

thrown out soil 0.1 to 0.9 m^3/ha) the weight is 0.2 to 0.3 ton per
ha (0.01 to 0.15% of the layer 0 to 20 cm).

Observations of the study areas showed ejections gradually
being covered by grass and becoming flat are visible four to five
years. In the steppe ejections of all ages cover 1 to 1.5% of the
area, and in the forests about 0.1%. The volume of all the soil
moved during this period constitutes in the steppe 0.15% of the
volume of soil in a layer of 0 to 20 cm, and in the forest about
0.01%.

INFLUENCE ON PHYSICAL AND CHEMICAL PROPERTIES OF THE SOIL

By digging and moving soil to the surface, *Spalax* changed the
physical properties and hydrothermic regime of the soil. Volumetric
weight of fresh ejections is 0.3 g/cm^3. This is 3 to 4 times less
than the volumetric weight of the upper horizon of virgin chernozems
and two times less than the volumetric weight of plowed land
(Afanaceeva 1966). Bare of vegetation, soil of the ejection is
strongly heated. In the summer during sunny days the maximum temperature on the surface of the ejection reaches 50°C, at the time
when on nearby grass areas it does not exceed 25 to 30°C. With
depth the temperature difference of reworked and virgin soil decreases. In the layer of 0 to 10 cm the temperature of the ejection
is higher by 10°C; in the layer of 10 to 15 cm it is higher by 5 to
6°C, and deeper the difference gradually disappears (Table 73). In
the upper horizons of the soil the amplitude of 24-hr fluctuation of
temperature also increases, which is particularly characteristic of
the steppe (Fig. 21).

Table 73. Temperature and soil moisture of fresh *Spalax* ejections
in the steppe (July, 1300 hours).

Depth (cm)	Temperature (°C)		Humidity	
	Ejection	Virgin[a]	Ejection	Virgin[a]
0	39.0	26.0	9.8	12.9
5	30.0	20.0	22.1	16.6
10	27.5	18.3	ND[b]	ND
15	23.0	17.5	22.0	15.6
20	13.0	17.5	ND	ND

[a] Data of P. T. Kokovina

[b] ND = no data

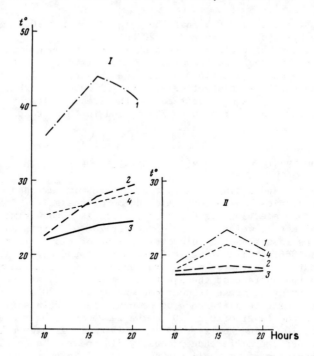

Figure 21
24 hour course of temperature in fresh ejections of mole-rats
(second 10 day period of August). I-steppe, II-forest; 1-surface
of ejection; 2-soil of ejection at depth of 5 cm; 3-the same,
at 10 cm; 4-surface of soil of the control section.

     The surface of fresh ejections is quickly covered by a crust
which prevents drying. At a depth of 5 to 20 cm the moisture of the
soil is higher by 7 to 8% (Fig. 22) than at the corresponding depth
of the virgin section (high moisture content of the soil of the
ejection is also connected with the lack of moisture loss by
transpiration).
     The major part of the *Spalax* home range is formed of foraging
passages, concentrated in the upper 20 to 30 cm layer of the soil.
From the general volume of the soil brought up yearly by *Spalax*
to the surface, 95% to 97% is from the humus horizon, primarily from
the layer of 0 to 30 cm, and only 3 to 5% come from carbonaceous
horizon.
     Making numerous passages, the *Spalax* mix the soil by carrying
to the surface material from deep layers, which are depleted of
humus and enriched by carbonates, and are characteristic of the
locations with ejections from deep nesting holes. In the soil
profile, the humus content of ejections from foraging passages reflects its content in the upper layer of the soil; on the top the
soil of the mound is from a depth of 20 to 30 cm, under it from a
depth of 10 to 20 cm, and so forth. Ejections and buried soil

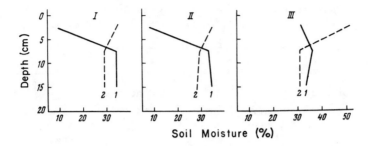

Figure 22
Soil moisture in ejections of mole-rats (second 10 day period
of August). I-unmowed sections of steppe; II-mowed sections
of steppe; III-forest glades; 1-ejection; 2-control.

differ not only in humus content, but also in fractional composition. In the soil reworked by *Spalax* the content of soluble fractions of humus increases. Fulvic acid content sharply increases
(especially in the ejections and the 20 cm soil layer under it),
and thus the relationship of humic acid:fulvic acid decreases
(Table 74 and 75).
        Soil profiles on the area colonized by *Spalax* are conspicuous
by multilayered molehills. Dark molehills formed of the soil brought
up from the humus horizon are seen to a depth of 1.5 to 2.0 m, and
sometimes even more; light mounds filled with carbonaceous loam are
spread throughout the entire humus horizon to its upper levels. In
the upper meter layer of the soil profile of steppe chernozem on a
$10 \ m^2$ area there is on the average 18 to 20 mounds with a total area
of 0.2 to $0.3 \ m^2$. However, it should be kept in mind that in the
humus horizon of the soil profile usually only the lighter molehills
are well distinguished, formed from the soil of the transitional and
carbonaceous horizons. The dark molehills, especially the old ones,
are almost indistinguishable. For this reason, the total area of
all the molehills is probably significantly greater.
        It is natural that the humus content of the molehills differs
from the surrounding soil. Thus, in the lower part of the humus
horizon the content of humus in dark molehills is 1.5% greater and
in the light molehills it is 2.0 to 2.5% less (level of significance
is 0.12 to 0.3). In the carbonaceous horizon all the molehills,
including the fresh ones, are rich in humus.
        Analyses have shown that by composition the humus of molehills
differs not only from the surrounding soil, but also from the soil
horizons from which the material was transferred. In all the molehills there is an increase in the relative content of humic acid
(primarily at the expense of non-hydrolyzed remains). It is characteristic that such a quantity is lacking in the entire thickness
of the humus layer of the unreworked soil of the meadow-steppe. The
greatest content of humic acid in the soil profile of the humus
horizons of unmowed sections of the steppe constitutes, according to
the data of V. V. Ponomareva and T. A. Nikolaeva (1965) 35.3% (at a
depth of 30 to 40 cm) and on the mowed sections 41.4% (at a depth of
66 to 70 cm). Fulvic acid content is less in the molehills from the

Table 74.   Distribution of humus and CO_2 of $CaCO_3$ in the soil profile through fresh *Spalax* ejections (% of dry soil).

Depth (cm)	Humus			CO_2 of $CaCO_3$		
	Control areas	Ejections		Control areas	Ejections	
		From forage passages	From forage passages		From forage passages	From forage passages
Layers of ejection above soil surface						
30–20	--	5.65	--	--	0.22	--
20–10	--	6.27	5.08	--	0.22	0.22
10–0	--	8.71	5.26	--	0.22	0.22
Soil layers under the ejection						
0–5	8.40	8.00	7.24	0.06	0.13	0.18
5–10	7.07	7.29	5.14	0.07	0.19	0.22
10–20	6.75	5.88	4.95	0.08	0.26	0.04
20–30	5.50	5.36	4.26	0.03	0.22	0.18
30–40	4.94	4.59	3.90	0.03	0.13	0.13
40–50	4.68	4.39	2.92	0.03	0.04	0.11
50–60	3.18	4.81	2.36	0.07	0.13	0.22

humus and transitional horizons, and in the molehills from the carbonaceous horizon it differs little from the content of the surrounding soil (Table 76).

Analogous changes of humus composition are exposed in the soil of foraging passages used by *Spalax*. Analyses showed that here the size of relationship of humic acid:fulvic acid is higher, than of the unreworked soil at a corresponding depth soil. Particularly, the quantity of humic acid under the passages strongly increases. In the 10 cm layer of the soil the relationship of humic acid:fulvic acid increases according to the measure of distance from the wall of the passage (Table 77 and 78). Thus, changes of the fractional composition of humus in the passages, both open ones and in the passages closed by the earth plugs, and in the soil profile through the ejection were dissimilar. There is a general increase of soluble material in the passages due to an increase in humic acid, and in the ejections and under them due to fulvic acid.

Table 75. Group composition of humus under fresh ejections (% of total C)[a].

Depth (cm)	C (% of soil weight)	Humic acids	Fulvic acids	Sum	Non-hydrolized remain	Humic acid / Fulvic acid
		Layers of ejection above soil surface				
15-10	4.14	34.7	31.0	65.7	34.2	1.12
10-0	4.86	36.4	32.8	69.2	30.8	1.19
		Soil layers under the ejection				
0-10	4.56 / 5.51	32.9 / 28.3	30.5 / 17.9	63.4 / 46.2	36.6 / 53.8	1.08 / 1.58
10-20	3.72 / 3.90	40.5 / 32.4	27.6 / 16.7	68.1 / 49.1	31.9 / 50.9	1.47 / 1.94
20-30	3.06 / 3.24	39.8 / 36.4	22.7 / 16.3	62.5 / 52.7	37.5 / 47.3	1.75 / 2.23
30-40	2.52 / 2.91	44.0 / 36.8	25.3 / 15.7	69.3 / 52.5	30.7 / 47.5	1.73 / 2.34
40-50	2.40 / 2.68	40.0 / 37.3	18.3 / 15.6	58.3 / 52.9	41.7 / 47.1	2.18 / 2.39
50-60	2.76 / 2.34	ND[b] / 38.9	26.3 / 16.8	ND / 55.7	ND / 44.3	0.56 / 2.31

[a] In the numerator is the humus composition in ejections (our data), in the denominator is the humus composition in undug soils (according to data of V. V. Ponomareva and T. A. Nikolaeva 1965).

[b] ND = no data.

We have noted that peculiarities in the composition of humus of reworked sections of the steppe are correlated with zoogenic changes of physical-chemical and biological processes occurring in the soil profile. Discovery of the essence of these changes is the subject of further investigations and goes beyond the competence of zoologists. At present we can only hypothesize that they are caused by the specificity of the hydrothermic regime of the reworked soil and the enriched organic material contained in the remains of forage and excretions of the animals. It is known that addition of organic fertilizer changes the composition of humus, and that the character of these changes (the relationship of humic acid:fulvic acid) depends on composition of the fertilizer (Visotskaya and Mikhnovski 1962, Kononova Aleksandrova and others 1964). With zoogenic litterfall come organic compounds to the soil that differ from the compounds coming from litterfall of plants (animal albumins in particular richer in nitrogen). In addition, animal excrement serves as a favorable substrate for the development of microorganisms and as a catalyzer of microbiological processes. This can be testified to by the sharp increase of intenstiy of soil respiration from the passages of *Spalax* and their plugs. Special experiments, conducted by the method of Shtatnova (Makarov and Matskevitch 1966), showed that in all the parts of the soil profile intensity of total CO_2 emission from the molehills is 1.3 to 3 times greater than from the

Table 76. Group humus composition in soil of molehills[a] (% of total C).

Depth (cm)	Sample	Humus (% for dry soil)	Humic acids	Fulvic acids	Sum	Non-hydrolized remains	Humic acid / Fulvic acid
60-70	Undug soil	3.72	32.8	31.4	64.2	35.8	1.05
	Soil from "molehills" with material from various horizons:						
	Humus	5.26	52.5	25.8	78.3	21.7	2.0
	Transitional	3.58	49.2	24.6	73.8	26.2	1.9
	Carbonaceous	1.48	38.5	35.2	73.7	26.3	1.1
130-150	Undug soil	1.10	20.6	38.9	59.5	40.5	0.53
	Soil from "molehills" with material from various horizons:						
	Humus	4.44	51.2	29.6	80.8	19.2	1.7
	Transitional	2.25	52.2	25.7	77.9	22.1	2.0
	Carbonaceous	1.39	40.0	35.3	75.3	24.7	1.1

a/ Analyses were carried out in laboratory of the Central Museum of Soil Science in the name of V. V. Dokuchaev under the guidance of V. V. Ponomareva.

Table 77. Humus composition in 10 cm soil layer around the passages of *Spalax* on fallow land (% of total C).[a]

Place of sample selection	Depth (cm)	Total C, % of soil weight	Humic acids	Fulvic acids	Humic acid / fulvic acid
Above the passage	10–20	3.15 / 3.90	41.6 / 32.4	15.2 / 16.7	2.9 / 1.9
On the sides of the passage[b]	20–30	2.91 / 3.20	38.5 / 36.4	12.2 / 16.3	3.1 / 2.2
Under the passage	30–40	2.61 / 2.90	46.3 / 36.8	7.7 / 16.3	6.0 / 2.3

[a] In the numerator is the humus composition in the passage walls, in the denominator, in the control sample.

[b] Average from determinations from both sides of passage.

surrounding soil, independent of their $CaCO_3$ content. Since roots and soil invertebrates were removed from the soil before the experiment, the intensive emission of CO_2 is connected with metabolic activity of microorganisms. (Table 79).

Additional changes of humus composition of reworked soil include increased content of calcium in the upper layers, and also increased organic material in the spring-summer period due to fresh grass buried by the ejections. The latter may be one of the reasons for formation of fulvic acid in the upper layers of the soil under fresh ejections (Tyurin 1965).

The materials presented show that the influence of *Spalax* on soil formation is highly variable. Chemical composition of the soil from the passage walls, the earth plugs, the molehills and ejections, are different and change over time. For this reason the total impact of *Spalax* on the soil-forming processes can be calculated only on the basis of soil analyses of the entire profile of the reworked sections. This allows us to make sample analyses from the soil cut in the permanent settlements of *Spalax*.

Due to the policy of preservation of the Reserve we were unable to make a number of soil cuts; only two cuts were made in the entire soil profile. In addition, three cuts were partially analyzed. For this reason the results are not of great precision. However, regularity of changes in chemical composition of the soil due to *Spalax* was revealed rather clearly. The cuts were situated from 15 to 40 cm from each other. As a control cut we used a cut near that described in detail by E. A. Afanaceeva (1966). Results of analysis showed modified distribution of humus and carbonate in the soil profile of the section reworked by *Spalax*. Carbonates are contained through the entire profile, while in the humus horizon of undisturbed soil they practically do not exist. In the humus horizon of

Table 78. Change of fractional humus composition at various distances from the passages of *Spalax* on fallow land (% of total C).

Depth (cm)	Distance from passage wall (cm)	Total C (% of soil weight)	Humic acids	Fulvic acids	Sum	Nonhydrolized remain	Humic acid / fulvic acid
Above passage							
8-10	8-10	3.21	41.1	12.1	53.2	46.8	3.4
12-14	4-6	3.12	42.3	15.1	57.4	42.6	2.8
16-18	0-2	3.11	42.4	18.3	60.7	39.3	2.3
On sides of passage							
	0-2	2.97	37.2	14.4	51.6	48.4	2.6
22	4-6	2.87	38.8	11.1	49.9	50.1	3.7
	8-10	2.82	39.5	11.2	50.7	49.3	3.5
Under passage							
25-27	0-2	2.94	40.8	9.2	50.0	50.0	4.4
29-31	4.6	2.46	48.8	8.5	57.3	42.7	5.7
33-35	8-10	2.44	49.2	5.3	54.5	45.5	9.3

Table 79.   Indicators of respiration intensity of typical chernozem soil
and of the passages and molehills in the mowed steppe.[a]

Depth (cm)	Sample	Boiling from HCl	Respiration mg CO_2/hr	Difference from control sample (%)
20-30	Control	None	0.16	
10-19	Mole hill light	Strong	0.49	306
15-22	light	Weak	0.39	244
21-28	dark	None	0.16	100
42-55	Control	None	0.36	
	Mole hill			
	dark	None	1.15	317
	light	Strong	1.02	283
150-156	Control	Middle	0.26	
	Mole hill in nesting chamber	Middle	0.47	180
183-187	Control	Middle	0.29	
167-178	Light mole hill	Strong	0.42	145
187-199	Light mole hill	Strong	0.38	131
210-220	Control	Strong	0.32	
	Dark mole hill	None	0.41	128

[a] For samples from a depth of 42-45 cm the calculation is carried out for
100 g of raw soil, for all others--for 50 cm^3. The values presented
are preliminary and can be used only for comparison of respiration
intensity of molehills and soil in which they are found.

the disturbed soil, in the layers through which the burrows pass,
the content of humus decreases by 0.7 to 3.5% and gross calcium
increases up to 4.3% (on the average by 2.5%). In the transitional
and carbonaceous horizons, the layers in which are located dark
"humus" molehills, contained 0.6 to 0.9% more humus and 2 to 4 times
less calcium (Table 80).

As a result of the penetration of passages and dark molehills
to a significant depth, the lower boundary of the humus horizon on
the areas disturbed by *Spalax* is 10 to 20 cm lower.[1] Simultaneously
the distribution of carbon, nitrogen, and calcium changes in the
profile of the chernozem humus. The reserve of humus in the humus
horizon decreases by 11% and in the transitional and upper section
of the carbonaceous layer it increases by 32%. The reserve of total
nitrogen in the upper 1 m layer increases by 41%. The reserve of

[1] For the humus horizon of thick chernozems humus content is characteristically more than 2% (Afanaceeva 1966).

gross calcium in the upper half of the humus horizon increases by 44% and in the lower horizon by 37% (Table 81).

At the same time the total reserves of carbon, humus, and calcium in a 1.5 m layer of the disturbed and virgin sections differ little. This points to the fact that in thick chernozems the digging activity of *Spalax* does not change the total reserve of major nutrients but effects their redistribution in the soil profile. The latter have great significance for soil formation and for biological cycling.

The role of *Spalax* in transfer and cycling of calcium is particularly great. It was not possible to calculate the exact quantity of calcium transferred annually by *Spalax*, since a significant part of the soil carried from the carbonaceous horizon remained in the old passages of the animals and our method did not permit determination of the age of molehills. For this reason, we were limited to calculations which would allow approximation of the role of *Spalax* in the cycling of calcium. In order to avoid over-estimation we consider that the increase of calcium in the root layer occurs only near the nesting passages where material is transported from the carbonaceous layer. The molehills (primarily from the carbonaceous and transitional horizons) occupy 2 to 3% of the area of the soil cut (at a layer of 0 to 100 cm). On the average in the steppe the sections with an increased content of calcium in the root zone occupy 2% of the top meter of the soil. On these sections the reserve of calcium (in the layer 0 to 50 cm) increases by 26 tons per ha (CaO by 36 tons per ha). In this case the increase of calcium reserve in the root-inhabited layer due to the vital activities of *Spalax* in the steppe should constitute on the average about 0.5 tons per ha.[2] This exceeds approximately by a factor of two the quantity of calcium annually absorbed from the soil of the meadow steppe by the total growth of phytomass (Afanaceva 1966).

In this way, in the meadow-steppe the quantity of calcium brought up by *Spalax* into the root layer is commensurate with the quantity put into the yearly cycle by vegetation, especially from the aboveground phytomass of grass stands into which there is put 0.04 tons per ha, according to the data of E. A. Afanaceeva. Obviously, to the earth mover belongs the essential role of replenishment of the reserve of calcium in the zone of intensive cycling, especially on the mowed sections of the steppe and the cultivations of the forage plants where a significant part of the ash elements is removed yearly from the system with the harvest. In disturbed chernozems composition of the humus changes noticeably. The size of the unhyrdolyzed fraction decreases, the total soluble material increases and the relative content of fulvic acid sharply increases. There also the content of nitrogen in the humus increases, mainly in the lower part of the humus layer. The latter is especially characteristic of areas with burrows from the nesting chambers. If the reserve of humus in the 50 to 100 cm layer on the areas with foraging and areas with nesting passages is almost the same, 175 and 170 tons per ha (on the control section, 203 tons per ha), then the content of nitrogen in humus which is 5% on the control

[2]Determination of CO_2 of carbonates in the soil of the molehills showed that the increase of calcium reserve is due to calcium carbonates transferred from the lower soil horizons.

Table 81. Change of gross reserve of humus, nitrogen, and calcium in disturbed soils of the unmowed steppe. [a]

Depth (cm)	Humus Reserve (t/ha)	Humus Difference (%)	C Reserve (t/ha)	C Difference (%)	N Reserve (5/ha)	N Difference (%)	CaO gross Reserve (t/ha)	CaO gross Difference (%)	C:N	N in humus (%)
0-50	368/334	-9	212/193	-9	19/22	+16	81/117	+44	11:2/8:8	4.85/6.59
50-100	203/173	-15	118/110	-7	10/19	+90	74/101	+37	11:8/5:8	5.00/10.90
400-150	65/86	+32	34/48	+26	Not determined/16		549/526	-4	Not determined/3:0	Not determined/Not determined
0-100	571/507	-11	330/303	-9	29/41	+41	155/218	+42	11:4/7:4	4.95/7.89
0-150	636/593	-7	368/351	-5	Not determined/57		704/744	+6	Not determined/6:2	Not determined/Not determined

a/ In the numerator, on the control section; in the denominator, on the disturbed section.

section reaches 7.9% on the section with foraging passages and 12.3% on the sections with nesting passages. Possibly this is connected with accumulation in the nesting passages of zoogenic nitrogen. The animals constantly use these passages and in them accumulates remains of forage and excrement serving as a substratum for the development of microorganisms.

CHANGES OF PLANT COVER

Spalax feeds chiefly on rhizomes, tubers, and tap roots of the steppe herbs and legumes. They especially eat spirea, milk gowan, sedge, dandelions, various types of clover and lucerne. From stomach contents of *Spalax* it was determined that an adult animal with a weight of 420 to 460 g eats during a 24-hr period about 20 g of forage and excretes approximately 5 g of excrement.[3] With an average number (1 to 3 animals per ha) during a year in the steppe they eat 7.2 to 21.6 kg per ha of rhizomes and roots, returning to the litter-fall 1.8 to 5.4 kg per ha of excrement. In the soil layer of 0 to 20 cm, where the majority of foraging passages of *Spalax* are located, growth of the belowground root stalks of herbs constitutes during the year 800 to 1600 kg per ha (approximate calculation according to the materials of A. M. Semenova-Tien-Shanskaya 1965). Thus, in this layer of the soil *Spalax* eat about 1.25% of the growth of the belowground phytomass of the indicated groups of plants.

To estimate the influence of digging activity of *Spalax* on the structure and productivity of plant cover, a geobotanical description of the stages of revegetation of ejections was made. Aboveground phytomass and the quantity of shoots on the ejections was determined. The data show that during the first year revegetation of fresh ejections is chiefly due to plant shoots of those plants surrounding or covering the ejections. The following year seedlings appear on the ejections.

The composition of vegetation on *Spalax* ejections differs from composition on the surrounding virgin section in the abundance of rhizome and root sucker plants, and also of ruderal types. Calciphilous plants, typical of the ejections from deeper holes of marmot and ground squirrel, are infrequent on the ejections of *Spalax*. They are seen only on ejections from the deep nesting chambers.

On the ejections in the meadow-steppe rhizome and root sucker plants predominate, those dominating the vegetative cover of the given section of the virgin steppe.[4] Especially numerous are spirea and bedstraw, observed on 44 to 50% of the ejections. Somewhat less important is brome grass, strawberry, and meadowgrass. Meadow rue and marshall knapweed are confined to the ejections. The second

[3]Here and further in the text is given dry weight of plants and excrement.

[4]The vegetative cover of the mowed sections of the meadow-steppe of the Central Chernozem Reserve is a mosaic; for this reason we compared the vegetation of ejections and the virgin section directly adjacent to them.

group of species characteristic of the ejections of *Spalax* is weeds
(*Potentilla*, sheepsorrel, strawberry, meadowgrass, and others).   On
the ejections they are more abundant and larger than in the virgin
steppe.   Often the ejections are distinguishable by the clump of
spreading sheepsorrel.   The weed and root sucker types are especially abundance on the ejections in the first stages of vegetative
development.

An analogous type of vegetation is characteristic of the overgrowing ejections on the herb-grass forest glades.   A basic difference is that in the steppe with a large variety of vegetation
(common and major species), only two species predominate on the
ejections, spirea and bedstraw; the remaining types contribute less
than 10%.   In the forests the same sharp difference between separate
types on the ejections is not observed (Tables 82 and 83).

Loosened moist soil and weak shading of fresh ejections are
very favorable for growth of seeds, especially in the steppe.   A
year after the appearance of ejections the quantity of sprouts of
various types of herbage (mainly rhizomatous weeds) on them is 6 to
9 times greater than on the nearby virgin section.   Conditions for
germination of seeds become less favorable with age.   Under two year
old ejections the quantity of sprouts is only 2 to 2½ times greater
than on virgin soil.   On the ejections in the forests shoots of
ground ivy predominate and the shoots of *Potentilla* are numerous,
but adult plants of these types are almost never seen.   In the case
of mature specimens shoots of forget-me-nots and chickweed are more
important than the shoots of strawberry, plantain, alfalfa, yarrow,
goutweed and most of the grasses (Table 84).

On the ejections in the oak groves there often appear shoots of
the main accompanying forest-forming species and undergrowth (oak,
pear, crab apple, blackthorn, cinnamon rose, buckthorn, steppe
cherry).   On the 2 year old ejections they are noted in 15 to 20% of
the cases.   Most often on the ejections there appear shoots of
blackthorn (on 8% of the ejections) and also pear and oak (on 3% of
the ejections).   On forest glades and on the periphery bordered by
the steppe cherry, almost all of the shoots of the cherry are confined to the ejections of *Spalax*.   Apparently the ejections are
ecological channels on which the woody and brush vegetation penetrates into the steppe meadows on the periphery and southern slopes
of the ravines.

INFLUENCE ON PRODUCTIVITY OF THE MEADOW-STEPPE

To estimate the biogeocoenotic role of *Spalax* it is necessary
to know the duration of changes caused by their digging activity.
On the study areas in the steppe during 4 years we marked new
ejections.   At the end of the fourth year in the ejections of all
ages we determined temperature and moisture of the soil, content and
composition of humus, and the production of grasses.   All determinations were conducted on the same ejections during the period of
maximum development of phytomass from five replicates for each age
group.

Physical properties of the soil of ejections and vegetative
cover on them is renewed rather quickly.   In one year the height of
ejections is reduced by half and in three years to one quarter.   In
this period the diameter of the base changes little.   The volume of

Table 82.   Vegetation on *Spalax* ejections in the mowed steppe
(cop. = abundant, sp. = medium, sol. = rare, un. = one).

Type	Ejections with given species (%)	Abundance on virgin[a]	Type of belowground organs[a]
Spirea	50	cop.	rhizome
Bedstraw	44	cop.	rhizome
Brome grass	25	cop.	rhizome
Meadow clary	24	cop.	tap root
Potentilla	24	sol.	root sucker
Sheep sorrel, weed	22	sol.	tap root ·
Strawberry	20	cop.	root sucker
Meadowgrass	19	cop.	rhizome
Meadowrue	16	sp.	rhizome
Marshall's knapweed	12	sp.-sol.	rhizome
Bindweed, weed	11	sp.-sol.	root sucker
Chickweed	11	sp.-sol.	cluster of roots
Milkgowan, weed	11	?	tap root
Jerusalem sage	10	sol.	tap root
Clover	10	sp.-sol.	rhizome
Violet	8	sol.	cluster of roots
Primrose	8	sp.	cluster of roots
Koeleria	5	sp.	sod
Medrey	5	cop.	tap root
Sandwort, weed	4	sp.	cluster of roots
Lychnis	4	sp.	cluster of roots
Vetch	4	sol.	rhizome
Yarrow	2	cop.	long rhizome
Spurge, weed	2	sol.	root sucker
Veronica, weed	2	sol.	rhizome
Plantain, weed	2	sp.	tap root
Geranium	2	sol.	rhizome
Sheep's fescue	2	cop.	sod
Valerian	1	cop.	cluster of roots
Quackgrass	1	sol.	rhizome
Lucerne	1	sol.	tap root
Solomon's seal	1	un.	rhizome
Forget-me-not, weed	1	cop.	cluster of roots
Sainfain	1	sol.	tap root
Pyrethrum	1	un.	tap root
Woodruff	1	sol.	tap root
Sedge	1	sp.	?
Bentgrass	1	sp.	fibrous

[a] According to data of A. M. Semenova-Tien-Shanskaya (1966).

Table 83. Vegetation on *Spalax* ejections in forest glades
(cop. = abundant, sp. = medium, sol. = rare).

Type	Ejections with given species (%)	Abundance on virgin[a]	Type of belowground organs[a]
Selfheal	60	cop.	cluster of roots
Strawberry	55	sp.-cop.	root sucker
Lucerne	50	sol.	rap root
Great Plantain, weed	45	sp.-sol.	tap root
Veronica, weed	45	cop.	rhizome
Yarrow	45	sp.-cop.	long rhizome
Bell-flower	40	sp.	tap root
"Grasses"	40	cop.	rhizome
Goutweed	30	cop.	rhizome
Sedges	30	sol.	rhizome
Plantago sp., weed	25	sp.	tap root
Oxeye daisy	25	sp.-cop.	short rhizome
Hawkweed	25	sp.-sol.	tap root
Red Clover	20	sol.	tap root
Forget-me-not, weed	15	sp.-cop.	cluster of roots
Bramble vetch, weed	15	cop.	long rhizome
Bedstraw	15	sp.	rhizome
Bistort	15	sol.	?
Crawling clover	10	sol.	rhizome
Potentilla, weed	10	sol.	short rhizome
Chickweed	10	sol.	cluster of roots
Hoary Plantain	5	sol.	tap root
Mountain Clover	5	sol.	tap root
Hedge Vetch	5	sol.	rhizome
Sowthistle, weed	5	sp.-sol.	tap root
Bunias, weed	5	sol.	tap root

[a] According to A. M. Semenova-Tien-Shanskaya (1966).

ejections after a year decreases to ½ and after 3 years to 10%. In
this way, a sharp decrease of volume is connected not with the
broadening of ejections, but with compaction, that is, with the
restoration of volumetric weight of the soil. The ejections were
quickly overgrown by grass. In 2 years the phytomass of the grass
stands on them reached 25 to 27%, and after 3 years reached 97% of
the aboveground phytomass of the steppe. On
the forest glades revegetation of ejections occurs still faster;
after 2 years the phytomass of the grass stand reaches 53% of the
phytomass of grass of the virgin sections. After 4 to 5 years on
these ejections a vegetative cover that is characteristic for the
basic phytocoenosis is restored (Fig. 23).
    Revegetation of ejections leads to a decrease of heat in the
upper layer of the soil and to redistribution of soil moisture. In
proportion to "the aging" of the ejection the soil temperature
decreases, moisture in the upper layer (0 to 2 cm) increases, and in
the root layer it decreases. The later is connected with the fact
that in relation to overgrowing and shading of the ejection

Table 84.   Abundance of shoots of various types of plants on *Spalax* ejections in forest glades (sol. = first, cop. = middle, sp. = few).

Type	Ejections with given species (%)	Abundance on virgin[a/]	Type of belowground organs[a/]
Ground Ivy, weed	100	sol.	rhizome
Selfheal	70	cop.	cluster of roots
Veronica, weed	50	cop.	rhizome
Potentilla, weed	40	sol.	short rhizome
Lucerne	35	sol.	tap root
Bell-flower	25	sp.	tap root
Forget-me-not, weed	25	sp.-cop.	cluster of roots
Oxeye daisy	25	sp.-cop.	short rhizome
Chickweed	25	sol.	cluster of roots
"Grasses"	20	cop.	rhizome
Strawberry	20	sp.	root sucker
Great Plantain, weed	15	sp.	tap root
Goutweed	15	cop.	rhizome
Hawkweed	15	sol.-sp.	tap root
Bistort	15	sol.	?
Crawling clover	10	sol.	rhizome
Yarrow	10	sp.-cop.	long rhizome
Multiflower buttercup	10	cop.	cluster of roots
Plantago sp., weed	5	sol.	tap root
Hoary Plantain, weed	5	sp.	tap root
Coronilla, weed	5	l.	root sucker
Primrose	5	sp.	cluster of roots
Sowthistle, weed	5	sol-sp.	tap root

[a/]According to A. M. Semenova-Tien-Shanskaya (1966).

evaporation from the surface decreases, but simultaneously loss of moisture by transpiration increases.

The humus reserve in the soil layer of 0 to 50 cm (in the ejection and below it) and its distribution in the profile is restored after one to 2 years, in proportion to revegetation of the ejection.

Deeper and more stable changes occur in humus composition, which can be judged by the relationship of soluble materials and non-hydrolyzed remainder and also by the relationship of humic and fulvic acids. Under the *Spalax* ejections the size of the non-hydrolyzed remainder decreases, and the total soluble material increases (chiefly due to fulvic acid). Under fresh ejections the relative content of fulvic acid is especially great in the soil of the ejection itself and in the layer of 0 to 20 cm under it. During 3 successive years the relative content of fulvic acid in the soil of the ejection decreases and under it, in the layer of 20 to 50 cm, increases due to the fact that distribution under profile of the upper half of the humus horizon is equalized. The content and

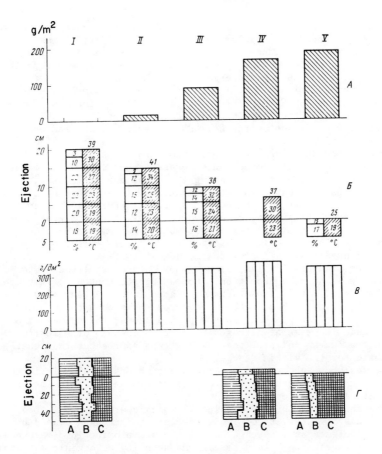

Figure 23
Soil and vegetation of various ages of ejections of mole-rats
(<<aging>> of ejections). I-ejection younger than one year;
II-the same, one year old; III-the same, 2 years old; IV-the
same, 3 years old; V-control. A-phytomass; B-hydrothermic
condition in soil of ejection and below it (humidity, %;
temperature, °C); C-reserve of humus in upper half of humus
horizon; D-fractional composition of humus in soil of ejection
and below it, %: a-humic acids; b-fulvic acids; c-insoluble
remainder.

distribution of humic acids in the dug-up soil during the period is
almost unchanged. Thus, during a 4 year observation the relationship of humus:fulvic acid decreased in proportion to the aging of
ejections and deviated more and more from that characteristic for
the virgin chernozem of the mowed steppe.
    The distribution of colonies of *Spalax* and the yearly volume of
digging activity by the animals allows us to hypothesize that the
entire upper horizon of the soil in colonies used by many genera-
tions of *Spalax* is reworked by them approximately every 1000 years,

and in the steppe on the average every 2000 to 5000 years. However, considering that the true volume of burrowing activity of *Spalax* is significantly greater, these numbers are underestimates. Besides single fresh ejections which appear in the virgin steppe during the time of spring and summer dispersal of the animals testifies to the fact that many sections, on which there are no ejections, are nevertheless populated by *Spalax*. The soil of these sections is pierced by passages, which the animals periodically and perhaps regularly use, creating an impact on the soil characteristics and the processes which flow in it.

Due to the quick restoration of aboveground phytomass on the ejections, the loss of production of grass stands on the burrowing areas is insignificant (no exceeding 1% of the annual growth). Also, the losses of humus in the excavated soils are very small. Even in the upper part of the humus layer differences in the content of humus between virgin and excavated soils of unmowed steppe are less than between the virgin soils of mowed and unmowed sections.

Thus, the vital activity of *Spalax* has little effect on the reserve of organic material of the meadow-steppe.

At the same time *Spalax*, as was shown above, exerts an important impact on humus composition, increasing the content of nitrogen and fulvic acid. The size of the C:N ratio in excavated soils is significantly lower than in the virgin soils (in both the unmowed and in the mowed steppe) and in the plowed lands, which indicates the zoogenic increase of nitrogen. The relationship of humus:fulvic acid in the dug-up soils of the mowed steppe approaches that characteristic for the virgin steppe.

As was shown above, *Spalax* also plays an essential role in the replenishment of calcium in the root layer of the soil, the major "zone" of biological cycling.

The changes of characteristics of thick chernozem connected with the digging activity of *Spalax* differ from changes caused by harvesting of meadow steppes. Hay mowing and plowing involve annual removal of vegetation. As a result the quantity of organic material decreases. This leads to losses of carbon, nitrogen and ash elements and to gradual impoverishment of the upper layer (0 to 50 cm) of the thick steppe chernozem (Afanaceeva 1964, 1966, Ponomareva and Nikolaeva 1965). The humus composition changes simultaneously. The decrease of fresh vegetation remains entering the soil decreases the content of fulvic acid and increases the relationship of humus: fulvic acid characteristic of plowed land (Fig. 24). At this time the size of C:N ratio, both in the mowed steppe and in plowed land, is almost unchanged, testifying to the fact that the rate of mineralization of carbonaceous and nitrogen parts of humus remains as before (Ponomareva and Nikolaeva 1965). Obviously, both perennial mowing and plowing change the thick chernozem of meadow-steppe in one direction, although the influence of plowing is greater. The activity of *Spalax* apparently facilitates restoration of the initial humus composition, characteristic of the thick chernozems of the meadow-steppe (Table 85). In this way, the biogeocoenotic role of the earth movers (rodents) is not to change the reserves of organic material but to augment its humification. Just as other basic components form the biogeocoenosis, these animals support its function, particularly in the role of soil formation.

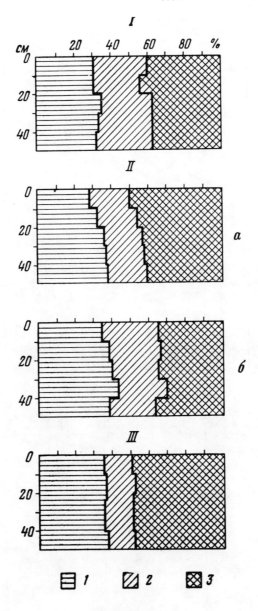

Figure 24
Fractional composition of humus in Chernozems of virgin sections
and sections cultivated by earth movers in the meadow steppe.
I-unmowed virgin steppe; II-mowed steppe: a-virgin sections;
b-cultivated sections; III-plowed fields. 1-humic acids;
2-fulvic acids; 3-insoluble remainder.

Table 85. Change of content and humus composition of thick chernozems caused by hay mowing, plowing, and activity of earth-movers (%). [a]

Depth (cm)	Humus			C:N			Humic:Fulvic acid		
	Unmowed steppe	Mowed steppe	Plowed field	Unmowed steppe	Mowed steppe	Plowed field	Unmowed steppe	Mowed steppe	Plowed field
0-10	$\frac{9.2}{8.9}$	$\frac{8.5}{7.4}$	6.0	$\frac{11.8}{7.0}$	12.0	11.9	1.07	$\frac{1.58}{1.11}$	2.14
10-20	$\frac{7.8}{7.3}$	$\frac{6.8}{6.7}$	5.8	$\frac{12.0}{9.9}$	11.5	11.9	1.26	$\frac{1.24}{1.38}$	2.23
20-30	$\frac{6.0}{5.9}$	$\frac{5.6}{5.8}$	5.3	$\frac{12.2}{9.8}$	11.9	12.6	1.27	$\frac{2.23}{1.59}$	2.33
30-40	$\frac{5.6}{5.2}$	$\frac{5.0}{4.9}$	5.8	$\frac{11.7}{9.8}$	12.9	12.6	1.19	$\frac{2.34}{1.50}$	2.23
40-50	$\frac{4.8}{3.5}$	$\frac{4.6}{4.0}$	4.4	$\frac{12.3}{10.8}$	12.7	12.2	1.05	$\frac{2.39}{1.49}$	2.13

[a] In the numerator, on virgin land; in the denominator, on sections with *Spalax* burrows.

164

II-5
Saprophages

The aboveground vegetative remains entering the soil annually with litter-fall serve as the basic source of elements in the forest-steppe ecosystem and some grass communities. Decomposition of vegetative litterfall is promoted by various factors of the environment, which can be divided into two categories: biogenic and abiogenic. Biotic mineralization is accomplished by the complex of saprophytic organisms--higher fungi, microflora and invertebrates. Abiogenic (physical-chemical) mineralization is a result of the impact on the vegetative remains of solar radiation, temperature, precipitation, gas composition of the lower layer of air and other factors.

A series of special investigations was devoted to the biotic destruction of dead vegetative remains. Experiments conducted in field conditions showed that a determining factor in the decomposition of plant (mainly forest) litterfall is the activity of soil animals (Kurcheva 1960, 1969, 1971, Karpachevski and Perel 1966, Edwards and Heath 1963, Crossley and Witkamp 1964). Until this time no attention was given to the study of the role of abiotic factors.[1] However, the first investigation conducted on the meadow-steppe of the Central Chernozem Reserve showed the contribution of abiogenic mineralization in the total decomposition of the steppe litter-fall is very great (Zlotin 1969a).

In 1967, 1968, and 1970 we carried out a series of experiments for comparative evaluation of the participation in mineralization of plant litterfall by the complex of microorganisms and various systematic groups of soil animals, and also of abiogenic factors. Major attention was given to determination of the roles of saprophages in the destructive processes occurring in the above-soil layer of the forest-steppe ecosystem.

In 1967 we studied mineralization of oak litterfall, in 1968 of litter-fall of the oak and grass steppe vegetation, in 1970 of the

[1]Years of investigation by G. F. Kurcheva (1960, 1965, 1969) in forest and grass ecosystems of the Central Chernozem Reserve were dedicated to the determination of the destruction role of biotic factors (microflora and saprotrophic animals).

oak, aspen, elm, and also of the steppe grasses and herbaceous vegetation. Experiments on decomposition of the forest litterfall were conducted in the watershed oak groves (in Dubroshina). With the goal of separating the impact on decomposition processes of zoogenic thinning of the upper cover of forests,[2] the study area selected was a forest situated on the edge of a small aspen area with only slightly damaged oaks, hence practically an undamaged section. The conditions of crown thinning in the various parts of the area differed insignificantly.

In the meadow-steppe the quadrat was situated on the watershed, previously mowed, which in 1967 was enclosed and removed from hay-mowing. About 70% of the weight of the herbage-grass litterfall which accumulated on this area was from grasses (*Bromus riparius* Rehm., *Agropyron repens* (L.) P. B., *Poa angustifolia* L.) and about 30% from herbs and legumes (*Achillea millefolium* L., *Adonis vernalis* L., *Vicia tenufolia* Roth., *Filipendula hexapetala* Gilib., *Trifolium pratense* L. and others). The litterfall, collected on the section of the protected unmowed steppe consisted almost exclusively of feather grasses (*Stipa stenophylla* Czem., *S. pennata* L.), of shore brome grass and bush grass; litterfall of herbs and legumes was very insignificant.

Duration of experiments was limited by the vegetation period, during which up to 60% of last year's litterfall is decomposed. In 1967 the experiment continued from 15 May through 23 September, in 1968 from 13 May through 15 October, and in 1970 from 26 April through 10 October. In the cold six months decomposition of litter-fall decreases sharply (only 10% to 20% mineralizes) and proceeds almost exclusively under the impact of physical-chemical factors, since the activity of the saprophytic organisms in this period sharply decreases.

The order of experiments was as follows. In the spring on the forest and steppe sections the quantity of last years litterfall remaining was determined. In order to obtain uniformity of material collected for the experiment the litterfall was sorted. Accidental admixtures were carefully removed. The litterfall was dried to a constant weight and placed in wooden frames 25 × 25 cm and 4 to 5 cm high. The weighed quantity of litterfall in the experiment cor-responded approximately to the spring reserve on a unit area. Below, the frames were covered with a Capron net with varying mesh size, and above, to prevent loss of litter-fall, with a very thin fish net with mesh of 3 × 3 cm. The mesh of the Capron nets was selected to allow access by determined sizes of organisms. Thus, with a mesh size of 10 mm all groups of reducers have access to the litterfall--microorgnaisms, micro- and mesofauna (earthworms, diplopods-myriapods, woodlouse, and large enchytraeids). With a mesh of 1.1 mm microorganisms and microfauna (nematodes, Collembola, enchitraeide, small earthworms) participated in decomposition of litterfall. With a mesh of 0.05 mm access to the litterfall from the saprophages is restricted to microorganisms. In this way, for the study of the biogenic decomposition of litterfall we conducted experiments of three types. In the last variant we applied in addition naphthalene which for prevention of penetration by animals.

[2]In the centers of mass reporduction of oak leaf roller the lit-terfall of the oak breaks down approximately two times faster.

It was sprinkled on the outside of the frame, and also scattered in a thin layer on the surface of the soil under the frame. During the experiment this protective barrier was regularly restored.

This method is a modification of the usual method of determination of the role of microflora in the decomposition of litterfall in which access by invertebrate-saprophages usually is prevented by enclosing litter-fall in small mesh Capron sacks with naphthalene or some other pesticide, to repel the animals. Naphthalene has been used in a way, so that the surface of the litterfall during the entire experiment was covered with a layer of this insecticide (Kurcheva 1965).

However, in recent years the application of this method has become doubtful since it essentially changes the natural conditions of decomposition of litterfall by distortion of some parameters of the external environment, including the hydrothermic regime and microbiological activity (Zlotin 1969a, Edwards, Reichle and Crossley 1970, Williams and Wiegert 1971). According to our observations, with contact application of naphthalene the speed of microbiological decomposition of vegetative remains decreases by 2 to 4 times. Besides this, naphthalene reflects solar radiation and lowers the temperature in the litterfall layer. The Capron bags act in the same way. The progress of decomposition in landscapes of southern exposure is especially retarded, where a large role in the decomposition of litter-fall is played by the physical factors of the environment.

In our experiments there was no direct contact of litter-fall with naphthalene. In this and the microbiological variant animals were rarely seen mainly large Collembola that accidentally fell into the frames from the grass canopy and very small tyroglyphoid mites.

In the experiments on determination of abiogenic decomposition, the plant litterfall was placed in the frame on a small mesh sieve surrounded by a barrier of naphthalene, and every 7 to 10 days was moistened with clean toluene. This reagent is usually applied by soil scientists for elimination of microbiological activity in samples of soil used in determination of the microfloral mobilization of mineral and organic compounds. At one time 80 to 150 ml toluene was used per frame. Painting is done at a sunny time in the second half of the day. At this time the wood is dry, and for this reason toluene well moistens its surface. In a few minutes toluene evaporates.

Toluene suppresses almost completely the trophic activity of microorganisms, which was confirmed by microbiological analyses on culture medium. In addition, observations on the evolution of carbon dioxide from the various types of forest and steppe litterfall moistened by toluene also showed that microbiological activity begins only after day 10 to 15 and then only in very limited amounts (not more than 10% of the activity in the control sample), providing that in this period there were no continuous rains. Abundant new additions of litter sharply decreased the effectiveness of toluene; then the activity of microflora in the litterfall regenerates itself during day 2 and 3. But even in this case toluene limits the microbiological activity by more than 50% during a 10-day period. For this reason during the rainy season painting should be conducted more often. The destruction of strips of cotton cloth[3] placed in the frame under the forest litter-fall was negligibly small in the experiment with toluene (2%), and with the admission of microorganisms it sharply increased (35%).

Toluene alone does not destroy the plant remains and does not change the natural course of mineralization. Thus, in the experiment with litterfall of oak and of steppe grasses, it was moistened 10 times by toluene at intervals of several days and weight did not decrease. Biochemical analyses of litterfall in the experiment with application of toluene did not reveal a sharp decrease in content even of such easily extracted organic compounds as fats.

Thus, four variants of field experiments characterized the mineralization of plant litter-fall under the chief forces of decomposition. The first variant represented the role of the entire complex of abiogenic factors. Three successive variants represented the biogenic decomposition of litterfall due to activity of three basic groups of saprophages: microorganisms, microfauna, and mesofauna.

The conditions for activity of various decomposition forces in all the experiments were sufficiently close to natural conditions. The lower edges of the frame did not hinder air exchange, and the thin net covering the frame above did not limit the penetration of precipitation and solar radiation. The lower surface of the frame fit close to the soil, which facilitated normal heat and moisture exchange between the litterfall and soil. The moisture content of litter-fall in all the variants of the experiments differed little.

The Capron sieve also did not disturb the conditions of decomposition. For confirmation of this hypothesis, the following experiment was conducted. Litterfall was placed on soil which had been sprinkled in a thin layer (2 to 3 cm) into the frame on top of the sieve. The results of this series of experiments coincided with the control variants without soil; the observed small differences were not statistically significant.

We believe that the applied method represents natural conditions of decomposition of litterfall. Changes in conditions of light due to disturbance of grass cover by the frames were the same in the forest and steppe experiments. Every variant included 4 frames, sometimes 3, which allowed statistical treatment of the results. Such repetition insured satisfactory precision; the error of the mean was usually 1 to 3% and the maximum did not exceed 12%. Variability of results from each variant was also small; the coefficient of variation was lower than 20%. The observed dispersion can be explained by irregularity in the distribution of invertebrate saprophages and by somewhat heterogeneous initial material. The latter is most essential in experiments with steppe litterfall, which includes both leaves and stems of grasses.

To determine the reliability of the differences between the variants of experiment with paired comparisons we used the t test. Differences between the factors of decomposition can be considered highly reliable in those instances where the t value was not lower than 2.3. In this case the level of significance of differences

---

[3]Our experiments showed that cotton cloth is broken down almost exclusively by the microflora. Physical factors and animal saprophages only slightly augmented this process.

approaches 0.05 and gives a probability of not less than 95%.
For estimation of the role of each individual factor the following
calculation was conducted. Total decomposition under the impact of
all abiotic and biotic factors was considered as 100%, and the
specific weight of each separate factor was calculated as a proportion of this.

Naturally, such an operation is conditional, since placing of
the frames presumed participation in each variant of all factors
present in the preceding ones. Such calculations do not account for
symbiotic relations beween microflora of the litterfall and invertebrates or for the influence of abiogenic treatment of plant litterfall on the trophic activity of saprophytic organisms. Determination
of actual role of various biotic factors in completely natural
conditions was not possible. However, determination of significant
differences between the separate factors in adjacent variants of the
experiment was completely competent. The latter is especially valid
for singling out such general categories of impact as abiogenic and
biogenic factors, which have a completely different nature. Besides
this, abiogenic decomposition in the experiments is thoroughly
separated.

THE ROLE OF SAPROPHAGES IN DECOMPOSITION
OF VARIOUS TYPES OF PLANT LITTERFALL

In the experiments in the forest ecosystem we used the litterfall of oak, aspen, and elm, and in the steppe the litterfall of
grasses and herb-grass litterfall.

Forest Litterfall. In the first variant of experiments on the
decomposition of oak leaf litterfall, which indicated abiotic
decomposition, the losses of weight constituted a total of only
4% to 8% during the various years of observation. With admission to
the litterfall of microorganisms, mineralization of oak leaves
noticeably increased. In this variant of the experiment the weight
of litterfall decreased in 1967 by 9%, in 1968 by 12%, and in 1970
by 11%. The reliability of the indicators of litterfall decomposition, obtained in these two variants of the experiment, was very
high in 1967 and 1970, but in 1968 it was significantly less (t =
1.4). The latter is explained by intensive fall precipitation that
year (in September, for example, there was more than 100 ml). Almost
daily rains facilitated preservation of the high moisture of litterfall, stimulating the activity of microorganisms and decreasing the
effectiveness of toluene.

Admisssion of microfauna to the litterfall sharply increased
the process of mineralization of plant remains. Decomposition of
oak leaves with participation of a complex of small worms and
arthropods was 17 to 25%. The difference in total decomposition
between this variant of the experiment and the variant with only
microorganisms, was highly significant.

With participation of invertebrate mesofauna in the decomposition of litterfall there is maximum decomposition of leaves.
This indicator, which characterized total decomposition of litterfall under the impact of all factors, varied insignificantly over
the years (33 to 35 %). The magnitude of total decomposition of
litterfall differed significantly from all preceding variants.

The variability in litterfall decomposition within different variants of the experiment during the time of our observations was not great, despite the differences noted in the hydrological regime (Tables 86 and 87).

Using the average for the three years of observation an each variant of the experiment, we can compare mineralization of oak litterfall with mineralization of litterfall of other woody species and steppe grasses. Experiments on decomposition of litterfall of aspen, started in 1970, showed similar results. The degree of aspen leaf decomposition increases with increase of the number of active factors (Table 88). The compared variants differ significantly from each other, with the exception of the abiotic and microbiologic variants.

Leaf decomposition of elm in different variants of the experiment on the whole is characterized by the same peculiarities which were

Table 86.   Decomposition of oak litterfall.[a]

Variant of experiment	Litterfall (g)		m (%)	Cv (%)	Decomposed litterfall		Compared variants of experiment	t-value
	Stored	Remaining			grams	%[b]		
				1967				
I. Abiotic decomposition	15	14.4 ± 0.13	0.9	1.8	0.6	4	I-IIa; I-IIb	4.3; 10.9
II. Biotic decomposition with addition of:								
a) microorganisms	15	13.7 ± 0.13	0.9	1.8	1.3	9	IIa-IIb; IIa-IIb	6.6; 3.8
b) microfauna	15	12.5 ± 0.13	1.0	2.1	2.5	17	IIb-IIc	2.6
c) mesofauna	15	10.0 ± 0.87	8.7	17.0	5.0	33	IIc-I	5.0
				1968				
I. Abiotic decomposition	10	9.2 ± 0.15	1.6	3.2	0.8	8	I-IIa; I-IIb	1.4; 5.9
II. Biotic decomposition with addition of:								
a) microorganisms	10	8.8 ± 0.25	2.8	5.6	1.2	12	IIa-IIb; IIa-IIc	3.7; 5.3
b) microfauna	10	7.5 ± 0.25	3.3	6.6	2.5	25	IIb-IIc	2.3
c) mesofauna	10	6.5 ± 0.35	5.4	10.8	3.5	35	IIc-I	7.1
				1970				
I. Abiotic decomposition	10	9.4 ± 0.14	1.5	3.2	0.6	6	I-IIa; I-IIb	2.8; 9.0
II. Biotic decomposition with addition of:								
a) microorganisms	10	8.9 ± 0.11	1.4	2.9	1.1	11	IIa-IIb; IIa-IIb	7.1; 7.0
b) microfauna	10	7.9 ± 0.09	1.2	1.9	2.1	21	IIb-IIc	4.1
c) mesofauna	10	6.6 ± 0.31	4.7	8.3	3.4	34	IIc-I	8.5

[a] m = error of the mean, Cv = coefficient of variation, litter-fall = dry weight.

[b] In each year every successive treatment includes all previous treatments.

Table 87. Some indicators of the hydrothermic regime.

Year	Time of conducting experiment (day/month)	Precipitation (mm)	Average temperature °C	Sum of temperatures above 0°C
1967	15 May - 23 April	166	16.8	2246
1968	13 May - 15 October	266	15.6	2323
1970	26 April - 10 October	252	15.8	2556

revealed for the litterfall of aspen and oak. A paired comparison of all the variants showed a high reliability of results. Litterfall of the elm disintegrates least of all under the impact of abiogenic factors, by 5%. In the micro-biological variant mineralization increased, but not significantly. The admission to litterfall of invertebrate microfauna leads to a strong increase of degree of decomposition. A more significant decomposition of litterfall is facilitated by participation of the invertebrate mesofauna, as a result of which total decomposition is 59% (Table 89).

Comparison of decomposition in different variants of the experiment among the three types of forest litterfall reveals mostly reliable differences. This permits determination of the significance of each factor acting in the mineralization of different materials (Table 90). From the data of Table 90 it follows that abiogenic factors account for 8 to 23% of the total decomposition of litter-fall. Correspondingly, the biogenic mineralization of plant remains constitutes 77 to 92%. In biogenic decomposition the most significant role belongs to representatives of the complex of mesofauna - the earthworms, myriapods - diplopods, and woodlice. The significance of microfauna is also rather important, but much less than the mesofauna. In the complex of microfauna the most active agents of decomposition of the forest litterfall, apparently, are the small bristle worms - Enchytraeidae, which in this variant of all experiments were maximum in number. The role of microorganisms in decomposition of leaf litterfall is minimal. The significance of microflora in all experiments turns out to be lower than the other biotic factors, and also than the abiotic factors. The data presented confirm the conclusion that the leading role is played by the soil invertebrate mesofauna in the mineralization of litterfall from species of trees (Kurcheva, 1971).

Steppe Litterfall. With mineralization of litter-fall of the steppe grasses, the the abiotic factors are of greatest significance. In the first variant of the experiment 21 to 24% of the litter-fall decomposed. In successive variants there was a slight increase in the degree of mineralization.

Thus, in experiments with participation of microorganisms the losses of weight of litterfall were 24 to 30%. The difference between this variant and the abiotic variant is highly significant.

Table 88. Decomposition of aspen litter-fall in 1970. [a]

Variant of experiment	Litterfall (g)		m (%)	Cv (%)	Decomposed litterfall		Compared variants of experiment	t-value
	Stored	Remaining			grams	% [b]		
I. Abiotic decomposition	10	9.4 ± 0.20	2.1	3.6	0.6	6	I-IIa; I-IIb	1.0 5.4
II. Biotic decomposition with participation of:								
a) microorganisms	10	9.2 ± 0.06	0.6	1.1	0.8	8	IIa-IIb; IIa-IIc	13.5 10.4
b) microfauna	10	8.3 ± 0.03	0.4	0.6	1.7	17	IIb-IIc	8.1
c) mesofauna	10	5.7 ± 0.33	5.9	10.2	4.3	43	IIc-I	9.8

[a] m = error of the mean, Cv = coefficient of variation, litter-fall = dry weight.

Table 89. Decomposition of elm litter-fall in 1970.[a]

Variant of experiment	Litterfall (g)				Decomposed litterfall		Compared variants of experiment	t-value
	Stored	Remaining	m (%)	Cv (%)	grams	%[b]		
I. Abiotic decomposition	10	9.5 ± 0.05	0.6	1.0	0.5	5	I–IIa; I–IIb	3.3 9.8
II. Biotic decomposition with participation of:								
a) microorganisms	10	9.1 ± 0.11	1.2	2.1	0.9	9	IIa–IIb; IIa–IIb	7.7 10.3
b) microfauna	10	6.9 ± 0.26	3.8	6.8	3.1	31	IIb–IIc	5.1
c) mesofauna	10	4.1 ± 0.48	11.7	20.0	5.9	59	IIc–I	11.7

[a] m = error of the mean, Cv = coefficient of variation, litter-fall = dry weight.

173

Table 90.   Participation of abiotic factors and various groups
of saprophages in the total decomposition of forest
litter-fall (%).

		Oak		Aspen	Elm
Variant of experiment	1967	1968	1970	1970	1970
I. Abiotic decomposition	12	23	17	14	8
II. Biotic decomposition under impact of:					
a) microorganisms	15	11	15	5	7
b) microfauna	24	37	29	21	37
c) mesofauna	49	29	39	60	48

With participation of microfauna the litter-fall is mineralized
by 28 to 32%. However, the difference between this variant and
the micro-biological variant during both years of observation (1968
and 1970) was less reliable (t = 1.5 to 1.7). It follows that the
role of saprophytic micro-arthropods (mites and Collembola), which
formed the major part of the microfauna in the meadow-steppe ecosystem, is not essential in the decomposition of grass litter-fall.

Admission to the litterfall of invertebrate mesofauna also has
little effect on increasing mineralization; in the fourth variant 32
to 33% decomposed. It was highly characteristic that the significance of invertebrate mesofauna, just as of micro-fauna, noticeably
increased in 1968 with the increased quantity of fall precipitation,
which facilitated a more active trophic activity of animals (Table
91).

Decomposition of the herbage-grass litterfall turned out to be
very similar to the mineralization of grasses. Just as in experiments with grass litterfall, the difference between microbiological
variants and mineralization with the participation of microfauna
was less reliable (t = 2.1). A paired comparison of all remaining
variants revealed a high reliability of differences (Table 92).

Despite differences in composition, the character of decomposition of both types of the steppe litterfall have a lot in common.
In the steppe decomposition of the aboveground dead phytomass occurs
chiefly under the impact of abiotic factors, which accounts for 66
to 73% of the total weight loss of litterfall. Biogenic mineralization is much less significant, 27 to 34%. Chief significance
among the biogenic factors belongs to the microorganisms (Table 93).

Table 91. Decomposition of steppe grass litter-fall.[a]

Variant of experiment	Litterfall (g)		m (%)	Cv (%)	Decomposed litterfall		Compared variants of experiment	t-value
	Stored	Remaining			grams	%[b]		
1968								
I. Abiotic decomposition	20	15.8 ± 0.15	0.9	1.8	4.2	21	I–IIa; I–IIb	2.4 4.6
II. Biotic decomposition with addition of:								
a) microorganisms	20	15.2 ± 0.20	1.3	2.7	4.8	24	IIa–IIb; IIa–IIb	1.7 3.9
b) microfauna	20	14.4 ± 0.25	1.7	3.3	5.6	28	IIb–IIc	2.4
c) mesofauna	20	13.6 ± 0.30	2.3	4.4	6.4	32	IIc–I	6.5
1970								
I. Abiotic decomposition	15	11.4 ± 0.24	2.1	4.2	3.6	24	I–IIa; I–IIb	3.6 4.1
II. Biotic decomposition with addition of:								
a) microorganisms	15	10.5 ± 0.06	0.6	1.2	4.5	30	IIa–IIb; IIa–IIc	1.5 2.8
b) microfauna	15	10.3 ± 0.12	1.1	2.2	4.7	32	IIb–IIc	1.2
c) mesofauna	15	10.1 ± 0.13	1.3	2.7	4.9	33	IIc–I	4.9

[a] m = error of the mean, Cv = coefficient of variation, litter-fall = dry weight.

Table 92. Decomposition of herbage-grass litter-fall in 1970.[a]

Variant of experiment	Litterfall (g) Stored	Litterfall (g) Remaining	m (%)	Cv (%)	Decomposed litterfall grams	Decomposed litterfall % [b]	Compared variants of experiment	t-value
I. Abiotic decomposition	10	6.7 ± 0.04	0.6	1.2	3.3	33	I–IIa; I–IIb	8.7 8.8
II. Biotic decomposition with addition of:								
a) microorganisms	10	5.9 ± 0.08	1.4	2.8	4.1	41	IIa–IIb; IIa–IIc	2.1 4.6
b) microfauna	10	5.6 ± 0.12	2.1	4.2	4.4	44	IIb–IIc	2.8
c) mesofauna	10	5.0 ± 0.18	3.6	7.3	5.0	50	IIc–I	9.2

[a] m = error of the mean, Cv = coefficient of variation, litter-fall = dry weight.

Table 93. Participation of abiotic factors and various groups of
saprophages in the general decomposition of steppe
litter-fall (%).

		Grass litterfall		Herb-grass litterfall
Variant of experiment		1968	1970	1970
I.	Abiotic decomposition	66	73	66
II.	Biotic decomposition under influence of:			
	a) microorganisms	10	18	16
	b) microfauna	12	6	6
	c) mesofauna	12	3	12

COMPARATIVE CHARACTERISTICS OF THE SAPROPHAGE
ROLE IN MINERALIZATION OF LITTERFALL IN FOREST
AND MEADOW-STEPPE ECOSYSTEMS

Comparison of results of field experiments and literature data
(Afanaceeva, 1966; Semenova-Tian-Shanskaya, 1960, 1966) indicates
similar rates of mineralization of forest and steppe aboveground
litterfall. During the warm season of the year about half of the
total reserve of winter litterfall is mineralized. Average values
of total decomposition for the various types of forest litterfall in the experiments is 45%, and of the steppe 42%. The most
intense decomposition was of elm leaves (59%) and the litterfall of
herb-grass steppe vegetation (50%). Minimum decomposition was noted
for the litterfall of steppe grasses, 32 to 33% and for the oak, 33
to 35%. The litterfall of aspen showed an intermediate rate of
decomposition, 43%.

Differences revealed in the rates of mineralization of litterfall of various types of plants are explained chiefly by dissimilar
biochemical and physical-chemical properties. Structure and the
degree of "softness" of litterfall affects decomposition as well as
forage quality. Paired comparison of integral rates of mineralization of litterfall of the various types reveals the following
(Table 94). Comparison of the rates of decomposition of woody
species, as with various types of steppe litterfall, shows they
are statistically significant. The difference in rates of mineralization of forest and steppe litterfall is not significant; the
leaves of the oak lose as much weight as the steppe grasses, and the
rate of decomposition of the leaves of elm and aspen does not differ
from the rate of decomposition of the steppe grass vegetation.

Thus, mineralization of plant litterfall in forest and meadow-
steppe communities of the forest-steppe zone proceed rapidly, and in
this case with similar rates. The most essential differences of the
forest-steppe ecosystem are in the types of decomposition factors,
and precisely in the relative importance of these driving factors.

Table 94. Significance of the t-criterion and reliability of difference between rates of decomposition.

Experiment	Litterfall	Compared experiments	t-criterion	Reliability of difference[a]
		Forest		
1	Oak	1-2	2.3	+
		1-3	4.4	+
		1-5	4.4	+
2	Aspen	2-3	2.8	+
		2-5	1.8	-
3	Elm	3-4	5.3	+
		3-5	1.8	-
		Steppe		
4	Grass	4-1	0.3	-
		4-2	2.9	+
5	Herb-grass	5-4	8.5	+

[a] The (+) plus sign notes differences significant at the 95% level, the (-) minus sign notes differences not significant at this level.

In the oak groves the major role belongs to the biogenic factors (87%) of the total litterfall decomposition), and the significance of physical-chemical mineralization is almost 8 times lower (13%). The steppe ecosystems, on the contrary, are characterized by a significant predominance of abiotic factors in decomposition. Under their impact 70% of the litterfall of grasses is mineralized.

An essential difference between forest and grassy communities is observed also in the participation of various biotic components. The role of saprophytic microorganisms in the steppe is two times greater than in the oak grove; they rework 17% of the steppe litterfall and in total 9% of the forest litterfall. One of the reasons for this difference is apparently dissimilar surface area of the steppe and forest litterfall. The total surface which can be occupied by colonies of microorganisms in the litterfall of the steppe grasses is much greater than in the same weight of leaves of trees. Experiments on "respiration" of different weight quantities of litterfall of steppe grasses and oak leaves, in laboratory conditions with similar temperature and moisture, showed that in the first instance the evolution of CO_2 is 1.5 times higher. From this we conclude there is a corresponding difference in the total microflora.

The role of invertebrate saprophages in decomposition of plant litterfall is significantly greater in the forest ecosystem. Micro- fauna rework 29% of the litterfall in the oak grove, and in the steppe 6%. There is a larger difference in the use of litter- fall by mesofauna; in the oak grove this group of saprophages ac- counts for almost 50% of the reduced litterfall, and in the steppe 7%.

The total participation of all animal saprophages in the de- composition of the aboveground litterfall in the steppe is six times less than in the forest. The dissimilar degree of destructive impact on plant litterfall by saprophagic invertebrates in the forest and meadow steppe ecosystems of the Central Chernozem Reserve was established earlier by G. F. Kurcheva (1971).

The difference in participation of invertebrate saprophages in mineralization of the steppe and forest litterfall is explained by the specific hydrothermic regime, which determines the conditions of activity and also the population structure of invertebrate saprophages. Forest and steppe ecosystems have a similar biomass of soil saprophages. However, in the steppe the litter, which on the mowed section is poorly developed, and also the upper half of the humus horizon are dry, which sharply limits the trophic activity of soil invertebrates. In addition, the absence of a thin layer of aboveground plant remains in the steppe fails to create the proper environment. For this reason there is lacking almost completely a semi-edaphic complex of saprophytic invertebrates, so characteristic for the forest ecosystems. The most typical representatives of this complex connected with the litter layer are the invertebrate micro- fauna--Collembola, mites, and enchytraeid worms, and also the meso- fauna--some types of earthworms, myriapods, woodlice, and larvae of insects.

A low abundance of microfauna in the litter of the mowed steppe indicates the insignificant participation of this group in decom- position of plant remains.

In the complex of the soil mesofauna invertebrates in the forest-steppe ecosystem various types predominate. In the oak groves there are numerous large and active earthworms, *Lumbricus terrestris* L., and also a specific litter, *Dendrobaena octaedra* Sav., which feed chiefly on the aboveground plant remains (Perel and Sokolov, 1964). In steppe communities *L. terrestris* is ex- tremely small in numbers, and *D. octaedra* is lacking; here these types are replaced by typical soil inhabitants *Eisenia rosea* Sav., *E. nordenskiöldi* Eisen, *Allolobophora caliginosa* Sav., which pri- marily use organic material of the soil (Bizova, 1965). Woodlice and large enchitraeids in this steppe are small in numbers. A significant role in the mineralization of the steppe litter-fall belongs to the Diplopoda, millipedes whose number in the oak groves constitute about 20 specimens per square meter. However, in the steppe the volume of work conducted by millipedes is essentially lower due to duration of the summer diapause limiting the period of their tophic activity.

Thus, participation of the soil animal saprophages in the decomposition of the aboveground plant litterfall and enrichment of the soil in mineral elements is highly essential in forest ecosystems, and on the mowed meadow-steppe their activity occurs chiefly in the soil layer of the community.

III
**Participation of Animal Populations in
Biological Cycling**

The data that have been presented, characterizing the bio-geocoenotic role of separate trophic groups of animals in forest-steppe ecosystems, allow some generalizations. The role of animal populations in biological cycling is manifested in two forms; animals implement the heterotrophic cycle by scattering and transforming organic material of primary production to other trophic levels of the ecosystem, and simultaneously they take a direct part in the regulation of the autotrophic cycle, actively influencing the natural factors affecting it.

The contribution of herbivorous animals to the heterotrophic cycle consists of utilization of a certain portion of the primary production, and can be estimated by the relationship between the zoomass and the annual growth and litterfall of phytomass.

In comparison to the production of plant cover, the biomass of phytophages is very small. In the meadow-steppe of the forest-steppe zone annual growth of the aboveground phytomass constitutes on the average three tons per hectare, of the belowground about 8 tons per hectare, while biomass of animal phytophages constitutes a total of 6 kilograms per hectare (dry weight). Approximately the same relationship between the total production of phytomass and biomass of herbivorous animals is observed in the forest-steppe oak groves (respectively 12 to 14 tons per hectare and 8 to 10 kilograms per hectare per year).[1]

Accordingly, the quantity of green mass consumed by these animals is small. Various groups of phytophages rework several percent during the year, and during years of outbreak not more than 25%, of the total growth of that fraction of phytomass with which they are trophically connected (Dinesman 1961, Vodopyanov 1971, Gebczynska 1970, Hansson 1971, Grodzinski 1971a, Kalela and Koponen 1971, and others).

The portion of the total production of vegetation (including inedible fractions of phytomass) eaten is still less; it constitutes

[1]During the years of mass reproduction of leaf-eating insects the biomass of phytophages in the oak groves can attain 60 kg/ha, dry weight.

2 to 4% and even during years of mass reproduction did not exceed 10%. Preliminary calculations, conducted for watershed ecosystems of the Central Chernozem Reserve, showed that the entire complex of phytophages of the meadow-steppe (including vertebrates and inverte-brates) utilizes about 700 kg of the vegetative mass, and in the oak groves about 600 to 1000 kg per hectare, which constitutes in both ecosystems 6% of the total primary production.

Detritus-feeding animals, in comparison with the complex of phytophages, use much more organic material. In various communities of the forest-steppe saprophages utilize during the warm six months 15 to 70% of the aboveground litterfall and about 10 to 20% of the root litterfall, or approximately 10 to 40% of the annual yearly litterfall.

However, estimation of the balance between biomass of herbiv-orous animals and primary production, and also between biomass of saprophages and plant litterfall, characterizes incompletely the role of animal populations in the ecosystem. A much greater impact is exerted by animals on the functioning of the ecosystem by modifying biological cycles.

Investigations of the exchange of material and energy in above-ground ecosystems are in the beginning stages. Only the processes of autotrophic cycling in the "plant-soil" system are relatively completely studied. According to the quantity of organic material transformed, this is the most important part of the biological cycle in terrestrial ecosystems. For this reason estimation of the role of animals in the autotrophic cycle is especially important.

The autotrophic cycle of the biological cycle includes two basic groups of processes: (1) the absorption of carbon by the photosynthesizing surface of plants from the atmosphere, and the absorption of nitrogen, ash elements and water from the soil by the root system and their transformation into phytomass, which deter-mines the yearly production "capacity" of the biological cycle; (2) the destruction of plant litterfall, the liberation of chemical elements included in it, their accumulation in the soil and a partial return to the atmosphere; these processes determine the speed of the biological cycle (Sukachev 1966, Rodin, Remezov and Bazilevich 1968).

Vital activity of animals, exerting a great influence on the geophysical and biotic factors of the external environment, leads to changes of intensity of production and decomposition processes, and collectively to changes of capacity and rate of the biological cycle.

III-1

The Role of Animals in the Production Processes

Participation of herbivorous animals in the function of the community is not limited to direct impact on the forage plants. Animals, as a rule, eat only a small part of the plant, but at the same this damage a significant quantity of the plant. For this reason, despite the second growth of the consumed trees and after-growth of grasses, their development is retarded for some time. This essentially changes the character of flow of production processes, not only in their susceptability to damage, but also in related trophic levels of the ecosystem.

INFLUENCE OF ANIMALS ON CONDITIONS OF ABSORPTION
BY PLANT COVER OF CARBON FROM THE ATMOSPHERE

Animal activity exerts a significant influence on a series of natural regimes affecting processes of assimilation that occur in the vegetative cover.

Radiation Regime. Phytophages usually use the nutritious growing parts of plants. As a result, the general assimilation surface of the damaged layers decreases; by 3 to 4 times in the grassy layer, in the woody layer (in the centers of outbreak) by 10's of times. Decrease, even brief, of the leaf surface involves essential changes of the radiation regime and conditions of illumination in the lower layers of the plant cover. Under the damaged canopy two to six times more solar radiation penetrates with a relatively larger portion of the photosynthetically active part of the spectrum. In the oak grove in the centers of leaf-eating insects conditions of illumination approach those characteristic of the open steppe. For this reason the thinning of the upper canopy by animal phytophages, increasing the flow of solar radiation, creates favorable conditions for the development of subordinate layers, where plants in the forest, as in some of the open communities, often are light limited.

Increase of solar radiation due to the thinning of the plant cover has an impact on microclimate of the ground layer of air and soil.

The Temperature Regime. Sections occupied by phytophages are warmed more strongly than those not so occupied. Large differences are observed on the surface of the soil and in the lower layer of air. Maximum temperature of the soil surface in the daytime is greater by 8 to 15°C on the section with animals and at night it is less by 0.5 to 2°C. The ground layer of air is warmed in the daytime by 1.5 to 2°C. As a result the 24-hour amplitude of temperature increases by 4 to 12°C, attaining in summer 23 to 25°C. Such zoogenic changes of the temperature regime apparently facilitate increased intensity of photosynthesis and at night decrease the cost of respiration which lowers the losses of the general production.

Moisture of the Air. Changes of the 24-hour course of temperature are accompanied by changes of moisture in the near-ground layer of air. In animal colonies in the daytime the moisture is less than on the unsettled sections and in the night and morning hours greater. Especially significant differences (up to 10%) are observed at night, which is connected with sharper 24-hour fluctuations of temperature in phytophage colonies, leading to saturation of the near-ground layer of air and abundant dew formation. Peculiarities of the hydrothermic regime of the near-ground layer of air, connected with the vital activity of animals, cannot help but be reflected in the intensity of physiological processes of plants, in particular their water regime. As is known, variations of air temperature by 1 to 3°C and moisture by 5 to 8% are accompanied by changes in intensity of transporation of the grassy plants by 10 percent or more (Gordeeva 1952, Evdokimova 1963).

The Gas Regime. One of the important factors determining productivity of the ecosystem is the concentration of CO_2 in the near-ground layer of air. In the aboveground ecosystem a major source of CO_2 is the soil litter layer.

The influence of animals on gas exchange and on the composition of the near-ground layer of air has been little studied. According to our determinations, 2 to 3% of the total flow of CO_2 from the soil is due to animals, in some instances (on weakly developed soil, abundantly settled by pedobionts) it attained 10%. In addition, the animal phytophages, changing in the process of their vital activities some biological and physical chemical characteristics of the soil and litter, have impact on the intensity of flow of CO_2 into the atmosphere.

Zoogenic litterfall and especially excrement of outbreak phytophages become centers of development of microorganisms, adding to diffusion of carbon dioxide. The intensity of emission of CO_2 from the litter when mixed with the excrement of the various types of phytophages, increases 2 to 5 times, and from the earth plugs (molehills) of the passages of the earth movers by one and one half to 3 times (in comparison with the undisturbed soil in which the molehills are found). The increased temperature of the litter and the upper horizons of the soil on the sections damaged by the phytophages enhance diffusion of CO_2 in the grass canopy layer. Animals feeding on the green parts of plants, while changing the relationship of biomass of roots which produce carbon dioxide to the aboveground parts which assimilate it, affect the increased concentration of CO_2 in the near-ground layer of air.

Besides this, the digging activity of animals changes aeration of the soil. The passages of the earth movers (of worms, rodents),

running through the entire thickness of the soil, facilitate more
intensive gas exchange between lower layers of the soil, saturated
with carbon dioxide, and the near-ground layer of air. In this way,
the activity of the animal phytophages significantly improves conditions of supply of carbon dioxide.

INFLUENCE OF ANIMALS ON CONDITIONS OF ROOT ACTIVITY OF PLANTS

Animals exert an important influence on the conditions of
absorption of moisture and mineral elements from the soil by roots.
The Water Regime of the Soil. Utilization of moisture in
forest-steppe ecosystems is determined mainly by the magnitude of
transpiration (Molchanov 1964, Afanaceeva 1966). The magnitude of
transpiration in plants is found to be directly dependent on the
mass and surface area of leaves. For this reason zoogenic decrease
of leaf surface area leads to a reduction of total transpiration and
insures preservation of moisture reserves in the soil. Such a
picture is observed in the oak groves with crowns defoliated by the
leaf eaters and also in the steppe ecosystems on sections occupied
by colonies herbivorous rodents. On these sections toward the end
of the vegetative period the water reserve in the root-inhabited
layer is 25% higher than in the nearby undamaged sections.
Defoliation of the crowns, thinning of the grass stands and
decrease of thickness of litter on sections colonized by phytophages, facilitates moistening of the soil by rains. In addition,
the lower layer of vegetation in colonies of animals receives a
large quantity of condensated moisture in the form of dew. All of
this insures a more favorable water regime for plants of the subordinate layers, and for this reason the vegetative period in it is
longer than on sections isolated from the phytophages.
Mineral Uptake. In humid communities the most significant role
in making minerals available belongs to the saprophagic animals and
microorganisms which implement mineralization of the vegetative
litterfall. They destroy the vegetative litterfall and organic
material of the soil, participate in the processes of synthesis of
chemical and biochemical compounds, and transform complex mineral
compounds into forms easily assimilated by the plants (Gilyarov
1939). Besides this, the activity of saprophages is accompanied by
emission into the surrounding environment of some soil fermentations
and biologically active growth-promoting materials (Atlavninite,
Dachulite and others 1966, Bagdanavichene 1969, Kozlovskaya and
Zaguralskaya 1972, and others). All of this stimulates development
of plants and facilitates increased productivity of the vegetative
cover.
An essential role in the process of mineral uptake by plants is
played by herbivorous animals. Their participation is expressed in
several ways: in bringing nitrogen and ash elements into the soil
with the zoogenic litterfall, in stimulating the decomposition
processes in litter and soil layers, and in bringing up mineral
elements from the lower horizons of the soil to the root inhabited
layer.
Zoogenic litterfall is chiefly from excrement of animals. In
it are included debris of plants and bodies of animals entering the
litter. Herbivorous insects (larva of beetles, caterpillars,
Orthoptera) eject with excrement 60 to 70% of the biomass of forage

consumed, small herbivorous rodents excrete about 20%, and the ungulate browse consumers excrete 25 to 40%. During the years of mass reproduction of leafeating insects the portion of zoogenic litterfall (mainly of excrement of oak leaf roller) constitutes about 10% of the net production of leaves in the oak groves, corresponding to the mass of autumn litterfall. Specific significance of zoogenic litterfall of the steppe phytophages (Orthoptera, rodents, larvae of Lepidoptera) in places of their mass accumulation attain 2 to 5% of biomass of the annual aboveground litterfall.

Zoogenic litterfall differs by having a high content of biogenic elements including nitrogen, phosporous, potassium, aluminum, sulphur, and silicon. Their quantity in the excrement of various types of herbivorous animals is 2 to 4 times greater than in the vegetative litterfall. In the debris of green leaves the content of nitrogen exceeds by 4 times, and in the body and exuviae of animals by 10 to 11 times its quantity in the autumn litterfall. In the outbreak centers of the oak leaf roller the quantity of nitrogen and phosporous entering with the zoogenic litter-fall is 35% of the amount brought in with the annual litterfall of oak leaves, and of potassium 26%.

Zoogenic litterfall is mineralized faster than plant litterfall. For this reason, as a result of vital activity of animals minerals easily assimilated by plants enter the biological cycle. Thus, during the years of mass reproduction of leafeating insects the quantity of nitrogen, phosporous and potassium entering the surface of the soil increases in the oak groves by 17, 21 and 13%. Replenishment of mineral elements of the soil is also facilitated by accelerated decomposition of litter during the years of mass increase of herbivorous animals.

A large role in the mineral uptake by plants is played by the phytophagous earth movers. They enrich the root layer of the soil by zoogenic nitrogen and, what is especially significant, by mineral elements brought up from the lower horizons. In ecosystems with a relatively shallow soil profile animals bring into the root layer of the soil a larger mass of mineral elements than plants (Abaturov 1966, Abaturov and Zubkova 1969).

In thick chernozems of the meadow-steppe a large role in replenishment of biogenic elements in the root layer is played by the vertebrate earth movers whose holes penetrate into the carbonaceous horizon. These animals mainly implement the movement of calcium and other minerals from the carbonaceous horizon into the humus. On watershed sections of the meadow steppe the quantity of calcium transferred by the earth movers into the root layer exceeds the quantity introduced by the total annual growth of phytomass.

In this way, animals exert great impact on a series of basic regimes of the production process. Zoogenic changes in radiation, gas and hydrothermic regimes, and also in conditions of water and mineral utilization, create favorable conditions for assimilating activities of plants.

III-2

The Role of Animals in Decomposition Processes

One of the integral growth indicators of the intensity of biological cycling is the speed of decomposition and mineralization of organic material included in the plant litterfall.

ANIMAL PARTICIPATION IN DECOMPOSITION OF PLANT LITTERFALL

Investigations begun in the U.S.S.R. on the initiative of M. S. Gilyarov and works of foreign investigators demonstrated the significance of soil-litter invertebrate animals, especially the mesofauna, in decomposition of litterfall in humid biogeocoenoses (Gilyarov 1939, 1967, Kurcheva 1960, 1965, 1971, Karpachevski and Peral 1966, Zlotin 1969a, Edwards and Heath 1963, Crossley and Witkamp 1964, Heath et al. 1966, and others). Thus, for example, in the forest-steppe oak groves 80 to 90% of the decomposition of aboveground plant litterfall which mineralized during the vegetative season is due to the activity of saprophages (of this about 50% is decomposed by the invertebrate mesofauna).

In steppe ecosystems the activity of animal saprophages also augments the process of litterfall decomposition, but in comparison with forest communities their role is not great. Specific weight of all invertebrates active in the mineralization of steppe litterfall does not exceed 20%. In steppe ecosystems (on mowed and pasture sections) there is very little litter, and for this reason a complex of semi-edaphic saprophytic invertebrates is almost lacking, the complex so characteristic of the oak groves. Although the numbers and biomass of saprophages in grassy forest and steppe communities is almost the same, in the steppe they are represented mainly by typical soil forms, which use chiefly organic detritus of the soil. Besides this, in the steppe ecosystem the litter and the upper half of the humus horizon dries out in the summer, and this limits the activity of soil invertebrates. Abiogenic factors have basic significance in the decomposition of the steppe litterfall and invertebrate saprophages, like the microorganisms, only speed up its decomposition.

A noted role in the decomposition process is played not only by saprophages, but also by herbivorous animals. Their contribution is chiefly in the change of decomposition regimes. Using a part of the phytomass growth in process of feeding, phytophages rework it and partially return it to the litterfall. As was pointed out above, the total quantity of the zoogenic litterfall (mainly excrement), even in years of very high numbers of animals, is small and constitutes only a few percent of annual aboveground litterfall of vegetation. However, the chemical composition and physical properties of the plant material, which went through the digestive tract of the animals, essentially change. In comparison with plant litterfall, excrement contains much more nutrient elements, less weakly-hydrolized compounds, and has a more narrow ratio of carbon to nitrogen. Besides this, excrement of phytophages, especially of the herbivorous insects, differs in structure by having hundreds of times more surface than the same mass of litterfall. The indicated physical chemical peculiarities of the zoogenic litterfall make it a highly favorable environment for intensive development of microorganisms. For this reason the admission of zoogenic litterfall on the litter activates microbiologic processes. As a result the plant litterfall, affected by microbiological decomposition, is more intensively reworked by invertebrate saprophages. The latter willingly use the excrement of the animal phytophages.

Consequently, admission into the litter of excrement of phytophages stimulates the activity of all the groups of saprophytic organisms and, as we showed in our experiments, significantly accelerates the mineralization of plant litterfall.

The zoogenic changes of the external environment also have important significance for the intensification of processes of destruction of litterfall. The increased moisture and temperature of the litter and of the upper horizons of the soil create favorable conditions for vital activity of saprophytic microorganisms and invertebrates. Their period of activity increases, and also their vertical distribution in the soil profile changes: they are concentrated in the upper layer, where the biological cycle is most active. In addition, the increase of light and heat in the lower layers strengthens the abiogenic destruction of litterfall.

Participation of phytophages in the decomposition processes is indicated by their influence on the speed of decomposition and accumulation of plant litterfall. In the aboveground layer of forest-steppe biogeocooenosis the accumulation of the dead plant remains predominates over their decomposition. This is characteristic both for the unmowed meadow steppe (Semenova-Tian-Shanskaya, 1966), and for the oak groves, where reserves of litter usually exceed by three to four times the annual litterfall of leaves. Decomposition of litterfall requires two to three years. The most intensive processes of decomposition of the dead plant remains occurs at the end of spring and beginning of summer.

The activity of the herbivorous animals causes mineralization of the dead organic remains to occur approximately twice as fast: during the vegetative season in the colonies of phytophages not less than 70% of the yearly quantity of litterfall is mineralized at a time when on the sections without colonies the total is about 30%. During periods of outbreak of leafeating insects almost the entire mass of litterfall is destroyed during the year, and there is practically complete renewal of the litter. In this case both in the

forest and in the steppe colonies of phytophages the period of most
intense mineralization shifts to the summer months. This leads to
the condition that nitrogen and ash elements, which are released
from the plant remians and excrement of phytophages during the same
vegetative season, are pulled into the biological cycle and participate in the processes of synthesis of organic material. In the
steppe toward the end of the vegetative period 71% of the nitrogen
and 36% of the ash elements are used for the second time for the
growth of grasses.

The earthmovers root eaters have great significance in the
transformation of organic material of the soil. This effect of
their activity has been studied very little; however, judging by the
changes in humus composition and the intensity of emission of carbon
dioxide from the soil on the excavated sections, it is possible to
hypothesize that the earthmovers play a definite role in the process of humus formation. In the humus composition of thick chernozems
of meadow-steppe, on the sections of perennial colonies of earth-
movers, the relative content of nitrogen and soluble fractions of
organic material (especially fulvic acid) increase. As a result of
this the relationship of carbon to nitrogen and of humic acid to
fulvic acid converges. The reasons for these changes are not yet
clear. One can only hypothesize that zoogenic impact on the intensity and character of processes in the soil have an effect on
the separate conditions of aeration and hydrothermic regime, and
also on the zoogenic enrichment of the soil by calcium and nitrogen.

III–3

Influence of Animals on Productivity of Ecosystems

Since the animals participate both in processes determining the formation of plant material and also in its decomposition, one can estimate their role in the biological cycle by the total impact on the magnitude of primary production, which is the integral characteristic of all production and destruction processes.

The general effect of zoogenic consumption of primary production includes losses of growing parts used by the animals as food, and of the losses connected with the deceleration of growth of damaged plants. The relationship of direct and indirect impact on primary production by various animal groups is not the same. Thus, for example, in the utilization of plant material grass-consuming animals have greater significance than the consumers of browse, due to the different speed of restoration of productivity of the grassy and woody parts. A corresponding relationship exists in the utilization of plant materials between plant sucking insects (aphids) and leaf-eaters (larvae). This is explained by the fact, that the larvae, in contrast to the aphids, greatly abbreviate the size of the photosynthetic apparatus of plants (Llewellyn 1972). Along with this, as was shown above, the losses of primary production utilized by the animals are usually significantly less than those losses which are connected with indirect impact. Thus, the biomass of the woody growth eaten by the consumers of perennial parts of the plants is 20 to 30% of the loss of phytomass brought about by the consequences of vital activity of these animals (Dinesman and Schmalgauzen 1967, Northcott 1971, and others).

Obviously, the characteristic disproportion in aboveground ecosystems between the biomass of primary producers and biomass of heterotrophs, expressed as the relationship between levels of trophic pyramids of Elton, is explained by the fact that the total impact of zoogenic consumption on phytomass growth is greater than the quantity used as food by phytophages.

Questions of total impact of animal populations on the plant cover and of size of total losses of primary production in various types of ecosystems have been studied insufficiently so far and are applicable only to the aboveground part of total phytomass. Judging by the little data in the literature, this size constitutes 20 to

40% (Ferguson 1968, Hendricks 1970, Northcott 1971). Our preliminary determination of the total zoogenic losses of primary production in the forest-steppe ecosystem also showed that they constitute
about 20%. This indicates the limiting maximum impact following
which is still preserved the stability of the natural ecosystem, if
it is in an equilibrium condition. This hypotheses is confirmed by
the data of investigations conducted in India on pastures in the
Teer Forest Reserve. For restoration of the productivity of these
pastures it was essential that the biomass of vegetation annually
destroyed by wild and domestic animals not exceed 25% of its annual
growth (Berwick and Jordan 1971).

The decrease of phytomass by phytophages in this region is
accompanied by changes of carbon assimilation and root uptake which
strengthen the development of other components of the ecosystem or
of structural parts of phytomass, and this to a certain degree
compensates for the general losses of community production.[1] For
this reason animal activity can be looked at as a peculiar relay,
implementing mutual activity of the various components of biogeocoenosis and capable of manifesting in it autoregularitory mechanisms.

Zoogenic production most completely manifests itself in complex
communities. Investigations of E. N. Ierusalimov (1965), and
Vorontzov, Ierusalimov and Mozolevskaya (1967), showed that during
the years of outbreak of leaf-eaters the observed decrease of
growth of damaged major woody species is compensated by increased
production of the accompanying woody and brush species, so that the
total growth of vegetation does not change. According to our
observations, in the centers of outbreak of oak leaf rollers in the
forest biogeocoenosis with a simpler two-layer structure, zoogenic
changes of the regime of productive processes under the canopy of
damaged tree stands facilitated increased productivity of the
grassy layer by more than a factor of two.

In the forest biogeocoenosis the increase of production of
grass in the outbreak centers compensates not only for the zoogenic
losses of growth of the damaged woody species but also completely
eliminates the decrease of total productivity for the entire woody
layer of the entire ecosystem due to unfavorable weather conditions.
In the grassy biogeocoenoses the phytophage activity facilitates
formation of complex multi-species communities, more stable under
the periodically changing conditions of the external environment.

In this way, in the aboveground communities the heterotrophs
are not only consumerss of production. They participate equally
with other natural components in support of the basic character-
isitics of the ecosystem (Isakov and Panfilov 1970).

Since the dominant part of the zoogenic losses of primary
production are connected with changes by animals of abiotic and
biological factors affecting growth and decomposition of plant
material, they can only conditionally be called losses. In reality
this is one of the characteristics of the community, connected with

---

[1]In order to judge the true significance of animals in production
processes, it is necessary to have data on the growth of all fractions of the phytomass, including the belowground parts. It is
known, for example, that the increase (or decrease) of production
of the green fraction is not always accompanied by a proportional
change of the biomass of roots.

the essential life processes. It determines productivity of the
ecosystem, and also the cycle of matter flowing in it.
    The above relates to the natural ecosystem in equilibrium. In
the biogeocoenosis changed by the activity of man, zoogenic loss of
harvest is significantly greater. Rodents alone lower the harvest
of the perennial grasses by 15 to 20%; on the felled areas they
destroy more than 50% of the seed harvest, and in the forest cultures up to 80'to 90% of the seedlings of the woody young stock
(Dinesman 1961). According to the data of the Food and Agricultural
Organization of the United Nations (FAO), the general losses of
harvest of agricultural crops connected with the activity of pests
was in 1967 about 35% (Poliakov 1972).
    The reason for large zoogenic losses in the ecosystems changed
by the anthropogenic impact is disturbance of the existing biogeocoenotic relationships: the change of structure of plant cover and
of animal populations and a sharp increase of abundance of separate
functional groups of heterotrophs.
    The increased impact of herbivorous animals on the vegetation
leads to sharp and often irreversable zoogenic succession,[2]
especially characteristic for the livestock regions with pasture
systems (Formozov 1929, Lavrenko 1956 Grazing in Terrestrial and
Marine Environments 1964; Merwe 1968). In recent decades zoogenic
changes have been of greater magnitude in the forest biogeocoenosis,
caused by the unregulated number of wild ungulates.
    Similarly, for a long time the opposite side of the mutual
relationship of animal and plant interactions of biogeocoenoses
has been known. The dropping out or sharp decrease of the number of
separate species and groups of animals also leads to succession,
causing disturbance of the structure of natural plant communities
and decreased productivity. I. K. Pachoski (1917) wrote that for
normal existence of steppes moderate grazing is necessary; in other
words "steppe vegetation is transformed into a kind of steady con-
glomerate of various forms of plants", and that "if steppe vegetation is allowed during an interval of time to leave equilibrium
it loses its normal character."
    Sharp changes of structure of the phytocoenosis and decreased
productivity are observed in grassy ecosystems with a history of
absolute protection. On protected sections of the Central Chernozem
Reserve, where wild herbivorous animals (ungulates, large rodents)
are absent, and grazing by domestic animals and hay mowing is not
conducted, a large quantity of dead plant remains accumulates forming
a thick litter, which disturbs the water and trophic regime of
plants (Semenova-Tian-Shanskaya 1966, Dokhman 1968). Decomposition
of the vegetation becomes poor. Herbs gradually disappear giving
place to some grasses (small reed, feather grass, quack grass) which
are not readily eaten by the animals. As a result, the number of
herbivorous insects and small rodents also decreases. Besides this,
the litterfall of these grasses decomposes significantly slower than
that of the wide leaf grasses and herbs. All this leads to a lowering
of the rate of biological cycling.
    Such completely protected steppe sections, besides the Central
Chernozem Reserve, have been established in steppe reserves of the
Ukraine (the Streletski Reserve, Khomutovski Steppe, Askania-Nova),

[2]It would be more correct to call them anthropozoogenic, since they
   are observed in communities which are changed by the activity of man.

and everywhere is observed an analogous "ungrazed" digression. But
when moderate grazing is conducted on the reserve unmowed sections
(as it is done in places in Askania-Nova) the relationship of the
production and decomposition processes is restored, and the steppe
acquires it's natural appearance.

For this reason explanation of changes in function of the
ecosystem resulting from removal of various groups of animals is one
of the essential and urgent problems of biogeocoenotic investigations.

The role of animal populations as a basic component of the biogeocoenosis, supporting its stability, is distinctly manifested in a
comparison of results of the influence of zoogenic and anthropogenic
factors.

In the forest-steppe all forms of economical use of natural
ecosystems (grazing, hay mowing, plowing) are accompanied by reduction of plant production, which leads to a decreased capacity of the
biological cycling in the soil-plant system and to reduction of the
reserves of organic material in the soil.[3] As a result of systematic
hay mowing or removal of harvest on agricultural lands a significant
part of the biogenic elements from the root layer was removed, which
in natural ecosystems return with the litterfall of the plants. The
same occurs on localities with strong overgrazing. With 50 years of
cultivation the humus reserves in the upper horizons of the thick
chernozem decrease by 25%; with haying and harvest of various agricultural products the anthropogenic ecosystems annually lose more
than 20% of the total quantity of ash elements contained in the
total growth of phytomass (Afanaceeva, 1966). Simultaneously,
the relationship of the humus components changes, which testifies to
disturbances of biological and physical-chemical processes of mineralization and synthesis of organic material of soil.

All this leads to a decrease in biological productivity and a
lowering of ecosystem stability. Zoogenic impact on the ecosystem,
as seen above, facilitates preservation of its characteristic
properties.

Another condition that supports the stability and equilibrium
of the ecosystem is the regularity of the perennial dynamics of
numbers of various functional groups of heterotrophic organisms. A
univeral property of equilibrium ecosystems is the tendency to
compensate for results of environmental impact by changes of population density (Slobodkin, Smith and Hairston 1967). Among the
mechanisms regulating the composition of populations, there is a
reverse relationship between density of population and the degree of
impact changing it's factors (mainly forage resources). On this is
based the preservation of equilibrium of the ecosystem.

From this it follows that in established ecosystems the dynamics
of numbers of herbivorous animals, especially of high density species,
is connected with the speed of restoration of the disturbed phytocoenoses. The observations showed that the faster plant cover and
productivity are restored, the more regularly can the number of
phytophages increase, and in this way the average level of their
abundance.

Thus, for example, in the meadow-steppe, where productivity of
the sections damaged by numerous herbivorous animals such as voles

[3]We have in mind anthropogenic impact, not accompanied by agro-
technical methods directed to the restoration of the soil fertility
and the increase of harvest of agricultural lands.

is already restored by following year, the number of rodents usually remains at a relatively high level, and annual fluctuations are insignificant. In semi-desert the vegetation on the localities colonized by these rodents is restored only after 3-4 years, the number of voles there is low, outbreaks are repeated in 7-10 years, and the amplitude of perennial fluctuations of numbers attain a multiple of 100. Short periods of increased numbers of voles alternate with lengthy periods of deep depression of density, during which time productivity of the ecosystem is restored. Analogous regularities are known also for other groups of phytophages (Forontzov 1936, 1948, Khodashova 1966).

Obviously, the structure of animal populations of ecosystems (in any case the relationship of the various trophic groups of herbivorous animals) is determined not only by the structure of the plant cover, but also by the rate of restoration of productivity of the various strata of the phytocoenosis. This is one of the reasons for the composition of abundance of animals feeding on annual and perennial parts of plants. Damage of perennial shoots continues to have an effect on the growth for several years, and for this reason the zoogenic pressure on the woody layer must be less than on the herbaceous layer.

Maximum zoogenic losses of primary production, the rate of restoration of the disturbed animal components of the system and the dynamics of numbers of animals undoubtedly are bilateral characteristics of the natural climax biogeocoenoses, determining their productivity and stability.

In this connection it is necessary to point out that the phenomenon of stability must be looked at in a dynamic context. Stability of community function is manifested in cycles of definite periodicity, changing with time. An example of such cycles is the alternation of dry and moist periods of variable duration, which are determined by the dynamics of solar activity. The degree of participation of animals, according to the various functional groups, is dissimilar during these periods. If we were to estimate the role of heterotrophs in transformation of organic material during moist and dry periods, then probably in the first case the most influential would be the complex of saprophytic organisms, and in the second the trophic chain of phytophages.

The above shows that heterotrophic organisms along with other natural components participate in creation of the structure of ecosystems and determine the mechanisms of their function.

For comparison of effectiveness of function of ecosystems as basic indices of their similarities or differences, we usually consider the level of biological productivity, the rate of decomposition processes and the reserve of dead organic matter in the soil. Watershed forest and steppe ecosystems of the central forest steppe of the mid-Russian uplands have very similar annual production of phytomass and almost similar levels of zoomass and abundance of microorganisms (Bondarenko-Zozulina 1955, Afanaceeva 1966, Grin, Rauner and Utekhin 1970, our data). In other words, the magnitude of general biological production in the forest and steppe are very similar. The intensity of decomposition processes also is approximately the same. For this reason both in the forest and in the steppe ecosystems soil is formed with similar reserves of humus.

The indicated characteristics of similarity in the general
functioning of watershed forest and steppe communities apparently is
explained by the fact that both ecosystems function in similar
conditions of physical and geochemical environment, receiving nearly
equal amounts of solar energy, precipitation and nutrients. Consequently, their total biological productivity differs little.

Thus, in quantitative balance of input and output, both systems
are essentially the same. At the same time the structure of these
ecosystems and mechanisms of processes occuring in them are not the
same. Forest and steppe ecosystems differ in structure of biomass
(by the relationship of fractions of phytomass and the functional
trophic groups of heterotrophs), by the effectiveness of use of
solar energy and moisture, and also by the type of decomposition
processes. In particular, one of the important differences between
these ecosystems consists of the different relationship of biotic
and abiogenic factors contributing to decomposition, which affects
the biochemical and geochemical transformation of organic material,
influencing the composition of intermediate and final products of
decomposition.

For a complete estimation of function of those or other communities it is insufficient to perform only balance determinations,
which characterize the "input" and "output" of the ecosystem. More
detailed investigations are necessary, which would allow charac-
terization of the types of function and would expose mechanisms of
mutual activity of internal components of the systems. In this
case, it should be remembered that the connections between various
structural components of the ecosystem, and also the type of the
biological cycle, is determined to a significant degree by the
activity of heterotrophic organisms. During years with high numbers
of herbivorous insects the biological cycle in the forest ecosystem
proceeds in a "mixed" fashion with approximately equal participation
of abiogenic and biogenic factors. In this period the forest
communities approach the steppe biogeocoenosis, according to the
regime of function, which indicates the ceaseless dynamic mutual
activity between their border coenoses, resulting in continuous
succession.

In conclusion, it should be said that the role of heterotrophs
in the biological cycling of the various communities, obviously, is
not the same. This is indicated by geographical differences in the
structure of animal populations (Chernov, Khodashova and Zlotin
1967, 1969b, Isakov and Panfilof 1969, Isakov, Zimina and others
1971), and also preliminary results of our investigation on the
study of the environmental modifying activity of animals in steppe
and semi-desert zones. Further study of the biogeocoenotic role of
animals must be directed to the explanation of geographic regularity
of their participation in the function of communities, both natural
and changed by the activities of man.

Bibliography

Abaturov, B. D. 1966. Influence of the digging activity of a mole (*Talpa europaea* L.) on the cycling of chemical matter in a forest biogeocenosis. Reports of the Academy of Science, USSR 168(4).

Abaturov, B. D., and Zubkova, L. V. 1969. Influence of small susliks (*Citellus pygmaeus* Pall.) on the water-physical characteristics of solonetz soils of the Trans-Volga peninsula. Soil Science No. 10.

Afanaseeva, E. A. 1947. The origin, composition and characteristics of large Chernozems of the Streletski Steppe. Reports of the Soil Institute in the Name of V. V. Dokuchaev, Vol. 25. Moscow-Leningrad, Publishing House of the Academy of Sciences, USSR.

Afanaseeva, E. A. 1964. Formation and regime of large Chernozems. *In* Chernozems of the Central Chernozem Oblast and Their Fertility. Moscow, "Nauka."

Afanaseeva, E. A. 1966. Chernozems of the Mid-Russian Upland. Moscow, "Nauka."

Afanaseeva, E. A., Golubev, V. N. 1962. Soil-botanical essay of the Streletski Steppe. Central Chernozem Government Reserve in the name of V. V. Alekhin. Kursk Book Publishing House.

Alekseenko, L. N. 1967. Productivity of meadow plants depending on the conditions of the environment. Literary Publishing House of the Leningrad University.

Amirkhanova, S. N. 1962. Nutrient matter in the leaves of healthy and weakened plant fodder of the odd silkworm. *In* Investigations of pest sources of forests in Bashkiria. Vol. 2, Ufa.

Aristovskaya, T. V. 1965. Microbiology of podzol soils. Moscow-Leningrad, "Nauka."

Arnoldi, K. V. 1965. The forest-steppe of the Russian Plain and its zoogeographical and coenologic characteristics based on insect studies. Reports of the Central Chernozem Reserve, Release 8, Voronezh, Publishing House Voronezh of the State University.

Arnoldi, K. V., and M. S. Ghilarov. 1963. Die wirbellosen im boden und in der streu als indikatoren der besonderheiten der boden und pflanzendecke der waldsteppen zone. Pedobiologia Bd. 4, H. 1/2.

Atlavinite, O., Ya. Dachulite, A. Grigyalis, and R. Shpokaukas. 1966. The influence of Oligochaeta on the biochemical characteristics of soil and on microorganisms. *In* Problems of soil zoology. Moscow, "Nauka."

Bagdanavichene, Z. P. 1969. Numerical change of microorganisms in the soil in connection with the vital activity of earthworms. *In* Problems of soil zoology. Moscow, "Nauka."

Bashenina, N. V. 1962. The ecology of the common field-vole and some features of its geographicl variability. Moscow, Publishing House of Moscow University.

Bazilevich, N. I., and L. E. Rodin. 1969. Geographical regularities of productivity and cycling of chemical elements in basic types of terrestrial vegetation. *In* General Theoretical Problems of Biological Productivity. Leningrad, "Nauka."

Bazilevich, N. I., A. V. Drozdov, and L. E. Rodin. 1968. Productivity of the plant canopy of the earth, general regularities of arrangement and connections with climatic factors. J. Gen. Biol. 29(3).

Bedeman, I. N., Z. G. Bespalova, and A. T. Rakhmanina. 1962. Ecological-geobotanical and agroreclaimed studies in the Kure-Araksinsk Lowland of Trans-Caucasia. Moscow-Leningrad, Publishing House of the Academy of Sciences of the USSR.

Belgovski, M. L. 1959. The tolerance of leaf rollers against low winter temperatures. Reports of the Forest Institute, Release 12, Moscow. Publishing House of the Academy of Sciences of the USSR.

Berwick, S. H., and P. A. Jordan. 1971. First report of the Yale-Bombay natural history society studies of wild ungulates at Gir Forest, Gujarat, India. J. Bombay Nat. History Soc. 68, N2.

Bizova, Yu. B. 1965. Dependence of oxygen consumption on the type of life and size of body in the example of earthworms (Lumbricidae, Oligochaeta). J. Gen. Biol. 26(5).

Bolshakov, A. F. 1961. Water condition of large Chernozems of the Mid-Russian Upland. Moscow, Publishing House of the Academy of Sciences of the USSR.

Bondarenko-Zozulina, M. I. 1955. Quantitative composition of soil microflora of the Central Chernozem Reserve. Reports of the Central Chernozem Government Reserve, Release 3, Kursk, Book Publishing House.

Chernov, Yu. I. 1967. Some peculiarities of structure of animal populations in the European part of the forest-steppe in the example of invertebrates. *In* Structure and Functional-Biogeocenotic Role of Animal Populations of Dry Land. Moscow.

Chernov, Yu. I., K. S. Khodashova, and R. I. Zlotin. 1967. Surface zoomass and some regularities of its regional distribution. J. Gen. Biol. 28(2).

Crossley, D. A., and M. Witkamp. 1964. Effects of a pesticide on biota and breakdown of forest litter. Trans. 8th Int. Congr. Soil Sci., Vol. 3. Bucharest.

Dimo, N. A. 1938. Earthworms in the soils of Central Asia. Soil
    Sci. No. 4.

Dinesman, L. G. 1961. Influence of wild mammals on the formation
    of tree stands. Moscow, Publishing House of the Academy of
    Sciences of the USSR.

Dinesman, L. G., V. I. Shmalgauzen. 1961. The role of moose in the
    cycling and transformation of matter in a forest biogeocenosis.
    Reports of the Forest Science Laboratory, Release 5, Moscow,
    Publishing House of the Academy of Sciences of the USSR.

Dinesman, L. G., and V. I. Shmalgauzen. 1967. The role of moose in
    the formation of primary forest productivity. Biology and hunting
    of moose, Vol. 3. Moscow, Russian Agricultural Publishing
    House.

Dokhman, G. I. 1968. Forest-steppe of the European part of the
    USSR. Toward knowledge of natural laws of the forest-steppe.
    Moscow, "Nauka."

Dokuchaev, V. V. 1883. Russian Chernozem. Report to the Imperial
    Free Economic Society. St. Petersburg.

Dukelskaya, N. M. 1932. The biology of the mole-rat and the problem
    of control. Reports on Plant Protection, Series 4, Vertebrates,
    Release 2. Leningrad.

Edelman, N. M. 1954. The influence of feeding conditions on the
    conversion of matter by the odd silkworm and winter moth.
    Reports of the All Russian Institute for the Protection of
    Plants, Release 6, Moscow-Leningrad, Agricultural Publishing
    House.

Edwards, C. A., and G. W. Heath. 1963. The role of soil animals in
    breakdown of leaf material. Soil Organisms. Amsterdam.

Edwards, C. A., D. E. Reichle, and D. A. Crossley. 1970. The role
    of soil invertebrates in turnover of organic matter and nutri-
    ents. Ecol. Studies. Analysis and synthesis, Vol. 1. Berlin.

Egorov, N. N., N. N. Rubtsova, and T. N. Solozhenikina. 1961. Oak
    leaf roller in the Voronezh District. Zool. J. 40(8).

Eigenson, M. S. 1948. Sun, weather, and climate. Leningrad,
    Hydro-Meteor Publishing House.

Eigenson, M. S. 1957. Notes on physical-geographic manifestations
    of solar activity. Lvov, Publishing House of Lvov University.

Eigenson, M. S., M. N. Gnevyshev, A. I. Ol, and B. M. Rubashev.
    1948. Solar activity and its terrestrial manifestations.
    Moscow-Leningrad, State Technical Publishing House.

Elagin, I. N. 1962. System of studying processes of the formation
    of the annual rings in oak. In Physiology of Arboreal Plants.
    Moscow, Publishing House of the Academy of Sciences of the
    USSR.

Eliseeva, V. I. 1959. A list of mammals and birds of the Central-
    Chernozem Reserve and some data on the phenology of their
    migrations and reproduction. Reports of the Central Chernozem
    Government Reserve, Release 5. Kursk, Book Publishing House.

Eliseeva, V. I. 1965. The distribution of mouse-like rodents in
    basic biotopes of the Central Chernozem Reserve and the dy-
    namics of numbers of leading types. Reports of the Central
    Chernozem Government Reserve, Release 8, Voronezh, Publishing
    House of Voronezh State University.

Eliseeva, V. I.   1967a.   A supplement to the list of mammals and
    birds of the Central Chernozem Reserve. Reports of the Central
    Chernozem Government Reserve, Release 10. Moscow, "Forest
    Industry."

Eliseeva, V. I.   1967b.   The fauna of lower terrestrial vertebrates
    of the Central Chernozem Reserve. Reports of the Central
    Chernozem Government Reserve, Release 10.

Eliseeva, V. I.   1968.   Animal world. Chapter in the book: Central
    Chernozem Government Reserve. Moscow, "Forest Industry."

Ermich, K.   1956.   Badania nad dynamika przyrostu grubości u *Pinus
    silvestris* L. i *Quercus robur* L. w ciagu okresu wegetacyjnego.
    Ekolog. Polska, Ser. A, 1956, t. 4, N 7.

Evdokimova, L. I.   1963.   Peculiarities of water expenditure on
    transpiration depending on the plants' water provision. *In*
    Water condition of plants in connection with the exchange of
    matter and productivity. Moscow, Publishing House of the
    Academy of Sciences of the USSR.

Ferguson, R. B.   1968.   Survival and growth of young bitterbrush
    browsed by deer. J. Wildl. Manage. Vol. 21, N 4.

Formozov, A. N.   1928.   Mammalia in the steppe biocenose. Ecology,
    Vol. 9, N 4.

Formozov, A. N.   1929.   Trampling of grazing land, its significance
    for steppe fauna and battle with pests. Nature No. 11.

Formozov, A. N.   1936.   Fluctuation of numbers of game animals.
    Moscow, Leningrad.

Formozov, A. N.   1948.   Small rodents and insectivores of the
    Sharin District of the Kostrom Region during the period of
    1930-1940. *In* Fauna and Ecology of Rodents. Moscow, Publish-
    ing House of the Moscow Society of Experimental Nature.
    (Materials for the Learning of Fauna and Flora of the USSR,
    new series, Dep. Zoology, Release 17 (32)).

Formozov, A. N.   1964.   Grazing in terrestrial and marine environ-
    ments. Sympos. British Ecol. Soc., Bangor, 11-14, April 1962,
    Ed. D. J. Crisp. Oxford.

Formozov, A. N., and I. B. Kiris-Prosvirnina.   1937.   Activity of
    rodents in pastures and hay mowings. Scientific notes of
    Moscow State University, Release 13, Biology.

Formozov, A. N., and A. G. Voronov.   1935.   Fundamental character-
    istics of rodent activity on pastures and hay mowing lands.
    Reports of the Academy of Sciences of the USSR. Vol. 3, No.
    8.

Formozov, A. N., and A. G. Voronov.   1939.   Rodent activity on
    pastures and hay mowing lands of western Kazakhstan and its
    economic significance. (Biotechnical Relations of Rodents to
    Vegetation). Scientific Notes of Moscow State University,
    Release 20, Biology, Moscow.

Frideriks, K.   1932.   Ecological fundamentals of applied zoology
    and entomology. Translated from German. Moscow-Leningrad,
    Agricultural Publishing House.

Fundamentals of Forest Biogeocenology.   1964.   V. N. Sukachev and
    N. V. Dylis (eds.). Moscow, Publishing House of the Academy
    of Sciences of the USSR.

Gebczyńska, S.   1970.   Bioenergetics of a root vole population.
    Acta Theriologica, Vol. 15, N 1-12.

Geiger, R.   1960.   Climate of the layer of air near the ground.
    Translation from English.   Moscow, State Publishing House for
    Foreign Literature.
Gerasimov, I. P., A. M. Grin, A. V. Drozdov, et al.   1972.   Periodi-
    cal problems of biogeocenology and results of reports of
    biogeocenotic permanent sites.   News of the Academy of Science
    of the USSR, Geographical Series No. 2.
Gertsik, V. V.   1955.   Influence of pasture on vegetation, humidity
    and soil structure.   Reports of the Central Chernozem Govern-
    ment Reserve, Release 4, Kursk, Book Publishing House.
Gertsik, V. V.   1957.   Some data on the role of precipitation in
    the vegetative period on replenishment of moisture reserve in
    the soil.   Reports of the Central Chernozem Government Reserve,
    Release 4, Kursk, Book Publishing House.
Gertsik, V. V.   1959.   Seasonal dynamics of humus in major Cherno-
    zems.   Reports of the Central Chernozem Government Reserve,
    Release 5, Kursk, Book Publishing House.
Gilyarov, M. S.   1939.   Soil fauna and life of the soil.   Soil
    Science No. 6.
Gilyarov, M. S.   1960.   Soil invertebrates as indicators of peculiar-
    ities of soil and vegetative canopy of the forest steppe.
    Reports of the Central Chernozem Government Reserve, Vol. 6,
    Kursk, Book Publishing House.
Gilyarov, M. S.   1967.   The development of soil zoology in the
    USSR.   Zoological Journal Vol. 47, Release 10.
Golubev, V. N.   1962.   Fundamentals of biomorphology of grassland
    plants of the central forest-steppe.   Reports of the Central
    Chernozem Reserve, Vol. 7, Voronezh, Publishing House Voronezh
    of the State University.
Gordeeva, T. K.   1952.   The rate of plant transpiration in the
    complex semi-desert interfluvial of the Volga–Urals.   Bot. J.
    Vol. 37, No. 4.
Grigoriev, A. A., and M. I. Budiko.   1959.   Classification of the
    climates of the USSR.   News of the Academy of Sciences of the
    USSR, Geographical Series No. 3.
Grigoriev, A. A., and M. I. Budiko.   1965.   The connection of heat
    and moisture balance with the rates of geographical processes.
    Reports of the Academy of Sciences of the USSR.   Vol. 162, No.
    1.
Grin, A. M., Yu. L. Rauner, and V. D. Utekhin.   1970.   Efficiency
    of utilization of radiation and moisture in forest–steppe
    ecosystems.   News of the Academy of Sciences of the USSR,
    Geographical Series No. 4.
Grodzinski, W.   1971a.   Energy flow through populations of small
    mammals in the Alaskan taiga forest.   Acta Theriologica, Vol.
    16, N 8–18.
Grodzinski, W.   1971b.   Food consumption of small mammals in the
    Alaskan taiga forest.   Annales Zoologia Fennici, Vol. 8, N 1.
Grudzinskaya, I. G.   1962.   Structure dependence of the annual ring
    of wood on the development of shoots of oak.   In Physiology of
    Arboreal Plants.   Moscow, Publishing House of the Academy of
    Sciences of the USSR.
Gubareva, V. A.   1970.   Chemical composition of precipitation
    penetrating through the crown, litter and soil.   Reports of
    Soviet Scholars at the International Symposium on the Influence
    of Forest on the External Environment, Moscow.   Vol. 2.

Hansson, L. 1971. Estimates of the productivity of small mammals in a South Swedish spruce plantation. Annales Zoologia Fennici, Vol. 8, N 1.

Heath, G. W., Arnold, M. K., Edwards, C. A. 1966. Studies in leaf litter breakdown. 1. Breakdown rates of leaves of different species. Pedobiologia, Bd. 6, H. 1.

Hendrichs, H. 1970. Schätzungen der Huftierbiomasse in der Dornbuschsavanne nördlich und westlich der Serengettisteppe in Ostafrika nach einem neuen Verfahren und Bemerkungen zur Biomasse der anderen pflanzenfressende Tierarten. Säugelier-kundliche Mitteilungen, Bd. 18, N 3.

Ierusalimov, E. N. 1965. Changes of growth in a mixed oak grove during consumption by leaf eating insects. News of the Higher Education Establishments. "Forest Journal," No. 6.

Isakov, Yu. A., and D. V. Panfilov. 1969. Zonal resource peculiarities of the animal world of the USSR. In Resources of the Animal World of the USSR. Results of Science. Geography of the USSR, Release 7, Moscow.

Isakov, Yu. A., and D. V. Panfilov. 1970. Basic aspects of the environment forming activity of animals. In Environment Forming Activity of the Animals. Materials for the Conference of December 17-18, 1970, Moscow.

Isakov, Yu. A., R. P. Zimina, L. N. Nikolaeva, and D. V. Panfilov. 1971. Production and structure of the animal populations of the major Caucasus landscapes and their landscape forming activity. In Biological Productivity and the Cycling of Chemical Elements in Vegetative Communities. Leningrad, "Nauka."

Ivanov, L. A., A. A. Silina, D. G. Zhmur, and Yu. L. Tselniker. 1951. Determining transpiration by the tree stand of the forest. Bot J., Vol. 36, No. 1.

Iveronova, M. I., and A. V. Yashina. 1971. The snow cover of the Streletski Section of the Central Chernozem Reserve. Reports of the Central Chernozem Government Reserve, Release 11, Moscow, "Forest Industry."

Kalela, O., Koponen, F. 1971. Food consumption and movements of the Norwegian lemming in areas characterized by isolated fells. Annales Zoologica Fennici, Vol. 8, N. 1.

Kaletski, A. A. 1967. The feeding of moose during the winter period and annual volume of food consumption. Biology and Moose Hunting, Vol. 3, Moscow, Russian Agricultural Publishing House.

Kamenetskaya, I. V. 1970. The phytomass and annual growth of pine (Pinus silvestris L.) in 30 year old pine trees of the southern Taiga. In The Formation of the Annual Ring and Accumulation of Organic Mass in Trees. Moscow, "Nauka."

Karmanova, I. V. 1970. The influence of exterior environmental factors on growth and productivity of undergrowth of some arboreal types. In Natural Renewal of Arboreal Types and a Quantitative Analysis of Its Growth. Moscow, "Nauka."

Karpachevski, L. O., and G. S. Perel. 1966. The role of invertebrates in the decomposition of forest litterfall. In Questions of Soil Biology. Moscow, "Nauka."

Khanislamov, M. G.   1963.   On conditions leading to outbreaks of
    needle and leaf eating pests.   Questions of Forest Protection,
    Vol. 2.   Materials for the International Conference for the
    Protection of Forests, Moscow.

Khodashova, K. S.   1960.   Natural environments and animals of clay
    semideserts of the trans-Volga.   Moscow, Publising House of
    the Academy of Sciences of the USSR.

Khodashova, K. S.   1966.   About geographical structural peculiari-
    ties of terrestrial populations of vertebrates.   *In* Regional
    Peculiarities of Population of Surface Animals.   Moscow,
    "Nauka."

Khodashova, K. S.   1970.   The influence of vertebrate-phytophages
    on the biological productivity and cycling of matter in forest-
    steppe landscapes.   *In* Environment Forming Activity of Animals.
    Materials for the Conference of December 17-18, 1970).   Moscow,
    Publishing House of Moscow State University.

Khodashova, K. S., Yu. I. Chernov, and R. I. Zlotin.   1967.   Struc-
    ture, dynamics and forms of influence of animal populations on
    the productivity of biogeocenoses of the Central Forest-
    Steppe.   *In* Structure and functional-biogeocenotic role of the
    animal population of dry land.   Moscow.

Khodashova, K. S., R. I. Zlotin, Yu. I. Chernov, and B. I. Eliseeva.
    1967.   On the role of animal populations in the biological
    cycling of matter.   *In* Geophysics of landscape.   Moscow,
    "Nauka."

Kirikov, S. V.   1959.   The changes of the animal world in natural
    zones of the USSR (18th-19th centuries).   The Steppe Zone and
    Forest Steppe.   Moscow, Publishing House of the Academy of
    Science of the USSR.

Kirikov, S. V.   1966.   Hunting animals, natural environment and
    man.   Moscow, "Nauka."

Kleshnin, A. F., and I. A. Shulgin.   1963.   About transpiration and
    temperature of plant leaves in conditions of solar lighting.
    In Water conditions of plants in conjunction with an exchange
    of matter and productivity.   Moscow, Publishing House of the
    Academy of Science of the USSR.

Knorre, E. P.   1959.   Seasonal peculiarities in the feeding state
    of moose in the Pechor Taiga.   Reports of the Forest Institute,
    Release 13, Moscow, Publishing House of the Academy of Science
    of the USSR.

Kobranov, N. P.   1925.   The forests of the Central Chernozem District
    and their investigation.   The Paths of Agriculture, No. 1-2.

Kokovina, T. P.   1967.   Towards the question of ash exchange in the
    oak-groves on large Chernozems.   Reports of the Central Cherno-
    zem Government Reserve, Release 10, Moscow, "Forest Industry."

Kononova, M. M., I. V. Aleksandrova, N. P. Belchikova, and N. A.
    Titova.   1964.   Humus of virgin and assimilated soils.   *In*
    Physics, chemistry, biology and minerology of soils of the
    USSR.   Reports to the 8th International Congress of Soil
    Scientists.   Moscow, "Nauka."

Kostin, S. I.   1960.   Climatic fluctuations in the central forest-
    steppe of the Russian Plain (according to an analysis of data
    on oak growth in thickness).   Scientific notes of the Voronezh
    Forest Technical Institute, Vol. 21, Voronezh.

Kovda, V. A.   1971.   The biosphere and humanity.   *In* The Biosphere
    and Its Resources.   Moscow, "Nauka."

Kozlovskaya, L. S., and L. M. Saguralskaya. 1972. The significance of invertebrates in the creation of fermented activity of the soils. *In* Basic principles of studying marshy biogeocenoses. Leningrad, "Nauka."

Kramer, P., and T. Kozlovski. 1963. Physiology of arboreal plants. Translated from English. Moscow, State Publishing House for Foreign Literatures.

Krasnitski, A. M. 1967. Composition, quantity and dynamics of litterfall in the oak groves of the Central Chernozem Reserve. *In* Geophysics of Landscape. Moscow, "Nauka."

Krivolutzky, L. A. 1962. Armoured mites (Oribatoidea) in the soils of the Streletski Section of the Central Chernozem Reserve in the name of V. V. Alekhin (Kursk District). Pedobiologia, Vol. 2, N 1.

Kryzhanovzki, K. V. 1954. The influence of light conditions on the growth of oak in a forest and in isolated cultures. Abstract of a candidate's Dissertation, Voronezh.

Kucheruk, V. V. 1963. The influence of grass-eating mammals on the productivitiy of the grass stand of the steppe and their significance in the formation of the organic part of steppe soils. Reports of the Moscow Society of Experimental Nature, Vol. 10. Biology, Biogeography, and Systematization of Mammals of the USSR. Moscow, Publishing House of the Academy of Science of the USSR.

Kulik, I. L. 1963. An experimental survey on the numerical conditions of mouse-like rodents in a large territory. *In* Organization and methods of counting the number of birds and harmful rodents. Moscow, Publishing House of the Academy of Sciences of the USSR.

Kurcheva, G. F. 1960. The role of invertebrates in the decomposition of forest litterfall. Soil Science No. 4.

Kurcheva, G. F. 1965. The degree of invertebrate participation in the process of decomposition of oak litterfall in the forest and the dependence of their activity on the weather conditions. Reports of the Central Chernozem Government Reserve, Release 8, Voronezh, Publishing House of the Voronezh State University.

Kurcheva, G. F. 1969. The role of soil invertebrates in the decomposition of grassland vegetation. *In* Questions of Soil Zoology. Materials of the 3rd All-Russian Conference, Moscow, "Nauka."

Kurcheva, G. F. 1971. The role of soil animals in the decomposition and humification of vegetative remains. Moscow, "Nauka."

Lavrenko, E. M. 1952. Microcomplexity and mosaic of vegetative cover of steppes as a result of vital activity of animals and plants. Reports of the Botanical Institute, Series 3, Geobotany, Release 8, Leningrad, Publishing House of the Academy of Sciences of the USSR.

Lavrenko, E. M. 1956. Steppes and agricultural lands in steppe locations. *In* Vegetative canopy of the USSR, Vol. 2, Moscow-Leningrad, Publishing House of the Academy of Science of the USSR.

Llewellyn, M. 1972. The effects of the lime aphid, *Eucallipterus tiliae* L. (Aphidae) on the growth of the lime *Tilia vulgaris* H. J. Energy requirements of the aphid population. J. Appl. Ecol., Vol. 9, N 1.

Makarov, B. I., and V. B. Matskevich. 1966. Methods for determining the composition of soil air and rate of gas exchange between the soil and the atmosphere. *In* Physical-chemical methods of studying soils. Adsorptive and isotopic methods. Moscow, "Nauka."

Malkina, I. S. 1964. Photosynthesis of plants under the cover of oak forest. *In* Permanent sites biogeocenotic studies in the southern subzone of the Taiga. Moscow, "Nauka."

Malkina, I. S. 1965. Photosynthesis of arboreal undergrowth under the cover of the forest. Bot. J. Vol. 50 No. 5.

Merwe, N. J., van der. 1968. Control of grazing and browsing in the National Parks. African Wild Life, Vol. 22, N 1.

Mina, V. N. 1954. Interrelation between arboreal vegetation and soils in some types of oak forest of the southern forest-steppe. Reports of the Forest Institute, Vol. 15, Moscow, Publishing House of the Academy of Science of the USSR.

Minimum Program for Determination of Biological Primary Productivity of Terrestrial Vegetative Communities (Project). Vegetative Resources, Vol. 3, Release 4.

Mitina, M. B. 1969. About the assimilation activity of the dominants of seasonal synusia in a cutover oak grove of the forest-steppe zone. *In* Mechanisms of interrelation of plants in the biogeocenosis of the Taiga. Leningrad, "Nauka."

Molchanov, A. A. 1964. Scientific fundamentals for managing oak grove of the forest-steppe. Moscow, "Nauka."

Molchanov, A. A. 1970. The change of width in the annual ring in connection with the change of solar activity. *In* Formation of the Annual Ring and Accumulation of Organic Mass in Trees. Moscow, "Nauka."

Molchanov, A. A., and V. V. Smirnov. 1967. Methods for studying the growth of arboreal plants. Moscow, "Nauka."

Mozolevaskaya, E. G. 1965. Harmful forest insects in reserves of the Middle Belt of the European part of the USSR and means of fighting them. Abstract of a Candidate's Dissertation, Moscow.

Northcott, H. 1971. Feeding habits of beaver in Newfoundland. Oikos, Vol. 22, N 3.

Ovchinnikova, S. L. 1969. Some peculiarities of ecology of the common mole-rat *Spalax microphthalmus* in the Chernozem Belt. Zoological J. Vol. 48, Release 10.

Pachosski, I. K. 1917. Description of the vegetation in Kherson Region. II Steppe. Kerson (materials for the study of soils and grounds of the Kherson Region, Release 13).

Pelikan, I., Svoboda, J., Kvet, J. 1971. Relationship between the population of muskrats (*Ondatra zibethica*) and the primary production of cattail (*Typha latiofolia*). Hydrobiologia, t. 12.

Perel, T. S., and D. E. Sokolov. 1964. A quantitative estimate of the participation of the earth worms, *Lumbricus terrestris* L., (Lumbricidae, Oligochaeta) in the reworking of the forest litterfall. Zoological Journal Vol. 43, Release 11.

Petrusewicz, K., and A. Macfadyen. 1970. Productivity of terrestrial animals. Principles and methods. Oxford-Edinburgh. IBP Handbook No. 13.

Plokhinski, N. A. 1961. Biometrics. Novosibirsk, Publishing House of the Academy of Science of the USSR.

Polyakov, I. Ya. 1972. Ecological fundamentals for protecting
    plants from pests. Ecology No. 4.
Polyakova, N. F. 1954. Correlation between mass of foliage,
    growth of wood and transpiration. Reports of the Academy of
    Science of the USSR. Vol. 96, No. 6.
Ponomareva, V. V., and T. A. Nikolaeva. 1965. Content and composi-
    tion of humus in Chernozems of the Streletski Steppe under
    various conditions. Reports of the Central Chernozem Govern-
    ment Reserve, Release 8, Voronezh, Publishing House of Voronezh
    State University.
Program and Methods of Biogeocoentoic Investigations. 1966.
    Moscow-Leningrad, "Nauka."
Ptushenko, E. A. 1940. Preliminary information about fauna of the
    vertebrates of the Streletski and Kazatski Steppes. Reports
    of the Central Chernozem Government Reserve, Release 1, Moscow.
Raskatov, P. B. 1948. The question of formation of annual rings
    in the oak. Scientific reports of the Voronezh Forest-
    Agriculture Institute, Vol. 10, Leningrad, State Forest
    Technical Publishing House.
Redulesku-Ivan, O. D. 1965. The role of rhizomatous grasses in
    the building of some communities and associations of the
    Streletski Steppe of the Kursk District. Abstract of Candi-
    date's Dissertation, Leningrad.
Risin, L. P. 1970. Influence of forest vegetation on natural
    renewal of arboreal types under the cover of the forest. In
    Natural Renewal of Arboreal Types and a Quantitative Analysis
    of Its Growth. Moscow, "Nauka."
Rodin, L. E., and N. I. Bazilevich. 1965. The dynamics of organic
    matter and the biological cycling of ash elements and nitrogen
    in basic types of vegetation of the globe. Moscow-Leningrad,
    "Nauka."
Rodin, L. E., N. D. Remezov, and N. I. Bazilevich. 1968. System-
    atic indications and dynamics of biological cycling in phyto-
    coenoses. Leningrad, "Nauka."
Schütte, F. 1957. Untersuchungen über die populationsdynamik des
    eichenwicklers (*Tortrix viridana* L.). Zeitschrift f. ange-
    wandte entomologie. Bd. 40, H. 1,3.
Semenova-Tian-Shanskaya, A. M. 1960. The dynamics of accumulation
    and decomposition of dead vegetative remains in the meadow-
    steppe and meadow coenoses. Bot. J. Vol. 45, No. 9.
Semenova-Tian-Shanskaya, A. M. 1965. Regularities of regional
    change of grassland types of vegetation of the Russian Plain.
    J. Gen. Biol. Vol. 26, Release 3.
Semenova-Tian-Shanskaya, A. M. 1966. The dynamics of steppe
    vegetation (example of studies of meadow-steppe and steppe
    meadow of the Central Forest-Steppe). Moscow-Leningrad,
    "Nauka."
Sergeev, P. N. 1953. Forest enumeration. Moscow-Leningrad, State
    Publishing House on Literature for Timber Industry.
Severtsov, N. A. 1950. Periodical phenomena in the life of wild
    mammals birds and reptiles of the Voronezh Region. Moscow,
    1855. Ibid. 2nd Edition. Moscow-Leningrad, Publishing House
    of the Academy of Science of the USSR.
Shafer, E. L. 1963. The twig count method for measuring hardwood
    deer browse. J. Wildl. Manage., Vol. 27, N 3.

Shvartz, S. S. 1967. General regularities which determine the role of animals in biogeocoenoses. J. Gen. Biol. Vol. 28, No. 5.

Shutyaev, A. M. 1964. Experimental study of geographic cultures of the English Oak in the Central Chernozem Reserve of the Kursk Region. Abstract of a Candidate's Dissertation, Voronezh.

Skriabin, M. P. 1946. Ancient cycles of natural conditions and forest vegetation of the forest-steppe. Reports of the Voronezh Government Reserve, Release 3, Moscow.

Slobodkin, L. B., Smith, F. E., Hairston, N. G. 1967. Regulation in terrestrial ecosystems and the implied balance of nature. Am. Nat., Vol. 101, N 918.

Smirnov, B. A. 1966. Ants in the protection of forest from the oak leaf roller. Forest Economy, No. 2.

Steger, O. 1960. Spätfröste und Massenwechsel von *Tortrix viridana* L. (Lep. Tortr.). Zeitschrift f. angewandte Entomologie, Vol. 46, N 2.

Sukachev, V. N. 1966. Fundamental concepts about biogeocenoses and general directions for their study. *In* Program and Method of Biogeocenotic Studies. Moscow, "Nauka."

Taranukha, M. D. 1952. Development of the odd silkworm depending on feeding and light. (Resume). Scientific Works of Entomology and Phytopathology, Vol. 3, Kiev, Publishing House of the Academy of Science of the USSR.

Tarkhanova, R. Yu. 1963. The relation of oak desiccation in the Ukraine with the Dutch disease of elm trees. Questions of Forest Protection, Vol. 2, Materials for the International Conference for the Protection of Forests, Moscow.

Tselishcheva, L. K., and E. K. Daineko. 1967. A survey of soils of the Streletski Section. Reports of the Central Chernozem Government Reserve, Release 10, Moscow, "Forest Industry."

Tselniker, Yu. L. 1967. Problems of studying the synthesis of organic matter by forest phytocoenoses. I. Radiation conditions of the forest. *In* Light Condition, Photosynthesis and Forest Productivity. Moscow, "Nauka."

Turchinskaya, I. A. 1963. The influence of leaf eating by the odd silkworm and other leaf eating pests on the growth of oak. Zoological J., Vol. 42, Release 2.

Tyurin, I. V. 1948. Composition and characteristics of the humus of the Chernozem in the Streletski Steppe. Reports of the Central Chernozem Government Reserve, Release 2, Moscow.

Tyurin, I. V. 1965. Geographical regularities of humus formation. *In* Tyurin, I. V. Organic Soil Matter and Its Role in Fertility. Moscow, "Nauka."

Vikhrov, V. E. 1954. Structure and physical-mechanical characteristics of oak wood. Moscow, Publishing House of the Academy of Science of the USSR.

Visotskaya, P. N., and V. K. Mikhnovski. 1962. The influence of green fertilization and peat on the content and group composition of humus in turf average-podzolized loamy soil. Soil Science No. 2.

Vodopyanov, B. G. 1971. Feeding of wild northern deer in the barren and Taiga Belts of the Stanov Plateau. News of Eastern Siberian Department of the Geographic Society of the USSR, No. 68.

Voronov, A. G.   1935.   Some observations on the activity of the
    common field-vole (*Microtus socialis*) in pastures of Dagestan
    Piedmont.   Bulletin of the Moscow Society of Experimental
    Nature, Biology Department, Vol. 44, Release 6.
Vorontsov, A. I.   1962.   Outbreaks of mass reproduction of forest
    insects in the Russian Plain during 100 years in connection
    with climate and weather.   Questions of Ecology Vol. 7, Kiev,
    "Higher Education."
Vorontsov, A. I.   1963.   Biological fundamentals of forest protec-
    tion.   Moscow, "Higher Education."
Vorontsov, A. I., E. N. Ierusalimov, and E. G. Mozolevskaya.   1967.
    The role of leaf-eating insects in a forest biogeocenosis.   J.
    Gen. Biol., Vol. 28, No. 2.
Vorontsov, A. I., M. A. Golosova, and E. G. Mozolevskaya.   1966.
    Criteria for a basis of chemical measures for battling leaf-
    eating insects.   *In* Questions of Forest Protection, Moscow.
Williams, J. E., Wiegert, R. G.   1971.   Effects of naphthalene
    application on a coastal plain broomsedge (*Andropogon*) com-
    munity.   Pedobiologia, Vol. 11, H. 1.
Winestein, B. A.   1949.   Entomofauna of oak leaf pests in field-
    protective plantings of the south of the Ukrainian SSR and its
    dependence on forest ecological-factors.   Zoological J.,
    Vol. 28, Release 6.
Winestein, B. A.   1950.   Leaf-eating pests of oak and their seasonal
    dynamics.   Zoological J., Vol. 29, Release 2.
Zalenski, O. V., T. P. Shtanko, and M. M. Ponomareva.   1961.   About
    plant photosynthesis of Central Kazakhstan.   *In* Materials of
    the Kazakhstan Conference on the Problem of "Biological Com-
    plexes of Regions of Recent Assimilation, Their National
    Utilization and Enrichment."   Moscow-Leningrad, Publishing
    House of the Academy of Sciences of the USSR.
Zholkevich, V. N., V. A. Kholler, and A. Ya. Rogacheva.   1964.
    About the relationship between respiration and heat return in
    growing leaves.   Reports of the Academy of Sciences of the
    USSR Vol. 158, No. 5.
Zlotin, R. I.   1967.   Outbreaks of the green oak leaf roller as
    stimulators of biological cycling in forest-steppe oak groves.
    In Structure and the Functional-Biogeocenotic Role of the
    Animal Population on Dry Land.   Moscow.
Zlotin, R. I.   1969a.   The role of invertebrate animals in the
    mineralization of plant litterfall.   *In* Questions of Soil
    Zoology.   Materials of the 3rd All-Russian Meeting.   Moscow,
    "Nauka."
Zlotin, R. I.   1969b.   Comparison of soil biocenoses of some natural
    and agricultural forest lands of the middle forest-steppe.   *In*
    Synontropization and domestication of animal populations.
    Materials for the meeting of November 19-20, Moscow.
Zlotin, R. I.   1969c.   Zonal peculiarities of biomass of soil
    invertebrates in open landscapes of the Russian Plain.   *In*
    Questions of Soil Zoology.   Materials of the 3rd All-Russian
    Meeting. Moscow, "Nauka."
Zlotin, R. I., and K. S. Khodashova.   1972.   The influence of
    excrement of herbivores on the rate of litterfall decomposition
    in the forest-steppe.   *In* Problems of Soil Biology.   Moscow,
    "Nauka."

Zlotin, R. I., N. I. Kalandadze, L. B. Koretskaya, and Yu. G. Puzachenko. 1970. Biological activity of forest soils. The 4th All-Russian Delegate Conference of Soil Scientists. Theses of Reports, Book 3, Alma-Ata.

Zozulin, G. M. 1955. The interrelation of forest and grassland vegetation in the Central Chernozem Government Reserve. Reports of the Central Chernozem Government Reserve, Release 3, Kursk, Book Publishing House.

Zozulin, G. M. 1959. The below-ground parts of the major species of grassland plants and Plakor Associations of the middle-Russian forest-steppe in connection with questions of formation of the vegetative canopy. Reports of the Central Chernozem Government Reserve, Release 5, Kursk, Book Publishing House, 1959.

APPENDIX TO ENGLISH EDITION

English, Latin, and Russian Plant Names

(Latin names were provided by Dr. K. S. Khodashova. English names are from Dony et al. (1974) or van Wijk (1911) or from Ussovsky (1967). Listed alphabetically by English common name for ease of reference from text.)

Spring Adonis	*Adonis vernalis*	Горицвет
Alder buckthorn	*Frangula alnus*	Крушина
Almond	*Amygdalus communis*	Миндаль
Aspen	*Populus tremula*	Осина
Bedstraw	*Gallium mollugo, G. verum*	Подмаренник
Bell flower	*Campanula bononiensis*	Колокольчик
Bindweed	*Convolvulus arvensis*	Вьюнок
European bird-cherry	*Padus racemosa*	Черемуха
Bistort	*Polygonum bistorta*	Раковая шейка
Bitter vetch	*Orobus* sp.	Сочевичник
Blackthorn	*Prunus spinosa*	Терн
Bush grass	*Calamagrostis epigeios*	Вейник
Multiflower buttercup	*Ranunculus polyanthemus*	Лютик многоцветковый
Wild (steppe) cherry	*Prunus fruticosa*	Вишня степная
Chickweed	*Stellaria graminea*	Звездчатка
Cinquefoil	*Potentilla argentea, P. alba*	Лапчатка
Clematis	*Clematis recta*	Ломонос
Red clover	*Trifolium pratense*	Клевер красный
Clover	*Trifolium* sp.	Клевер
Crawling clover	*Trifolium repens*	Клевер ползучий
Mountain clover	*Trifolium montanum*	Клевер горный
Composite	*Compositae*	Сложноцветные
Coronilla	*Coronilla varia*	Вязель
Cow parsley (chervil)	*Anthriscus sylvestris*	Купырь

213

Cow wheat	*Melampyrum nemorosum*	Марьянник
Crab apple	*Malus praecox*	Яблоня
Dandelion	*Taraxacum officinale*	Одуванчик истиные
Dewberry	*Rubus caesius*	Ежевика
Elder	*Sambucus* sp.	Бузина
Elm	*Ulmus scabra*	Ильм
Elm	*Ulmus* sp.	Вяз
Forget-me-not	*Myosotis suaveolens*	Незабудка
Geranium	*Geranium sanguineum*	Геран
Goutweed	*Aegopodium podagrica*	Снать
Quack grass	*Agropyron intermedium*	Пырей ползучий, средний
Bent grass	*Agrostis syreistschikowi*	Полевица
Smooth brome grass	*Bromus inermus*	Костер безостый
Straight brome grass	*Bromus erectus*	Костер прямой
Brome grass	*Bromus riparius*	Костер береговой
Wide-leaf grasses	*Bromus, Agropyron* and *Helictotrichon*	Злаки широколистные
Oat grass	*Helictotrichon pubescens, H. schellianum*	Овсец
Feather grass	*Stipa pennata, S. stenophylla*	Ковыль
Narrow-leaf grasses	*Stipa, Festuca, Poa,* and *Koeleria*	Злаки узколистные
Meadow grass	*Poa angustifolia*	Мятлик
Ground ivy	*Glechoma hederacea*	Будра
Guelder-rose (Viburnum)	*Viburnum opulus*	Калина
Hawkweed	*Hieracium* sp.	Ястребинка
Hawthorne	*Crataegus curvisepala*	Боярышник
Hazel nut	*Corylus avellana*	Лещина
Honeysuckle	*Lonicera* sp.	Жимолость
Inula	*Inula* sp.	Девясил

Jerusalem sage	*Phlomis tuberosa*	Зопник
Knapweed	*Centaurea marshalliana*	Василек
Koeleria	*Koeleria gracilis*	Тонконог
Lily of the valley	*Convallaria majalis*	Ландыш
Linden	*Tilia* sp.	Липа
Liverleaf, Hepatica	*Hepatica nobilis*	Перелеска
Longleaf	*Falcaria vulgaris*	Резак
Lucerne, alfalfa	*Medicago falcata*	Люцерна
Lungwort	*Pulmonaria obscura*	Медуница
Tartarian maple	*Acer tataricum*	Клен татарский
Norway maple	*Acer platanoides*	Клен платановидный
Meadow clary	*Salvia pratensis*	Шалфей
Meadow-rue	*Thalictrum minus*	Василистник
Medrey	*Thymus marschallianus*	Чебрец
Milkgowan	*Leontodon hispidus*	Кульбаба
Mullein	*Verbascum* sp.	Коровяк
Nettle	*Urtica* sp.	Крапива
Pedunculus (English) oak	*Quercus robur*	Дуб черешчатый
Oxeye daisy	*Leucanthemum vulgare*	Нивянник
Wild pear	*Pyrus communis*	Груша
Plantain	*Plantago lanceolata*	Подорожник ланцетоносный
Plantain	*Plantago major*	Подорожник большой
Plantain	*Plantago media*	Подорожник средний
Potentilla	*Potentilla argentea*	Лапчатка
Potentilla	*Potentilla alba*	Лапчатка
Primrose	*Primula veris*	Примула
Pyrethrum	*Pyrethrum corymbosum*	Ромашник

Raspberry	*Rubus idaeus*	*Малина*
Cinnamon rose	*Rosa cinnamomea*	*Шиповник*
Dog rose	*Rosa canina*	*Шиповник*
Rowan	*Sorbus aucuparia*	*Рябина*
Sainfoil	*Onobrychis arenaria*	*Эспарцет*
Sandwort	*Arenaria sp.*	*Песчанка*
Sedge	*Carex sp.*	*Осока*
Selfheal	*Prunella sp.*	*Черноголовка*
Sheep's fescue	*Festuca sulcata*	*Типчак*
Sheep sorrel	*Rumex acetosella*	*Щавелек*
Smallreed	*Calamagrostis arundinacea*	*Вейник лесной*
Solomon's seal	*Polygonatum officinale*	*Купена*
Sow thistle	*Sonchus arvensis*	*Осот*
Spindle (European prickwood)	*Evonymus europaeus*	*Бересклет европейский*
Warty spindle (prickwood)	*Evonymus verrucosus*	*Бересклет бородавчатый*
Spirea (dropwort)	*Filipendula hexapetala*	*Таволга*
Spurge	*Euphorbia sp.*	*Молочай*
Strawberry	*Fragaria vesca*	*Земляника*
Strawberry	*Fragaria viridis*	*Клубника*
Valerian	*Valeriana rossica*	*Валериана*
Veronica	*Veronica sp.*	*Вероника*
Hedge vetch	*Vicia sepium*	*Горошек заборный*
Bramble vetch	*Vicia tenuifolia*	*Горошек тонколистный*
Vetch	*Vicia sp.*	*Вика*
Violet	*Viola sp.*	*Фиалка*
Warty cabbage	*Bunias orientalis*	*Свербига*
Willow	*Salix caprea, S. livida*	*Ива*
Woodruff	*Asperula sp.*	*Ясменник, Асперула*
Yarrow, milfoil	*Achillea millefolium*	*Тысячелистник*

References for Plant Names

Dony, J. G., F. Perring, and C. M. Rob. 1974. English names of wild
    flowers. Butterworths, London. 121 p.

Ussovsky, BN. 1967. Comprehensive Russian-English agricultural dictionary.
    Pergamon Press. 470 p.

van Wijk, H. L. Gerth. 1911. A dictionary of plant names. Vol. I.
    Martinus Nijkoff, The Hague. 1444 p.

Index

About the Editor

NORMAN R. FRENCH is Professor of Biology at Colorado State University where he has taught since 1969. Prior to that date he taught at the University of California, Los Angeles, Michigan State University, the University of Utah, the University of Nebraska, and the University of Illinois.

Professor French completed his undergraduate work in zoology at the University of Illinois in 1949, and received the M.S. degree in biology from the University of Colorado, and the Ph.D. in ecology from the University of Utah. He is currently a Senior Ecologist at the Natural Resource Ecology Laboratory at Colorado State University.

Dr. French's major interests are ecosystem analysis, computer modeling and simulation, population dynamics, and zoogeography. He is the author of numerous papers in these areas and is the editor of *Perspectives in Grassland Ecology.*

DATE DUE

PRINTED IN U.S.A.